Byron's Poetic Experimentation

Byron's Poetic Experimentation

Childe Harold, the Tales, and the Quest for Comedy

Alan Rawes

Ashgate

Aldershot • Brookfield USA • Singapore • Sydney

Published by

Ashgate Publishing Ltd
Gower House, Croft Road,
Aldershot, Hampshire GU11 3HR
England

Ashgate Publishing Company
131 Main Street
Burlington, Vermont 05401
USA

Ashgate website: http://www.ashgate.com

ISBN 0 7546 0171 4

British Library Cataloguing-in-Publication Data
Rawes, Alan
  Byron's poetic experimentation: Childe Harold, the tales, and the quest for comedy. –
  (The nineteenth century series)
  1. Byron, George Gordon Byron, Baron, 1788-1824 – Criticism and interpretation
  2. Byron, George Gordon Byron, Baron, 1788-1824. Childe Harold
  I. Title
  821.7

US Library of Congress Cataloging-in-Publication Data
Rawes, Alan
    p.   cm. – (Nineteenth century series)
  Includes bibliographical references (p.) and index.
  1. Byron, George Gordon Byron, Baron, 1788-1824. Childe Harold's pilgrimage.
  2. Byron George Gordon Byron, Baron, 1788-1824 – Technique. 3. Byron, George Gordon Byron, Baron, 1788-1824 – Humor. 4. Experimental poetry, English – History and criticism. 5. Humorous poetry, English – History and criticism. 6. Comic, The, in literature. I. Title. II. Nineteenth century (Aldershot, England)
  PR4357 .R39 2000
  821'.7-dc21   00-042046

Printed and bound in Great Britain by MPG Books Ltd, Bodmin, Cornwall

0= 185797850

Contents

The Nineteenth Century

General Editors' Preface

The aim of this series is to reflect, develop, and extend the great burgeoning of interest in the nineteenth century that has been an inevitable feature of recent decades, as that former epoch has come more sharply into focus as a locus for our understanding not only of the past, but also of the contours of our modernity. Though it is dedicated principally to the publication of original monographs and symposia in literature, history, cultural analysis, and associated fields, there will be a salient role for reprints of significant texts from, or about, the period. This, we believe, distinguishes our project from comparable ones, and means, for example, that in relevant areas of scholarship we both recognize and cut innovatively across such parameters as those suggested by the designations 'Romantic' and 'Victorian'. We welcome new ideas, while valuing tradition. It is hoped that the world which predates yet so forcibly predicts and engages our own will emerge in parts, as a whole, and in the lively currents of debate and change that are so manifest an aspect of its intellectual, artistic, and social landscape.

Vincent Newey
Joanne Shattock
University of Leicester

Acknowledgements

First and foremost, I would like to thank Bernard Beatty, to whom my debt is immense. My warmest gratitude also goes to Cathy Rees and Barbara Smith for their invaluable help, to Karl Simms and Nick Davis for their aid with parts of this study in its early stages, to Arthur Bradley for his unstinting generosity and wise counsel, to Professor Vincent Newey for his advice and encouragement, to Alec McAulay, Ruth Peters, and Cathrin Vaughan for all their help and for their patience, and to my reader at Ashgate for numerous helpful comments and suggestions.

This study was initially made possible financially by the British Academy, for which I am extremely grateful. It was sustained throughout by the support of my wife, Louie, and I dedicate this book to her.

Part of chapter 1 first appeared in the *Keats–Shelley Journal* 48 (1999) and is reprinted with the permission of the editor. A version of part of chapter 4 appeared in the *Byron Journal* 27 (1999) and is reprinted with the permission of the editor. A version of part of chapter 5 appeared in the *Aligarh Critical Miscellany* 9:2 (1996) and is reprinted with the permission of the editor.

Introduction

Byron is back in fashion. While Deconstruction neglected him, New Historicism has brought him back to the centre of the critical arena. The emphasis the latter places on social, historical, and ideological contexts has clearly led Byron studies into new and fecund territories. Despite its local cogency, however, I cannot wholeheartedly embrace New Historicism's privileging of historical and ideological contexts over the imaginative and aesthetic. Byron's poetry continues to reward the study of its artistic aims and achievements *per se*, and there is much that still needs to be fully understood about Byron's poetry which is necessarily overlooked by many of his latest critical admirers.

For Byron is more impressive as a poet than he has sometimes been given credit for. He is pulled to all of the basic poetic forms of narrative, drama, and lyric, and to the full generic range of comedy, tragedy, satire, and the pastoral. Few writers have Byron's scope, but then few writers have the ambition that we find in Byron's verse. This is especially evident, I think, in the first half of Byron's poetic career: in the drive to experiment with and explore, to draw on and master, the new ways of imagining and new kinds of writing towards which his imagination drew him.

The following study is concerned with precisely this ambitious experimentation. It has been discussed before, and at length, by Robert Gleckner in *Byron and the Ruins of Paradise*, and the present study owes a fundamental debt to that book. Gleckner argues that in Byron's drive to explore new ways of imagining and writing, we see him 'forging a frighteningly dark and coherent vision of man and life' while 'struggling to develop the most effective form to embody that vision'. Accordingly, Gleckner reads the Byron 'canon' as a 'fascinating history of struggle for form'.[1] But Gleckner's work is now more than thirty years old, and advances a main argument that many critics have distanced themselves from.[2] It is

---

1   *Byron and the Ruins of Paradise* (Baltimore: Johns Hopkins University Press, 1967), pp. xv, 254 (hereafter referred to as *Ruins*).

2   Jerome McGann, for example, 'cannot agree' with Gleckner's 'controlling idea' (*Fiery Dust: Byron's Poetical Development* (Chicago: Chicago University Press, 1968), p. ix), while Michael Cooke tells us that Gleckner's study 'differs from the synthesis that is to be sought' in his own work (*The Blind Man Traces the Circle* [Princeton: Princeton University Press, 1969], p. x, hereafter referred to as *The Blind Man*). More recently, Vincent Newey says that Gleckner's 'view must be handled with care' ('Authoring the Self: *Childe Harold* III and IV', in *Byron and the Limits of Fiction*, ed. by B. Beatty and V. Newey [Liverpool: Liverpool University Press, 1988], p. 177), but Philip Martin is Gleckner's harshest critic. He calls Gleckner's response to *Childe Harold* I and II 'perverse', criticizes his 'rhetoric', and implies that Gleckner's account of *Don Juan* 'projects into it themes and concepts' that are not there (*Byron: A Poet Before His Public* [Cambridge:

perhaps time we reconsidered Byron's relation to some of the forms in which he wrote and on which he drew.

I begin this study with cantos I and II of *Childe Harold's Pilgrimage* and move forward chronologically through Byron's major poetry to *Childe Harold* IV. The study ends by touching briefly on *Beppo*. There are four reasons for this chronological procedure and these particular limits.

Firstly, the study is chronological because it is interested in Byron's movement into and between kinds of writing and ways of imagining. We will be looking at local examples of this within Byron's poems, but also at the larger transitions which run through them, and a chronological study is the best way of looking at the latter.

Secondly, we begin with cantos I and II of *Childe Harold* because in them we see Byron consciously attempting, for the first time, to discover a way forward out of modes of composition which had become habitual and constricting. Before 1809, when Byron began *Childe Harold*, his poetic output was made up of either short lyrics or longer satires, but in *Childe Harold* I and II, Byron was looking for a form that would, as he says himself, following Beattie: 'give full scope to my inclination' (*Childe Harold's Pilgrimage* I and II, Preface, 35). Clearly, short lyrics and satires had not offered him this scope. The first two cantos of *Childe Harold* are my starting point, then, because they inaugurate the exploration of multiple possibilities that I am principally interested in here.

Thirdly, this study is framed by cantos I and II of *Childe Harold* and *Beppo* because, as I hope to demonstrate, the former lead into, and the latter brings to a close, a battle for supremacy in Byron's work between a powerful attraction to the tragic, and what progressively reveals itself to be a comic impulse. The experimentation of *Childe Harold* I and II pushed Byron's verse in the direction of what George Steiner has described as 'the tragic vision of life',[3] and in the tales which followed Byron became entrenched in, and entrapped in, his own Romantic version of this vision. But as 'tragedy' imposed its own absolute limits on his imagination, so Byron sought, as Morse Peckham was the first to point out, a way of pushing beyond those limits, and a prolonged struggle ensued.[4] The tragic polarity exerted a tenacious pull on Byron's imagination, and his preliminary efforts to detach his writing from that pull proved unsustainable and ended in failure. The achievement of a sustained comic idiom in *Beppo*, however, announces his ultimate success.[5]

Finally, this study engages with the period between *Childe Harold* I and

---

Cambridge University Press, 1982], pp. 10, 107, 173).

[3]   *The Death of Tragedy* (London: Faber and Faber, 1961), p. 9.

[4]   See *Beyond the Tragic Vision: The Quest for Identity in the Nineteenth Century* (New York: George Braziller, 1962). For Peckham, Byron's poetry first attempted to 'grasp utterly the implications of total negation' (p. 102) generated by the tragic subject's 'alienation from man and nature' and 'guilt before man and the universe' (p. 103). But it goes on, says Peckham, to seek, and ultimately find, a 'resolution' of these 'problems' (p. 103) in the 'amor' (p. 106) of 'comic and ironic indifference' (p. 107).

[5]   A clear and easy path back to tragedy is established on the other side of *Beppo*, but the present study will not be concerned with this.

II and *Beppo* because *Childe Harold's Pilgrimage* is Byron's major site of experimentation. We will be following this experimentation in chapters devoted almost entirely to each instalment of the poem, corresponding to its publication history. In a sense, then, this study is dominated by *Childe Harold*. The chapters concerned with it will not, however, offer a reading of *Childe Harold* as a single work. I will be looking closely at the play-offs and negotiations between different kinds of writing and imagining which make up much of *Childe Harold*, but I will be situating each canto's exploration of possibilities within the larger development of Byron's poetry. I will be discussing how each canto moves Byron forward from what precedes it, and how each instalment of *Childe Harold* plays a role in the genesis of the poetry which follows it. Three things will be of particular importance here: *Childe Harold*'s part in the making of Byron's early tragic narratives, its part in the genesis of the comic *Beppo*, and its pivotal role in making Byron's fraught transition between these possible.

It is for these reasons, then, that this study is structured as it is. Let us now turn to *Childe Harold* I and II, where Byron first begins to try and endow with form the full scope of his inclination, and from there follow Byron's progress through to the transition between *Childe Harold* IV and *Beppo*, where the basic modes of his later poetry are all finally uncovered.[6]

---

6   This is not to deny that there are further stages of experimentation after *Beppo*. Indeed, experimenting remained habitual to Byron, and alongside his classical tragedies, for example, we have the openly experimental *Cain*, *Heaven and Earth*, and *The Deformed Transformed*.

CHAPTER ONE

'Mix'd in One Mighty Scene with Varied Beauty Glow'

In many of the poems we will be looking at, Byron entertains and tries to synthesize a number of contradictory ideas about the nature of poetry.[1] The first place where these contradictions are allowed full scope, and indeed almost write the poem, is in cantos I and II of *Childe Harold's Pilgrimage*. This is accordingly where we begin.

In 1813, Byron famously wrote:

> I by no means rank poetry or poets in the scale of intellect – this may look like Affectation – but it is my real opinion – it is the lava flow of the imagination whose eruption prevents an earth-quake.[2]

Byron often used poetry as a kind of cathartic self-therapy, venting not only a boiling imagination, but heated emotions. For instance, *The Waltz* vented 'the prudishness of his libertinism' and the 'pangs of the lame watcher on the sidelines of London and provincial balls'.[3] In cantos I and II of *Childe Harold*, this cathartic use of poetry is insisted upon. In stanza 91, for example, 'unavailing woe / Bursts from my heart' (*CHP* I, 927–928).

Yet the idea that emotional outpourings are a legitimate source of poetry is also ridiculed in *Childe Harold* I and II. When Harold pours his 'last "Good night"' to 'the elements' (*CHP* I, 117), he is made to look ridiculous. Indeed, his outburst is offered as a burlesque of a particular kind of poetry rather than an example of it. Similarly, in the midst of Cadiz's 'jubilee' (*CHP* I, 693), Harold pours forth an utterly inappropriately gloomy 'lay' (*CHP* I, 835) and once more looks slightly ludicrous. We can say, then, that the first instalment of *Childe Harold* is 'in touch with a number of contradictory viewpoints' even about its own procedures.[4] Correspondingly, the poem is difficult to describe, though not to read, because it is

---

[1] The title of this chapter is taken from canto I of *Childe Harold's Pilgrimage*, line 251. Hereafter quotations from *Childe Harold's Pilgrimage* will be followed in the text by the abbreviation *CHP* and the relevant canto and line numbers. All quotations from Byron's poetry are taken from *The Complete Poetical Works of Lord Byron*, ed. by Jerome J. McGann, 7 volumes (Oxford: Clarendon Press, 1980–1993), hereafter referred to as *Works*.

[2] Letter to Annabella Milbanke of 29 November 1813, in *Byron's Letters and Journals*, ed. by Leslie A. Marchand (London: John Murray, 1973–1982), vol. III, p. 179. All quotations from Byron's letters will be taken from this edition, hereafter referred to as *BLJ*.

[3] Leslie Marchand, *Byron: A Biography* (London: John Murray, 1957), p. 371.

[4] Bernard Beatty, 'Lord Byron: Poetry and Precedent', in *Literature of the Romantic Period 1750–1850*, ed. by R. T. Davies and B. G. Beatty (Liverpool: Liverpool University

constantly inventing itself, bringing into being the point of view from
which it *might* be conceived but never from which it *must* be conceived. It
lives in its own presentness and each Spenserian stanza becomes the
realization of the moments that constitute that present.[5]

This openness to invention is a form of generation, but it is also a way of
trying to move forward into new possibilities. *Childe Harold* I and II explore
new ways of writing and imagining, and progress without a fixed sense of
where they will lead to, or of what they will become. This opening chapter
will, in trying to describe that progress, echo the poem's openness to what is
new and disruptive. While we will be guided by the question, 'What kind of
poem does Byron finally write?', we must postpone any attempt at a
comprehensive answer until the end of the chapter. For now, we will limit
ourselves to describing the succession of 'moments that constitute' the poem's
present.

As we begin to read the poem, that reading is conditioned by the title. It
does two things. Firstly, it leads us to expect a narrative poem centred on
Harold.[6] Secondly, it leads us to expect a particular kind of narrative. The
words 'Pilgrimage' and 'Childe', in conjunction with the subtitle, clearly
evoke the tradition of romance. William H. Marshall describes its procedures
as follows:

> the protagonist of the verse romance is sent upon a mission, the fulfilment
> of which will prove his courage and other qualities needed for moral
> survival: the end of the pilgrimage must be the test itself.[7]

Press, 1976), p. 115 (hereafter referred to as 'Poetry and Precedent'). The poem does not only
oscillate between employing poetry as an emotional pressure valve and mocking such uses of
poetry. It also oscillates between being a lyrical account of Byron's actual journey and a
narrative account of Harold's fictional one.

[5]   Brian Nellist, 'Lyric Presence in Byron from the *Tales* to *Don Juan*', in *Byron and
the Limits of Fiction*, p. 41 (hereafter referred to as 'Lyric Presence').

[6]   Harold has long been the subject of debate. Though the present chapter is not
primarily concerned with that debate, it should be noted that critics often hold diametrically
opposed views of his status as a character. McGann, for example, argues that Harold is 'an
object-self in a confessional poem', an 'ego-projection' (*Fiery Dust*, p. 69). Conversely,
Peter Thorslev holds that Harold is 'inspired by literature not life': 'The traditional literary
figure of Harold in cantos I and II is ... a potpourri ... of the characteristics of ... the Child of
Nature; the Gothic Villain ... the accursed Wanderer; the Gloomy Egoist ...; the man of
feeling.' (Peter L. Thorslev, *The Byronic Hero: Types and Prototypes* [Minneapolis:
University of Minnesota Press, 1962], p. 138.) My own view is more in sympathy with
Thorslev's, for reasons that should become clear as the chapter progresses.

[7]   William H. Marshall, *The Structure of Byron's Major Poems* (Philadelphia:
University of Philadelphia Press, 1962), p. 36 (hereafter referred to as *Structure*). Of course,
pilgrimage *per se* does not involve a final test but a reward: often a glimpse of the New
Jerusalem. Harold receives no such reward, though the final stanzas of *Childe Harold* IV, in
which the poet-figure and Harold look out at the ocean, may be a conclusion that in some
ways is meant to correspond formally as a secular alternative to, for example, Christian's
arrival at the Celestial City in *Pilgrim's Progress*. Certainly, at the end of canto II, *Childe
Harold* is a long way from any such arrival or reward, and the poem thus far gives no
suggestion that it might be heading in any such direction. Pilgrimage, too, is specifically for

Harold does not fulfil these conditions, and we quickly realize, on reading the opening stanzas, that we are not going to get this kind of narrative. Harold does not embark upon a mission, but simply 'for change of scene' (*CHP* I, 54). If anything, Harold's journey is an escape rather than a quest.

Why, then, does Byron set up the expectation of a romance narrative only to disappoint that expectation? The title claims for the poem an allegiance with a particular tradition, that is, with the imitations of Spenser's stanza that were common in the eighteenth century, such as *The Castle of Indolence* and *The Minstrel*.

The allegiance implicitly claimed by the title is explicitly claimed by the Preface:

> The stanza of Spenser, according to one of our most successful poets, admits of every variety. Dr. Beattie makes the following observation: 'Not long ago I began a poem in the style and stanza of Spenser, in which I propose to give full scope to my inclination, and be either droll or pathetic, descriptive or sentimental, tender or satirical, as the humour strikes me; for, if I mistake not, the measure which I have adopted admits equally of all these kinds of composition'– Strengthened in my opinion by such authority, and by the example of some in the highest order of Italian poets, I shall make no apology for attempts at similar variations in the following composition; satisfied that, if they are unsuccessful, their failure must be in the execution, rather than in the design sanctioned by the practice of Aristo, Thomson, and Beattie. (*CHP* I and II, Preface, 32–44)

Byron's project is that of Beattie: 'variety', 'variation', 'all ... kinds of composition', to 'give full scope to my inclination', and Byron claims his poem belongs with those of 'Aristo, Thomson, and Beattie'. But as Bernard Beatty suggests, Beattie and Thomson are 'exemplars ... more in theory than in fact'. While these precursors 'suggest possibilities', they only began to 'realize the varied possibilities of the form'.[8] Byron's aim is to fully realize those possibilities.

His means to this end, however, are not those of Beattie and Thomson. *The Castle of Indolence* is an allegorical and moral romance narrative. The Knights of Art and Industry triumph over the Wizard of Indolence. *The Minstrel*, on the other hand, is a psychological narrative, which traces 'the progress of a Poetical Genius, born in a rude age, from the first dawning of fancy and reason'.[9] As we shall see, *Childe Harold's Pilgrimage*, though it contains narrative elements, is not really a narrative in either of these senses. Furthermore, while its opening stanzas are structured as narrative, as the poem progresses this structure is pushed to one side, and replaced with a looser lyric

---

sinners. The opening stanzas do seem to suggest that we are reading the story of a sinner's spiritual progress, but this suggestion, though never entirely put aside, is quickly overwhelmed by others.

[8]   Beatty, 'Poetry and Precedent', pp. 129–130.

[9]   James Beattie, Preface to *The Minstrel*, in *The Minstrel, in Two Books: With Some Other Poems* (Edinburgh and London: [n.pub.], 1771; repr. London: [n.pub.], 1784), p. xi.

form. The first instalment of *Childe Harold* is a 'medley',[10] a 'collection of lyrics'.[11]

Canto I begins, then, by acknowledging the poem's eighteenth-century precedents and situating the poem in the context of the particular tradition it continues. But it also begins by announcing Byron's desire to do something new within that tradition. The title, and to some extent the first few stanzas, lead us to anticipate a romance narrative, possibly a knightly narrative, along the lines of Spenser filtered through, say, Beattie. The poem's refusal to fulfil the expectation thus generated articulates Byron's determination to do something new and different.

Nevertheless, Byron did not begin with a clear and fixed plan of the poem he was writing. Much more obvious is a clear sense of the kinds of poem he did not want to write. For example, Harold's character and imminent departure quickly generate a narrative which seems to be tracing 'a therapeutic movement toward a better self than the one he was at the outset'.[12] Harold begins 'Sore given to revel and ungodly glee' (*CHP* I, 15), but becomes 'sore sick at heart' (*CHP* I, 46) in stanza 6, and eager to 'flee' his 'fellow bacchanals' (*CHP* I, 47). Yet Byron fends off this kind of narrative progression almost as soon as it takes shape.[13] His narrator's attitude oscillates between optimism and contempt, or as Richard Cronin puts it, 'between sympathy and disapproval',[14] but a sarcastic and mock-heroic portrayal of Harold runs through his narration which ironizes the suggestion that Harold aches to be a 'better self'.[15] This can be heard in the extract below, especially in the pause stressed by a semicolon at the end of line 33.[16] It holds the reader's expectation, aroused by the phrase 'Worse than adversity', only to answer that expectation with bathos:

---

[10]   Beatty, 'Poetry and Precedent', p. 129.

[11]   Nellist, 'Lyric Presence', p. 43.

[12]   McGann, *Fiery Dust*, p. 69.

[13]   Indeed, for Stuart Curran, Harold 'is fictional ..., but there is no fiction for him to enter upon' (*Poetic Form and British Romanticism* [New York and Oxford: Oxford University Press, 1986], p. 151). Byron, we might suggest, wilfully denies Harold a fiction at the commencement of a poem that is concerned with what Curran calls 'the universal decay of fictions' (p. 155). However, *Childe Harold*'s achievement, Curran argues, is to become 'a living monument' (p. 155) to 'creative inventiveness' (p. 151): a monument that triumphs, finally, over the decay it laments.

[14]   'Mapping *Childe Harold* I and II', in *Byron Journal* 22 (1994), p. 18.

[15]   An ironic tone may have been obvious to contemporary readers of *Childe Harold* I and II from the very outset, and signalled by a detail that does not have, for late twentieth-century readers, the ironic resonance that it had, according to McGann, for early nineteenth-century readers. Harold is described as 'a shameless wight' in stanza 2, and McGann argues that the word 'wight ... carries its own ironic history'. McGann tells us that by 'the time the word reaches the nineteenth century ... its romance meaning ... is continually threatened by an ironic undertone'. This 'emerges quite clearly in the influential opening stanzas of Byron's *Childe Harold*, Canto I, where the ironization of the romance usage is complete'. For McGann's argument in full, see *The Beauty of Inflections: Literary Investigations in Historical Method and Theory* (Oxford: Clarendon Press, 1985), p. 34, n. 26.

[16]   In 1813, Byron wrote to John Murray, asking 'do you know any body who can *stop* – I mean *point* – commas & so forth – for I am I fear a sad hand at your punctuation' (letter of 26 August 1813, in *BLJ* III, p. 100). The possibility that someone other than

But long ere scare a third of his pass'd by,
Worse than adversity the Childe befell;
He felt the fullness of satiety. (*CHP* I, 32–34)

On occasion, the narrator even seems to feel contempt, indeed outright dislike, for Harold, as in these lines:

Ah, happy she! to 'scape from him whose kiss
Had been pollution unto aught so chaste;
Who soon had left her charms for vulgar bliss,
And spoil'd her goodly lands to gild his waste,
Nor calm domestic peace had ever deign'd to taste. (*CHP* I, 41–44)

Byron fends off one kind of narrative with another, or rather, he fends off the idea of a narrative of spiritual growth with the idea of a narrative of villainy, in which the hero moves on only because satiated, and moves on only to further villainous exploits and 'ungodly' acts:

And now Childe Harold was sore sick at heart,
And from his fellow bacchanals would flee;
'Tis said, at times the sullen tear would start,
But Pride congeal'd the drop within his ee:
Apart he stalk'd in joyless reverie,
And from his native land resolv'd to go,
And visit scorching climbs beyond the sea;
With pleasure drugg'd he almost long'd for woe,
And e'en for change of scene would seek the shades below. (*CHP* I, 46–54)

The opening lines here suggest a movement towards a 'better self', but the words 'sullen', 'pride', 'stalked' carry forward the suggestion of villainy.[17] Even though the narrator distances himself from these suggestions, reporting them as a rumour (''Tis said'), he does not refute them. Indeed, a degree of contempt creeps into his own voice: 'with pleasure drugg'd'. Does he also hint at the possibility of future villainies when he says that Harold 'almost long'd for woe'? It is not clear, but this is my point. One possibility is held at bay by others. And in the final Alexandrine, while Byron stresses Harold's desire to 'change', move on, leave the 'scene' of bacchanalia, we also see that Harold would be prepared to do anything for a change. The image Byron picks to describe the lengths to which Harold's desire to escape 'ungodly glee' will go is Hell.

Though it is difficult to pick out just how many ideas are coming together here, we can isolate two of them. We can see that Byron checks the idea of spiritual growth with the idea of villainy. But it is equally significant that he

---

Byron may have punctuated his poems should be borne in mind whenever we offer an analysis of that punctuation, though it should be also stressed that Byron would have seen the punctuation and approved it and, despite his disclaimer of expertise, was concerned with such details.

[17]   Thorslev goes as far as to suggest that pride is 'almost a hallmark' of 'the Gothic Villain' (*The Byronic Hero*, p. 134).

fends off the idea that Harold is a villain by hitting a note of unambiguous sympathy:

> Yet oft-times in his maddest mirthful mood
> Strange pangs would flash along Childe Harold's brow,
> As if the memory of some deadly feud
> Or disappointed passion lurk'd below:
> For his was not that open, artless soul
> That feels relief by bidding sorrow flow,
> Nor sought he friend to counsel or condole,
> Whate'er his grief mote be, which he could not control. (*CHP* I, 64–72)

We are naturally intrigued by these 'strange pangs', and by the closure of 'none this knew'.[18] The reader is curious and holds on to the possibilities offered, especially 'disappointed passion': it picks up on the earlier hint that 'he lov'd but one, / And that lov'd one, alas! could ne'er be his' (*CHP* I, 39–40) which was smothered by the suggestion that her escape had been a lucky one. Here the hint resonates, because of the words 'sorrow', 'grief', and the suggestion of isolation, which runs over into the next stanza: 'And none did love him' (*CHP* I, 73). These things call out for a sympathy usually denied a villain,[19] and we recall that he 'loath'd ... in his native land to dwell' not only because he is satiated with pleasure, but because it is 'more lone than Eremite's sad cell' (*CHP* I, 35–36).

It is important to emphasize that this note of sadness, loneliness, and lovelessness opens up a new range of possibilities, and sets up various kinds of new expectations. When anticipated from the standpoint of this stanza, the poem no longer seems likely to be a catalogue of villainy, for example. We modify our expectations accordingly, and a number of possibilities suggest themselves: a 'therapeutic movement' into a better existence, certainly, and perhaps one that will end in the discovery of love, or in a reconciliation to his loneliness. Or again, the poem could pan out, say, into a narrative that follows Harold's state as it darkens and his isolation is accentuated by travel. Either

---

[18]   A fellow traveller for a time, John Galt, described Byron's appearance on the first occasion he saw him as follows: 'His physiognomy was prepossessing and intelligent, but ever and anon his brows lowered and gathered; a habit, as I then thought, with a degree of affectation in it, probably first assumed for picturesque effect and energetic expression; but which I afterwards discovered was undoubtedly the occasional scowl of some unpleasant reminiscence: it was certainly disagreeable – forbidding – but still the general cast of his features was impressed with elegance and character.' (*Letters from the Levant* [London (n.pub.), 1813], p. 50, quoted in Marchand, *Byron: A Biography*, p. 194). Galt's first instinct may have some truth in it. The scowl he notes quickly found its way into the first appearance of the Byronic hero, as we see here. The effect Byron's scowl produced in onlookers, and which Byron clearly knew it produced, ensured that it remained a distinguishing feature of the Byronic hero from Harold to Conrad, Lara, Manfred, and Fletcher Christian.

[19]   The Byronic hero, of which Harold is a prototype, is, almost by definition, a sympathetic villain. There were a number of other prototypes of course, especially Schiller's *Der Raüber*, a text well known in England in 1809–1810, and one which Byron 'admired' (McGann, *Works* III, p. 446)

way, Harold's significance at this point seems to be emotional and psychological, and we anticipate a journey that will be significant on these grounds: depicting a process of rejuvenation, spiritual growth, or deepening despondency. Indeed, the following two stanzas seem to settle the poem into one of these possible narratives, soliciting our sympathy and moving us to Harold's departure without offering some new viewpoint from which to read Harold, and from which to anticipate the journey to come.

The poem seems to have discovered a kind of stability, then. But it does not rest in it. Byron's drive to experiment, to explore untried possibilities, soon reasserts itself. In stanza 13, Byron begins once more to fend off closure, and the limitations on his 'inclination' imposed by any one narrative. Just as we begin to be confident that we know how to read Harold correctly, the degree of stylization to which Byron subjects him becomes so overt that we start to lose that confidence. Harold is perilously close to becoming an object of ridicule. On leaving England, Harold 'did fling' (*CHP* I, 113) his fingers over a harp, which 'he at times could string' (*CHP* I, 110) and which he just happens to have with him. All the verbs here are what would have been seen, fifty years later, as melodramatic: 'He seiz'd his harp' (*CHP* I, 110) and 'pour'd' his 'last "Good night"' to 'the elements' (*CHP* I, 116). Harold's 'last "Good night"' contributes to a scene in which we are asked to imagine a boat load of people who 'sate and wept, / And to the reckless gales unmanly moaning kept' (*CHP* I,108–109).

What is it to take Byron seriously here, with Harold apparently reduced to a 'melodramatic' sentimentalist who, overcome with emotion at leaving his native country, seizes his harp? This from a soul that could not find relief, we are told in stanza 8, by 'bidding sorrow flow'? We find ourselves again unsure of how to respond to Harold, and unsure of where Byron's invention is leading him. The kind of narrative we are reading is precariously open to change, and the ballad that follows accentuates the poem's uncertainty about its own direction. On the one hand, the capitalization of 'Good night' and the melodrama of 'last', 'seiz'd', and 'fling' signal the quasi-burlesque nature of the ballad, which takes as the immediate object of its parody, '"Lord Maxwell's Good Night", in the Border Minstrelsy, edited by Mr. Scott' (*CHP* I and II, Preface, 25–26). On the other hand, though the ballad is certainly a parody of a certain kind of sentimental poetry, it is not only this. Certain details suggest an undercurrent of feeling and solicit our sympathy:

> Enough, enough, my little lad!
>   Such tears become thine eye;
> If I thy guileless bosom had
>   Mine own would not be dry. (*CHP* I, 154–157)

The patronizing and complacent voice does not smother the echo, in 'If I thy guileless bosom had' of 'his was not that open artless soul / That feels relief by bidding sorrow flow'. It seems after all that Harold has not given up his customary self-restraint, and that he is not letting his sorrow flow, despite all appearances to the contrary. This, and the fact that Harold seems to suddenly interrupt the page, give 'Enough, enough' a slight sense of urgency, as if Harold is in danger of losing his self-control – of becoming genuinely overcome with emotion – which he is determined not to do. Does the ballad begin as an emotional outpouring, but rapidly mutate into a kind of self-parody used as a defence against emotion?

The sense of repressed emotion emerges again in stanza 9, with the line 'And now I'm in the world alone' (*CHP* I, 182). On the face of it this is untrue since the ballad is a dialogue between Harold, the page, and the yeoman. Doubtless Byron took for granted the idea of an aristocratic sensibility that would not be shared by the menials who accompany Harold. That sensibility is, perhaps, rather exaggerated in this ballad, but we are reminded that Harold's recent decision to marginalize himself, to 'flee' his 'fellow bacchanals' has led to the journey he is now embarking upon. 'And now I'm in the world alone' echoes, once again, stanza 8, and the fact that Harold possesses no 'friend to counsel or condole'. Perhaps more importantly, the phrase recalls the fact that 'none did love him'. These echoes give the phrase a degree of poignancy.

Even when Harold arrives on the Continent, then, the poem has still not decided how to present him, or fixed on the kind of narrative he will occupy. Harold is both a sympathetic character and a ludicrous one. Indeed, potentially, he is a villain. We might be reading a narrative of emotional maturation and spiritual growth, or one of deepening despondency. We might find the poem becomes a sort of rake's progress or a villain's adventures. Nothing is yet fixed, and all of these seem possible. It seems that Byron himself had not yet decided what kind of poem he was writing, indeed, rather than come to a decision, we have seen him fend off closure and limitation. In the opening stanzas, we see Byron exploring the fictive possibilities offered by the idea of a young aristocrat embarking on a long foreign journey. He could develop all or any of these possibilities later. There was no need, at this point, to close Harold down, and the poem does little more than toy with various ideas that Byron clearly did not want to follow up, at least in isolation.

This calculated indecision is maintained when Harold arrives in Lisbon. Neither he nor the poem answer any of the expectations set up in the opening stanzas, but rather go on to explore a different mode of procedure. Harold becomes a sort of *Citoyen du Monde*, surveying 'as from "a tower upon a headlong rock" (*CHP* III, st. 41), the world of dispute and turmoil below'.[20] The poem seems to dispense with narrative and become a travelogue, sketching landscapes, offering political comment, and offering a sort of travel-guide for 'easy chair' (*CHP* I, 347) travellers:

> Then slowly climb the many-winding way,
> And frequent turn to linger as you go,
> From loftier rocks new loveliness survey,
> And rest ye at our 'Lady's house of woe'. (*CHP* I, 252–255)

These stanzas give us a foretaste of the kind of poem *Childe Harold* I and II will eventually become. The mode here is lyrical in that it offers a single speaker expressing his own observations and thought processes in the first-

---

20   Jerome McGann, *The Romantic Ideology: A Critical Investigation* (Chicago and London: University of Chicago Press, 1983), p. 138.

person. Moreover, stanzas 15 to 26 display something like the variety of 'kinds of composition' Byron claims to be aiming at in the Preface. In stanzas 15 to 26 that variety is projected through the figure of Harold, who offers description (stanza 19), travelling advice (stanza 21), and satire (stanza 25) 'as the humour strikes' him. However, this is still only a foretaste of what is to come. The poem does not continue in a lyrical mode, but shifts back to narrative in stanza 27, as the narrator reappears to assess the significance of the movement of consciousness the poem has just dramatized:

> So deem'd the Childe, as o'er the mountains he
> Did take his way in solitary guise:
> Sweet was the scene, yet soon he thought to flee,
> More restless than the swallow in the skies:
> Though here awhile he learn'd to moralize,
> For Meditation fix'd at times on him;
> And conscious Reason whisper'd to despise
> His early youth, misspent in maddest whim;
> But as he gaz'd on truth his aching eyes grew dim. (*CHP* I, 315–323)

The narrator reappears in the phrase 'So deem'd Harold', and tells us that we have been just been reading, in stanzas 15 to 26, a dramatization of Harold's consciousness. Yet, as Peter Thorslev suggests, the preceding stanzas dramatize 'sentiments peculiarly unfit for the Childe'.[21] He goes on to say that in stanza 27, Byron 'apologizes'.[22] If not quite an apology, there may well be an element of Byron covering his tracks here. Byron's habit of 'letting things happen'[23] as he writes has resulted in a 'transformation'[24] of Harold's character. He now seems to feel obliged to explain that transformation, retrospectively, by telling us that the 'the dissipated young cynic portrayed in the first few stanzas' has,[25] while looking on Spain, 'learn'd to moralize'. This shows a concern that Harold should be a credible fiction – that he should be consistent as a character. To ensure this credibility, Byron reintroduces the idea that the poem witnesses to a process of emotional maturation and 'a movement towards a better self'.

As we have seen, this idea was brought into play, but then fended off, earlier in the poem. Byron now brings it back into play to fend off Harold's disintegration as a fiction. Harold began 'Sore given to revel and ungodly glee', but moved on to 'flee' his 'fellow bacchanals'. Now we have a further step in this process of emotional or psychological maturation, as 'conscious Reason whispered to despise / His early youth'.

Though he may well have felt obliged to suggest this kind of progression, however, Byron clearly did not want to follow it up, or to limit himself to simply writing this kind of poem. Even while he is explaining what has gone before with the idea that Harold is 'growing up', he is fending off the

---

21   Thorslev, *The Byronic Hero*, p. 129.
22   Ibid., p. 130.
23   Nellist, 'Lyric Presence', p. 42.
24   Thorslev, *The Byronic Hero*, p. 130.
25   Ibid., pp. 129–130.

limitations which that idea imposes on what is to come. In other words, the idea is expedient but dangerously limiting. So, while asserting that Harold 'gazed on truth', Byron also insists that 'his aching eyes grew dim'. 'Reason whisper'd to despise his misspent youth', but only 'whisper'd'; Harold 'learn'd to moralize', but only 'for a while', and meditation fixed on him only 'at times'. Harold's response to reason, meditation, morality, indeed to the process of maturation which seems to have begun, is to 'flee':

> To horse! to horse! he quits, for ever quits
> A scene of peace, though soothing to his soul:
> Again he rouses from his moping fits,
> But seeks not now the harlot and the bowl.
> Onward he flies, nor fix'd as yet the goal
> Where he shall rest him on his pilgrimage;
> And o'er him many changing scenes must roll
> Ere toil his thirst for travel can assuage,
> Or he shall calm his breast, or learn experience sage. (*CHP* I, 324–332)

'Letting things happen' has led Byron to imply a psychological progress where he wants none. Having acknowledged that progress, he has Harold suddenly resist it by quitting the scene that inspired it, and fixes him somewhere between restlessness and his old satiation with 'the harlot and the bowl'. Byron again adjusts the way in which we read Harold, offering us a new viewpoint from which to look at him. And this manoeuvre once more fends off a kind of poem Byron does not want to write. By interpolating into Harold's character something of the eternal wanderer, Cain, Byron fixes Harold, for a moment, as simply 'restless': flying onward though with no fixed goal, driven simply by a 'thirst for travel'.

From this kind of fixity, possibilities open up rather than close. Harold's narrative can end when Harold's thirst for travel is assuaged 'or' when his breast is calm 'or' when he has learnt 'experience sage'. Alternatively, Harold can become a full-blown Cain, an eternal wanderer. Byron can keep in view all the possible narratives he set up at the beginning of the poem: a 'therapeutic movement' towards a happier existence, or at least a more resigned, calmer one; emotional maturation, or a 'movement towards a better self' achieved when he has learnt experience. But stanzas 27 and 28 effectively add another possible narrative structure, and another viewpoint on Harold: the eternal wanderer, cursed simply and forever to move on.

We have been watching Byron experiment with, and fend off, various narratives and, in the early stages of canto I, the impulse towards narrative is dominant.[26] However, we have touched upon another, lyrical, impulse in these early stanzas, and as the canto progresses this lyrical impulse comes more and more to dominate and structure the poem. As it does so, it pushes the whole business of narrative to the margin of the poem, and Harold becomes less and

---

[26]   We should nevertheless note the effect of reading 'To Ianthe' on reading the poem as a whole. From the outset there is a lyrical expectation, even if it is held off until stanza 15.

less important. As always, the poem pushes beyond any limitations it discovers, even the narrative limits it seemed to accept at the outset.

The shift out of narrative and into lyric starts in stanza 29, where the narrator begins, for the first time, to digress away from the subject of Harold. To begin with, this digression does not break away from Harold's narrative but remains anchored in it: Harold 'wends through' (*CHP* I, 345) his narrator's digression and his narrative frames and contains it.[27] But it is through digression that canto I of *Childe Harold* breaks away from narrative and moves into a lyrical mode. Between stanzas 29 and 34, the narrator appears simply to delay the narrative by digressing. After stanza 34, however, there is a natural pause, as he exhausts the subject of his digression, or rather, reaches the end of a free-flow of associated ideas. It would be natural, therefore, for him to return to Harold after this pause and, indeed, we might expect him to do so because at this point we have every reason to feel that we are reading a narrative poem. However, the narrator extends his digression rather than return to Harold's narrative, and it is precisely at this point that digression begins to take over the poem. The poem breaks clear of narrative and establishes a sequence based on lyricized engagements. Harold's narrator breaks clear of the limiting role of a narrator.

The jump from a narrative to a lyric mode is made conspicuous by the apostrophe that opens stanza 35: 'Oh, lovely Spain! renown'd romantic land!' (*CHP* I, 386). As Jonathan Culler suggests, 'the lyric is characteristically the triumph of the apostrophic',[28] but it is not just Byron's use of the apostrophe that marks his practice as increasingly lyrical, though Byron does repeatedly turn from his audience of readers and address the object observed, so that the poem is often 'not heard but overheard'.[29] A host of other features mark *Childe Harold* I and II as lyrical. The poem's style, for example, while original, is also in the tradition of the Greater Ode, the characteristic style of which, as Cowley put it, is a 'falling from one thing to another after an enthusiastical manner'.[30]

Another specifically lyrical feature of *Childe Harold* I and II is that they present us with 'a determinate speaker, whom we are invited to identify with the author himself, whose responses to the local scene are a spontaneous overflow of feeling and displace the landscape as the centre of poetic

---

[27]   That is to say that Byron's digression at this point serves to '"fill in" the narrative space separating the hinge functions' or 'hinge-points of the narrative' (Roland Barthes, 'Introduction to the Structural Analysis of Narratives', in *Image-Music-Text*, trans. by Stephen Heath [Glasgow: Fontana, 1977], p. 93).

[28]   Jonathan Culler, *The Pursuit of Signs: Semiotics, Literature, Deconstruction* (London and Henley: Routledge and Kegan Paul, 1981), p. 149.

[29]   Northrop Frye, *The Anatomy of Criticism: Four Essays* (Princeton: Princeton University Press, 1957), p. 5. This overheard quality is, for Frye, the defining feature of the lyric, in which the poet characteristically 'turns his back on his audience' (p. 271). According to Frye, the lyric is a genre that avoids 'the mimesis of direct address' (p. 293).

[30]   Quoted in David Lindley, *Lyric* (London and New York: Methuen, 1985), p. 14.

interest'.[31] Byron uses 'spatial, temporal and personal deictics' to transform the poem's narrator into 'a meditative persona' and 'the poem is presented as the discourse of a speaker who, at the moment of speaking, stands before a particular scene'.[32] The poem creates the impression of a consciousness spontaneously responding to, and thinking about, the scenes before him, and it is in this sense that the mode of the poem becomes definitively lyrical. Indeed, the 'ambiguous, even contradictory, attitudes' that run through the sections on Spain 'in quick succession' go a long way towards creating the impression of immediacy,[33] and the sense that we are watching 'a moving picture' of Byron's 'reactions' to Spain.[34]

This 'meditative persona' dominates canto I from stanza 35 until the end. As the sections on Spain progress, he offers incidental laments over Spain's fate and throws scorn and lashing irony at the architects of that fate, in a 'collection of lyrics' that explore 'the implications of images supplied' by Byron's journey through Spain.[35] As he does so, he moves inexorably towards a melancholic gloom that increasingly manifests itself as cynicism. It reaches a climax in stanza 42:

> There shall they rot – Ambition's honour'd fools!
> Yes, Honour decks the turf that wraps their clay!
> Vain Sophistry! in these behold the tools,
> The broken tools, that tyrants cast away
> By myriads, when they dare to pave their way
> With human hearts – to what? – a dream alone.
> Can despots compass aught that hails their sway?
> Or call with truth one span of earth their own,
> Save that wherein at last they crumble bone by bone? (*CHP* I, 450–458)

---

[31]   M. H. Abrams, 'Structure and Style in the Greater Romantic Lyric', in *The Correspondent Breeze: Essays on English Romanticism* (New York and London: Norton, 1984), p. 90.

[32]   Jonathan Culler, *Structuralist Poetics: Structuralism, Linguistics and the study of Literature* (London and Henley: Routledge and Kegan Paul, 1975), p. 167.

[33]   McGann, *Fiery Dust*, p. 49. Byron's various attitudes to war are especially contradictory: 'The 39 stanzas describing the war, out of the 93 which compose this canto, show a constant wavering of judgement, for the poet fluctuates between condemnation and enthusiastic celebration. His divided attitude is condensed in the oxymoronic apostrophe: "Oh Albuera! glorious field of grief"' (Diego Saglia, 'Spain and Byron's Construction of Place', in *Byron Journal* 22 [1994], p. 36). Saglia goes on to argue that 'Spain and the Peninsular War ... stir up a host of difficulties which Byron tries to spell out in writing' (p. 36).

Richard Cronin argues in a similar vein, but goes a step further than Saglia. According to Cronin, 'the problem of how the events' in Spain 'should be looked at' is 'the problem that the canto addresses' ('Mapping *Childe Harold* I and II', p. 20).

[34]   McGann, *Fiery Dust*, p.49. In the Preface, Byron tells us that, though the sections on Spain 'were composed from the author's observations' there (*CHP* I and II, Preface, 3–4), the poem was 'begun in Albania' (*CHP* I and II, Preface, 2). In 1817, Byron wrote: 'But I can't describe because my first impressions are always strong and confused – & my Memory *selects* & reduces them to order – like distance in the landscape – & blends them better – although they may be less distinct' (letter to John Murray of 9 May 1817, in *BLJ* V, p. 221).

[35]   Nellist, 'Lyric Presence', p. 46.

Canto I moves from being a narrative poem that centres on a fictional character, Childe Harold, to a lyrical poem that uses its narrator to dramatize a consciousness besieged by melancholy, but struggling to fight it off. Initially, the narrator tries to dismiss that melancholy by simply moving on to some other subject: 'Enough of Battle's minions!' (*CHP* I, 468). The first three lines of stanza 45 dismiss both the 'game of lives' (*CHP* I, 469) and the 'fame' (*CHP* I, 469) his own 'worthless lays' (*CHP* I, 467) offer, which 'will scarce reanimate their clay' (*CHP* I, 470). However, the poem goes on to dramatize a tension between, on the one hand, sentiment, sympathy, and emotional response, and on the other hand, the desire to remain detached and objective. Such detachment proves elusive. While it seems, in stanza 44, that the poem is on the verge of detaching itself from 'Battle's minions', the thought that 'thousands fall to deck some single name' (*CHP* I, 471) reawakens the scorn of stanza 42, which now mutates into the sneering cynicism and damning irony of the second quatrain: the dead may as well die in war as prove their country's shame by living, or by dying in some domestic feud.

Cynicism retains its hold and seems strong enough to overwhelm any attempt to fight clear of it. The determination to do so remains, though. In stanza 45, for example, the narrator turns back to Harold: 'Full swiftly Harold wends his lonely way' (*CHP* I, 477). Byron hoped, presumably, to move the poem on from the melancholy prospect of war, which dominates the section on Spain, by returning to the story with which he began. The word 'swiftly' certainly seems to articulate a desire to move on, and yet almost immediately the narrator is distracted back to the prospect of war. Even in Seville, 'Soon, soon shall Conquest's fiery foot intrude' (*CHP* I, 480). Resigning himself, the narrator attempts to achieve some degree of detachment by retreating into clever, allegorical, but, most importantly, abstract images. Yet even this retreat is haunted by the idea of 'worthless lays'. The narrator cannot become entirely detached from the consciousness of 'the coming doom' (I, 486), and his retreat into increasingly satirical abstractions is finally undermined by the implications of the word 'kind' (*CHP* I, 494) at the end of stanza 46. 'Reality' intrudes via a sort of pathos, and ultimately his retreat into an allegorical idiom turns into an articulation of the gloom he had been trying to escape.

In fact, the poem continues to use its narrator to dramatize a battle against melancholic, cynical gloom through to stanza 54. But the narrator breaks free of this gloom here, for a time at least. He recollects the 'Maid of Saragoza',[36] and the recollection seems to cheer him up. She offers a sufficiently unusual and impressive instance of 'glory' to distract him, at last, from his contemplations of 'grief' (*CHP* I, 459). This 'Spanish maid' (*CHP* I, 558) leads in turn to the recollection of 'Spain's maids' (*CHP* I, 585), and, by stanza 58, eulogy has replaced elegy and nostalgia has replaced cynicism.

All this demonstrates how completely a lyric persona has taken centre stage, even by stanza 58. Harold is pushed to the margin. The poem no longer seems to be a narrative at all, or, more precisely, it seems to be something more than the narrative it contains. When the narrator does return to the subject

---

[36] Byron goes on to talk more about the 'Maid' in a prose note to the poem. He tells us that when 'the author was at Seville she walked daily in the Prado, decorated with medals and orders, by command of the Junta' (*Works* II, p. 189).

of Harold in stanza 82, Harold has become simply one subject among many which occur to him as he writes. By stanza 59, in which he tells us that: 'now / I strike my strain' (*CHP* I, 604–605), the poem belongs to its speaker, who remains our focus of attention until the end of the canto. We watch him as he strikes his strain, so to speak. And the poem has shifted not only from being a narrative sequence to being a lyrical one. It has also moved into a loco-descriptive mode. By stanza 63, the poem's 'theme' (*CHP* I, 644) is no longer Harold, but

> ... the land, the sons, the maids of Spain;
> Her fate, to every freeborn bosom dear. (*CHP* I, 641–642)

Though it begins as a narrative, then, canto I of *Childe Harold's Pilgrimage* develops into an extended lyric, or perhaps more accurately, 'a collection of lyrics', relatively early on. On the one hand, this 'collection of lyrics' explores 'the implications supplied by the European journey' Byron took between 1809 and 1811. On the other hand, it dramatizes a consciousness in the act of recalling, responding to, and writing about, a series of scenes abroad. Byron's insertion of stanza 91, on the death of John Wingfield, in which 'woe / Bursts from' his lyric persona's 'heart' (*CHP* I, 927–928) testifies to the extent to which that persona has been fixed at the centre of the poem, and to the extent to which the poem has moved away from a narrative mode, and into a lyrical one.

However, while we might say that this seems to be an accurate account of the poem's development, we would also have to say that it is an incomplete one. The poem manifestly evolves away from narrative, but Byron does not relinquish Harold and narrative altogether. Though Harold is increasingly only of marginal importance, the poem is still formally a narrative account of Harold's journey:

> Here is one fytte of Harold's Pilgrimage:
> Ye who of him may further seek to know,
> Shall find some tidings in a future page,
> If he that rhymeth now may scribble moe. (*CHP* I, 945–948)

Throughout canto II, the poem offers 'tidings' of Harold, reporting the progress of his journey, and canto I is not simply 'one fytte' of his journey in a notional sense. It has followed his progress from England to Lisbon, his journey through Spain to Seville, and at the end of the canto he is waiting at Cadiz to be urged 'across the wave' (*CHP* II, 137) to Gibraltar in canto II.

Let us turn back to Harold, then, and Byron's continued development of him at the margin of the poem. After a long absence, during which the poem's narrator has moved to the foreground, Harold reappears in stanza 82. Even here, well into the poem, Byron is shaping and reshaping, 'inventing' his hero, and still deciding what viewpoint he is going to adopt and what kind of narrative, if any, Harold is going to occupy. Harold is 'now ... unmov'd' (*CHP* I, 812) by love. The 'now' dates back to his satiation, so that we are not to deduce that any further change has come over Harold in the meantime. A more recent change is suggested in the lines that follow:

> And lately had he learn'd with truth to deem
> Love has no gift so grateful as his wings:
> How fair, how young, how soft soe'er he seem,
> Full from the fount of Joy's delicious springs
> Some bitter o'er the flowers its bubbling venom flings. (*CHP* I, 814–818)

This is the beginning of a reconciliation to the fact that 'he lov'd but one / And that lov'd one, alas could ne'er be his'. Harold is still bitter, but the implication seems to be that his own love is waning: 'Love has no gift as grateful as his wings'. It is the word 'grateful' that is most telling. There is a degree of relief in it that suggests the flight of a passion which is burdensome because unrequited.

At the beginning of the poem, the hint that Harold leaves England to recover from a failed love affair is swamped by the suggestion that his kind of 'love' is a 'pollution' and short-lived: he would have 'soon ... left her charms for vulgar bliss'. Here the idea is brought back into play. The first stage of Harold's recovery is a movement from idealism to a sort of stoic realism, heard especially in the last two lines of the previous quotation. The second stage is exhaustion:

> But Passion raves herself to rest, or flies;
> And Vice, that digs her own voluptuous tomb,
> Has buried long his hopes, no more to rise. (*CHP* I, 823–825)

Harold's love is waning, his passion nearly at rest. This is not far from the 'calm' suggested as one possible end of Harold's journey. Once again, however, as soon as the poem seems to be adopting a particular line, it changes direction. Harold's recovery, incomplete as it is, stops here, and proves to be no recovery at all:

> Pleasure's pall'd victim! life-abhorring gloom
> Wrote on his faded brow curst Cain's unresting doom. (*CHP* I, 826–827)

Byron suddenly shifts from the idea of a slow recovery, to the idea of permanent despondency. As he does so, Harold's 'doom', that is, Byron's final decision, at least for the purposes of *Childe Harold* I and II, as to Harold's nature as a character and the kind of narrative he will occupy, emerges. He stands as 'hopeless', 'life-abhorring', and 'curst' simply to wander, to share 'Cain's unresting doom'. Harold's first journey, as it finally discloses itself, is not after all significant on emotional or psychological grounds, at least not in the sense of being a narrative of increasing despondency, of slow recovery, or of a 'movement towards a better self'. His character in *Childe Harold* I and II is finally formed by the satiety which began his restlessness: he remains 'Pleasure's pall'd victim', and is defined as a character only by that same restlessness. The 'secret woe' (*CHP* I, 841) he bears is 'not love, it is not hate, / Nor low Ambition's honours lost' (*CHP* I, 845–846), but

> ... that settled, ceaseless gloom
> The fabled Hebrew wanderer bore;

That will not look beyond the tomb,
  But cannot hope for rest before. (*CHP* I, 852–855)

The role Byron finally invents for Harold in *Childe Harold* I and II, then, is that of a 'gloomy wanderer' (*CHP* II, 137). This may be part of a strategy to lift the gloom away from the increasingly lyricized and foregrounded narrator, who, as we have seen, battles against his own melancholy. Byron may well have been hoping to project some of that melancholy on to Harold, and so to some extent free-up the narrator. And once Byron has closed Harold down, so to speak, his narrative is not a quest, but simply an account of his gloom-laden wanderings. From this point on, much of what we hear of Harold is simply that he 'saw ... The glittering minarets of Tepalen' (*CHP* II, 491–492); 'pass'd the sacred Haram's silent tower'(*CHP* II, 496); 'saw' (*CHP* II, 586); 'did address / Himself to quit' (*CHP* II, 613–14); 'was receiv'd a welcome guest' (*CHP* II, 628); 'at little distance stood / And view'd' (*CHP* II, 640–641). After stanza 29 of canto I, Harold shows very little interest in, or evidence of being changed by, anything he sees or experiences. His thematic contribution to canto II is well described by Byron in the Addition to the Preface. He shows

> that early perversion of mind and morals leads to satiety of past pleasures and disappointment in new ones, and that even the beauties of nature, and the stimulus of travel (except for ambition, the most powerful of all excitements) are lost on a soul so constituted, or rather misdirected. (*CHP* I and II, Addition to the Preface, 88–92)

According to the Preface, Harold's wanderings offered Byron a loose but coherent structure into which he could insert his own experience. Not, in the end, through Harold himself, however. Harold is, in some ways, a fictional projection of Byron, but it is the figure of Harold's narrator that Byron finally fixed on as his poetic persona. Harold's narrative provided a structure into which Byron could slip commentary, digressions, and observations in the gaps between Harold's departures and arrivals.[37] But Harold is, ultimately, no more than 'A fictitious character ... introduced for the sake of giving some connexion to the piece' (*CHP* I and II, Preface, 11–12).

Indeed, it eventually seems as if Byron is running two quite distinct poems alongside one another: a narrative account of Harold's journey and a lyric account of his own. It is tempting to say that his aim in doing so was to find a way of facilitating and including material and experiences that would perhaps have to be excluded if he were to choose one kind of poem, and if he were to employ only one poetic persona. But equally, if Byron was to keep the poem open to a variety of impulses, he needed to contain various kinds of response and various kinds of mood that threatened to swamp the poem and exclude other responses and moods. Fixing Harold as a sort of Cain-like tourist, a despondent spectator ever driven to find new scenes at which to spectate, was,

---

[37]   If we wilfully read the poem simply as Harold's narrative, Byron's digressions take on the formal significance of Barthes's 'catalysers', each of which 'accelerates, delays, gives fresh impetus to the discourse' ('Introduction to the Structural Analysis of Narratives', pp. 94, 95).

I suggest, a way of using Harold to free the narrator, a little, from the gloom that was finding its way into the poem.

We can find some support for this suggestion if we try and peer into that 'nearly inaccessible zone where the possibility of a work's existence is being decided'.[38] We are helped in this by knowing that at an early stage in the poem's composition, Byron had very different ideas for Harold, even at this point. For some reason, Byron pointedly altered those earlier plans, making Harold a figure of melancholy isolation rather than, as appears to have been the idea, a figure of rejuvenation and sexual contentment. The remnants of such a plan can still be found in stanza 84:

> Still he beheld, nor mingled with the throng;
> But view'd them not with misanthropic hate:
> Fain would he now have join'd the dance, the song;
> But who may smile that sinks beneath his fate?
> Nought that he saw his sadness could abate:
> Yet once he struggled 'gainst the demon's sway,
> And as in Beauty's bower he pensive sate,
> Pour'd forth this unpremeditated lay,
> To charms as fair as those that sooth'd his happier day. (*CHP* I, 828–836)

Harold moves closer once more to the world he fled in England, feeling the urge to rejoin 'the dance, the song'. The narrator treats this temptation with his tongue rather in his cheek: despite sinking 'beneath his fate', despite his 'sadness', Harold can still manage to sing a song to a beautiful woman. Nevertheless, Harold is moving back in from the margin of society. The song Harold originally sang after stanza 84 was 'The Girl of Cadiz'.[39] It began:

> Oh never talk again to me
>   Of Northern charms and British ladies;
> It has not been your lot to see,
>   Like me, the lovely Girl of Cadiz. (1–4)[40]

If we read this as part of the poem's fictional narrative, Harold's recovery now seems complete. His love of one 'British lady' had been waning, his passion coming to rest, and Harold had withdrawn into a state of restless detachment. Now his ex-paramour is eclipsed by the Girl of Cadiz, who possesses 'charms as fair as those that sooth'd his happier day'. A new love and a new passion replace the old, and Harold is revitalized by a girl

---

[38]   This is where Paul de Man claims that the criticism of George Poulet 'reaches as by instinct' ('The Literary Self as Origin: The Work of Georges Poulet', in *Blindness and Insight: Essays in the Rhetoric of Contemporary Criticism* [London: Methuen, 1983], p. 97).

[39]   It might be argued that by inserting songs into the poem, Byron is offering the main body of the poem as something distinct from lyric. Yet, as we have seen, the main body, too, becomes increasingly, if perhaps covertly, lyrical.

[40]   Quotations from 'The Girl of Cadiz' are taken from *Works* I. Line references are given after the quotations in the text.

> ... that meets your love
> Ne'er taunts you with a mock denial,
> For every thought is bent to prove
> Her passion in the hour of trial. (33–36)

Harold, we surmise, has rediscovered his own passion too, while the hint of sexual freedom in the last two lines of this quotation might suggest, if viewed from a particular perspective, that Harold has returned, revitalized, to being 'Sore given to revel and ungodly glee'. All this indicates a very different history for Harold from the one we read in the final version of the poem. And our brief look at 'The Girl of Cadiz' supports the idea that Byron had in mind, among other things, a narrative in which Harold moved from being loved by none to finding at least some kind of contentment in lovemaking. Byron's sudden change of heart, and his decision to replace 'The Girl of Cadiz' with 'To Inez', suggests, however, that he came to see Harold as a way of articulating the poem's growing sense of despondency: in this case at least, as he wrote that despondency in, he decided to do so through Harold. Equally, the narrator's struggles against that despondency demonstrate the need to find some way to contain it, or of channelling it off. Harold's fate was sealed.

And yet Byron did not finally succeed in disengaging the narrator from the pervading sense of gloom which ultimately overwhelmed the poem. Indeed, Harold and his narrator, far from ending the poem as very different personalities, end the poem as very similar ones, as McGann has demonstrated.[41]

This does not mean that we are wrong to suggest that at some time during the poem's composition, Byron wanted to concentrate its gloom in the figure of Harold, and to use the narrator to experiment with other moods, idioms, and to articulate other kinds of responses and experiences. The narrator does, after all, delight in the maids of Spain, revel in the fact that he is actually looking at Parnassus, and look on the festivity of Istanbul with no small degree of pleasure. We have already seen that Byron's plans for *Childe Harold* I and II were constantly evolving even as he was writing. Nevertheless, if at one time Byron projected the narrator's gloom on to Harold, in order to free the narrator so that other kinds of experience could be projected through him, he did a U-turn, so to speak, when making his final corrections and additions to *Childe Harold* I and II. These corrections and additions, as McGann argues, did much to transform the poem into a record of 'the step-by-step process of Byron's "Consciousness awaking to her woes"':[42] a record projected entirely through Byron's highly lyricized narrator-figure.

Let us turn to the later stages of the evolution of *Childe Harold* I and II, then. Even while *Childe Harold* is in many ways derived from various non-lyrical topographical and panoramic precursors, it eventually fixes a lyrical persona at its centre. And it is significant in terms of our discussion that though Byron may for a while have had other plans, he decided to use that lyrical persona to dramatize an 'awaking' to 'woes'. In this departure from the

---

[41]   McGann was, I think, the first critic to point out that in stanza 97 of canto II, 'the narrating poet's mood and opinions distinctly echo Harold's' (*Fiery Dust*, p. 70).

[42]   McGann, *Fiery Dust*, p. 105, quoting *CHP* I, 941.

tradition to which the cantos look back, we see Byron beginning to look to more contemporary precursors, and beginning to explore other new ways of writing. Byron's handling of his lyric persona, as he becomes more and more occupied with his 'woes', suggests that he looked to the Romantic Lyric tradition for models of procedure. This may seem unlikely when we think of Byron as a writer of lyrics *per se*. Byron belonged to the Restoration lyric tradition of song rather than that of extended meditation – a tradition which came down to him through, among others, Thomas Moore. Yet, much of what M. H. Abrams describes as characteristic of the 'Greater Romantic Lyric' is also characteristic of the first two cantos of *Childe Harold*:[43]

> Some of the poems are called odes, while others approach the ode in having lyric magnitude and a serious subject, feelingly meditated. They present a determinate speaker in a particularized, and usually a localized, outdoor setting, whom we overhear as he carries on, in a fluent vernacular which rises easily to a formal speech, a sustained colloquy, sometimes with himself or with the outer scene, but more frequently with a silent human auditor, present or absent. The speaker begins with a description of the landscape; an aspect or change of aspect in the landscape evokes a varied but integral process of memory, thought, anticipation, and feeling which remains closely involved with the outer scene. In the course of this meditation the lyric speaker achieves an insight, faces up to a tragic loss, comes to a moral decision, or resolves an emotional problem.[44]

Even the most cursory reading of *Childe Harold* I and II shows us that many of the lyrical sequences which constitute the cantos 'approach the ode' in the manner described by Abrams. They present us with a determinate speaker who is localized at various places in Spain, Greece, Albania, and Turkey, and many begin with description but develop into articulations of 'memory, thought, anticipation, and feeling' in a way similar to Wordsworth's lyrics. The cantos are a 'sustained colloquy' with Europe, its history, landscape, art and present. And while that colloquy is conducted in a manner that is closer to Thomson's *Seasons* than it is to Wordsworth's lyrics,[45] Byron publicly 'faces up to a tragic loss', indeed, to a series of tragic losses. Finally, like the speaker of 'Tintern Abbey', or 'This Lime Tree Bower my Prison', the speaker of

---

[43] The term 'Greater Romantic Lyric' is Abrams's. See 'Structure and Style in the Greater Romantic Lyric'. Abrams claims that 'Byron ... did not write in this mode at all' (p. 76). McGann, on the other hand, has suggested that 'Byron did write on the mode' but 'took considerable liberties with the form'. McGann also suggests that *'Childe Harold's Pilgrimage* has a number of set piece passages that correspond to the form' of the Greater Romantic Lyric ('Byron and the Anonymous Lyric', in *Byron Journal* 20 [1992], p. 44, n. 14) and I want to build on this suggestion here.

[44] 'Structure and Style in the Greater Romantic Lyric', pp. 76–77. See also McGann's description of the 'conventions' of this distinctive lyric form in 'Byron and the Anonymous Lyric' (p. 36).

[45] We should also note, however, that Byron, like Wordsworth, read and was influenced by Gray, who contributed to the process by which the topographical poem became lyricized.

Childe Harold I and II is obliged to make moral decisions about the scenes he observes, to articulate those decisions, to revise them and reform them.

Cantos I and II of *Childe Harold*, then, employ various procedures more usually found in poems like 'The Eolian Harp', 'Frost At Midnight', 'Tintern Abbey', and 'Ode: Intimations of Immortality', and there is a real sense in which we can read cantos I and II of Byron's poem as we read the Greater Romantic Lyric, despite the obvious differences of scale and form.[46] Is this similarity merely a coincidence? I suggest not, for it is entirely possible that Byron was consciously experimenting with the mode of the Greater Romantic Lyric in *Childe Harold* I and II.[47] He had read and reviewed Wordsworth's *Poems* of 1807, which included 'Ode: Intimations of Immortality', and in that review he had praised *Lyrical Ballads*, which, of course, concluded with 'Tintern Abbey'.[48] He went on to experiment extensively with Wordsworthian modes of procedure in *Childe Harold* III.

There his experimentation takes on board the idealism of Wordsworth's poetry. In *Childe Harold* I and II, however, while Byron may have adopted some of Wordsworth's procedures, he rejects what we might call the ideology which underpins Wordsworth's practice as a poet. Indeed, the overall direction taken by *Childe Harold* I and II is, I suggest, a direct result of this part adoption and part rejection of Wordsworthian practice. Let us look briefly at the model of Wordsworth.

The issue which concerns Wordsworth most frequently in his lyric verse is a present feeling of being alienated, excluded even, from the universal harmony offered by the 'natural milieu' by which his mind was 'fostered' in childhood.[49] This feeling of alienation can have many causes, one of which is a burdensome awareness of political and/or social ills. This is the case in 'Tintern Abbey', as McGann powerfully demonstrates in *The Romantic Ideology*.[50] McGann, who here reads the poem from a quasi-Marxist position, goes on to argue that Wordsworth overcomes his entanglement in a political present by replacing 'an image and landscape of contradiction', namely that between cottage dwellers and vagrants, 'with one dominated by "the power / Of Harmony"(48–9)'. We do not need to share the Marxist perspective of *The Romantic Ideology* to recognize the validity of this insight. Wordsworth's

---

[46]   As a sequence of Spenserian stanzas, cantos I and II of *Childe Harold's Pilgrimage* are markedly different from the majority of these lyrics. Coleridge and Wordsworth do not usually use stanza forms at all in their lyrics, and when they do it is most often the Royal stanza. See, for example, 'Dejection: An Ode' and 'Resolution and Independence'.

[47]   Karl Kroeber argues that the whole of *Childe Harold* 'belongs to the category of the Romantic journey poem and is in several ways like Wordsworth's *Prelude*'(*Romantic Narrative Art* [Madison, Milwaukee and London: University of Wisconsin Press, 1966], p. 137). Byron, of course, could not have read *The Prelude*, but as Abrams points out, *The Prelude* is 'an epic expansion of the mode of *Tintern Abbey*' ('Structure and Style in the Greater Romantic Lyric', p. 79), which Byron had read. McGann specifically compares the mode of *Childe Harold* I and II and the mode of *The Prelude* in *Fiery Dust* (see pp. 32–35).

[48]   For Byron's review of Wordsworth's *Poems* (1807), see *Lord Byron: The Complete Miscellaneous Prose*, ed. by Andrew Nicholson (Oxford: Clarendon Press, 1991), pp. 8–10.

[49]   Abrams, 'Style and Structure in the Greater Romantic Lyric', p. 79.

[50]   McGann, *The Romantic Ideology*, pp. 85–92.

strategy, as McGann rightly says, is to 'not fill the eye of the mind with external and soulless images, but with "forms of beauty"(24) through which we can "see into the life of things"(50)'.[51]

Such a transcendence of ills is also available, for Wordsworth, when those ills are not political. A physical dislocation from nature during which the self is trapped in the city is also recalled in 'Tintern Abbey'. In this case, the immediate situation is forgotten in favour of the memory of moments like that described in the poem. Much of Wordsworth's poetry, and virtually all of his shorter lyric poetry, is made up of such 'spots of time' by which 'our minds / Are nourished and invisibly repaired' (*The Prelude* [1805], XI, 257, 263–264), even in the recollection of them.[52]

If we put 'Tintern Abbey' alongside cantos I and II of *Childe Harold*, we quickly see that however different the two poems are, they are both centred in a sense of alienation and both look to moments of communion with the natural world as a means of transcending that alienation. The alienation both poems describe, we might say, is that of belonging to a present that has lost its connection with the 'glorious' past, whether personal or cultural, which preceded it. In *Childe Harold* I and II, perhaps more overtly than in Wordsworth's poetry, it is particularly the alienation of living in 'the ruins of history and of culture',[53] but in moments very like Wordsworth's 'spots of time', Byron considers the prospect of transcending even his overt sense of historical ruin. Such moments are recalled in stanza 25 of canto II:

> To sit on rocks, to muse o'er flood and fell,
> To slowly trace the forest's shady scene,
> Where things that own not man's dominion dwell,
> And mortal foot hath ne'er, or rarely been;
> To climb the trackless mountain all unseen,
> With the wild flock that never needs a fold;
> Alone o'er steeps and foaming falls to lean;
> This is not solitude; 'tis but to hold
> Converse with Nature's charms, and view her stores unroll'd. (*CHP* II, 217–225)

Is Byron inviting us to recall the kind of poetic transcendence offered by Wordsworth? If not, he is clearly toying with, or 'meditating upon',[54] an idea of escaping into a transcendent communion with nature that is very close to the Wordsworth paradigm. In a Wordsworth lyric, precisely this kind of experience would be transformed into 'a sufficient aesthetic whole',[55] an instance and demonstration of one of Wordsworth's basic ideological premises, namely, that 'consciousness ... can set one free of the ruins of

---

[51]   Ibid., p. 86, quoting 'Tintern Abbey'.

[52]   All quotations from *The Prelude* (1805) are taken from *The Prelude 1799, 1805, 1850: Authoritative Texts, Contexts and Reception, Recent Critical Essays*, ed. by Jonathan Wordsworth, M. H. Abrams, and Stephen Gill (New York and London: Norton, 1979). Book and line references are given after quotations in the text.

[53]   McGann, *The Romantic Ideology*, p. 91.

[54]   McGann, 'Byron and the Anonymous Lyric', p. 37.

[55]   Abrams, 'Style and Structure in the Greater Romantic Lyric', p. 82.

history and culture',[56] indeed, free of 'aught of heavier or more deadly weight' (*The Prelude* [1805], XI, 261).

But it is at this point that we see Byron depart from Wordsworth, for having moved into a distinctly Wordsworthian poetic territory, Byron goes on to distance himself from it. Rather than isolate a moment of visionary insight and offer it as evidence of an ability to transcend the 'weight' of existence, Byron places the recollection of spiritual 'converse' with the natural world alongside the recollection of its opposite. For Byron, to write about moments of 'transcendental' experience is insufficient, aesthetically or otherwise, and *Childe Harold* I and II do not isolate and hold up such moments. Instead, they follow them up, as in stanza 26, with the solitude of being in crowds:

> But midst the crowd, the hum, the shock of men,
> To hear, to see, to feel, and to posses,
> And roam along, the world's tir'd denizen
> ...
> This is to be alone; this, this is solitude! (*CHP* II, 226–234)

When Wordsworth recalls similar 'lonely ... hours of weariness' ('TA', 25–27) in 'Tintern Abbey',[57] he insists that he can, by means of memory, escape such weariness: through the 'blessed mood' ('TA', 37) bestowed by the memory of visionary moments, 'the weary weight / Of all this unintelligible world, / Is lightened' ('TA', 39–41). In cantos I and II of *Childe Harold*, on the other hand, Byron insists on the very kinds of experience that Wordsworth claims to have transcended. Why?

One possible answer to this question is that Byron recognized that while Wordsworth's poetry insists on the idea of a permanently available means of escaping the weariness of existence, it never completely escapes that weariness. In 'Tintern Abbey', for instance, Wordsworth recalls the restorative influence of memory as it has 'Oft' manifested itself 'in lonely rooms' ('TA', 25). That word 'Oft' obscures but also inadvertently preserves moments when 'sensations sweet' ('TA', 27) did not come, when 'pleasure' ('TA', 31) could not be recalled, and when the comforting sense of universal 'harmony' ('TA', 48) eluded him. Nor does the poem completely fend off the haunting knowledge that there are more moments to come when Wordsworth will need consoling.

Indeed, Wordsworth's poetry never really solves the problem of being repeatedly subjected to moments when consolation is needed. Nor does Wordsworth deal with his own memory of those times, darkly hinted at but no more, when memory failed to console and rejuvenate him. Poems like 'The

---

[56] McGann's position in *The Romantic Ideology* is that this is 'the grand illusion of every Romantic poet'. He goes on to argue that the 'idea continues as one of the most important shibboleths of our culture, especially – and naturally – at its highest levels' (*The Romantic Ideology*, p. 91).

[57] All quotations from 'Lines written a few miles above Tintern Abbey' are taken from *The Poetical Works of William Wordsworth*, ed. by E. de Selincourt, vol. II (Oxford: Clarendon Press, 1944). Line references are given after quotations in the text, and are prefaced by the abbreviation 'TA'.

Ruined Cottage', 'Tintern Abbey', and 'Ode: Intimations of Immortality' do not articulate such moments. They work for this very reason.[58]

Similarly, the social, historical, and political matters that seem to impinge on Wordsworth's consciousness at the beginning of 'Tintern Abbey' are simply eclipsed, or as McGann argues, displaced.[59] One set of associations suggested by the landscape is temporarily replaced with another, and social and political matters are pushed to one side and ignored. Wordsworth, we might say, offers a visionary solution to problems he does not confront, and avoids dealing with society, politics, and history by turning away from them and resisting their encroachment of his consciousness.[60]

Did Byron recognize this in Wordsworth's verse, and in *Childe Harold* I and II does he insist on what Wordsworth evades in answer to that evasion? The cantos certainly 'reopen the horizon of feeling' where Wordsworth's poetry closes it down,[61] while history 'intervenes with increasing urgency as the cantos develop'.[62] And though Byron's 'commitment to unlimited experience',[63] and his faithfulness to history and to various political causes all help to explain his insistence on those areas of human experience that Wordsworth's poetry avoids, they do not explain it entirely. For in that insistence we also hear a rejection of the idea that humanity can transcend the 'weary weight' of its personal, political, and historical existence. In cantos I and II of *Childe Harold*, consciousness is thrown back on to a sense of its own deprivation and alienation, and on to 'the ruins of history and culture', despite

---

[58]   As James Soderholm points out, however, lines 49–50 of 'Tintern Abbey' do seem to articulate a moment of sudden doubt in the very idea that Wordsworth's 'memories of the Wye are as spiritually profound, even redemptive, as he had believed' ('Dorothy Wordsworth's Return to Tintern Abbey', in *New Literary History* 26:2 (Spring 1995), p. 311). But, as Soderholm goes on to argue, this doubt is only allowed into the poem very briefly and in the lines that immediately follow, 'conventional apostrophe revitalizes' Wordsworth, reassuring him of the 'soundness of his beliefs' (p. 311).

[59]   For McGann's reading of the poem, and his demonstration of Wordsworth's 'strategy of displacement' (p. 90), see *The Romantic Ideology*, pp. 85–92.

[60]   'Many recent critics of "Tintern Abbey" use the poem ... to highlight' Wordsworth's 'resistance to the social' (Soderholm, 'Dorothy Wordsworth's Return to Tintern Abbey', p. 314) and clearly there is such a resistance in 'Tintern Abbey'. Nevertheless, Soderholm recalls 'early critics' of the poem (like Robert Langbaum, Geoffrey Hartman and Harold Bloom) who saw a 'socializing' of Wordsworth's 'private' experience in the poet's address to his sister at the end of the poem (p. 314). And while much recent criticism has seen 'the turn to Dorothy as lacking the social dimension earlier critics were happy to acknowledge' (p. 314), Soderholm offers an interesting case in support of the idea that Wordsworth's address to his sister, if not a gesture towards society at large, is 'an authentic gesture at the social world' Dorothy 'represents' (p. 316).

[61]   McGann, 'Byron and the Anonymous Lyric', p. 33.

[62]   Curran, *Poetic Form and British Romanticism*, p. 153. In canto I, the fate of Spain replaces Harold as the poem's 'theme' (*CHP* I, 644), while in canto II, the 'woes' of Greece 'pervade' the poet's 'strain' (*CHP* II, 751). And even when he is set upon describing the 'merriment' (*CHP* II, 747) of Istanbul, and certainly absorbed by its festivity, Byron cannot fend off the thought, nor is he prepared to leave it out of the poem, of hearts which 'lurk' among the jollity and which throb with the 'secret pain' (*CHP* II, 775) of the 'true-born son of Greece' (*CHP* II, 783).

[63]   McGann, 'Byron and the Anonymous Lyric', p. 33.

visionary moments and the sense of transcendence they bring with them. For Byron, the mind cannot hold on to, or recall at will, moments of communion, or moments of insight into 'the life of things'. It is always doomed to return to its own alienation bereft of the comfort found in such moments:

> ... clay will sink
> Its spark immortal, envying it the light
> To which it mounts, as if to break the link
> That keeps us from yon heaven which woos us to its brink. (*CHP* III, 123–126)

These lines from *Childe Harold* III read like a direct answer to the Wordsworthian claim that 'consciousness ... can set one free' of 'aught of heavier or more deadly weight', and it is an answer which is implicit throughout *Childe Harold* I and II. Where Wordsworth's Greater Romantic Lyrics stop just short of this inevitable sinkage, breaking the 'spots of time' they lyricize 'out of time',[64] *Childe Harold* I and II firmly fix those 'spots of time' in the march of time. The cantos follow consciousness as it moves beyond these moments of vision, or of forgetful transcendence, refusing to endorse the idealistic Wordsworthian notion that consciousness can rest in, or gain permanent access to, visionary transcendence. Instead, *Childe Harold* I and II testify to the idea that 'the weight / Of Earth' always 'recoils upon us' (*CHP* IV, 464–465):

> ... he who there at such an hour hath been
> Will wistful linger on that hallow'd spot;
> Then slowly tear him from the 'witching scene,
> Sigh forth one wish that such had been his lot,
> Then turn to hate a world he had almost forgot. (*CHP* II, 239–244)

In this instance, Byron's movement beyond a visionary 'spot of time' results in 'a shocking inversion of the conventional romantic topos of nature'.[65] And we might argue that, as part of Byron's 'lyric satire style', such movements beyond visionary moments play a significant part in the 'satire upon a normative mode of romantic writing' that McGann sees at work in that style.[66] But in his simultaneous rejection of Wordsworthian idealism and adoption of various Wordsworthian procedures, Byron also found a poetic idiom that in many ways helped to facilitate the 'variety' he was seeking. Like Wordsworth, Byron could write lyrical sequences in a meditative mode which foregrounds the speaker and which creates the impression of moving freely and intimately with the 'thought ... and feeling' of that speaker. But where Wordsworth necessarily limits himself to a single experience, or to the achievement of a particular mood, Byron's lyricism can and does move

---

[64]   Abrams, 'Style and Structure in the Greater Romantic Lyric', p. 81.
[65]   McGann, 'Byron and the Anonymous Lyric', p. 37. 'In simplest terms', McGann goes on to say, 'Byron's passage through a romantic meditation on nature does not conclude in a Wordsworthian "tranquil restoration" but in a characteristically Byronic turn to passion and savagery' (p. 37).
[66]   Ibid., p. 30.

perpetually between multiple experiences and multiple moods. Here, in one sense, is the freedom to 'give full scope to my inclination'.

Oddly, then, Byron discovers one kind of poetic freedom while insisting on human limitation. As we have seen, Byron follows consciousness into, but also beyond, the moments of vision allowed it, and as he does so, dramatizes a kind of inevitable return to a sense of solitude and alienation that is bereft of the consolations glimpsed in momentary intimations of universal harmony. For Byron, at the end of *Childe Harold* I and II, there is no escaping or transcending that solitude and alienation. Thus, while it is in the crowd that we know and suffer solitude, we can only ever 'almost' forget it, even in moments of communion with 'Nature'. And ultimately we have to turn back to our solitude. Similarly, despite the fact that both the narrator of *Childe Harold* I and II and the Harold of *Childe Harold* III can people 'the stars' (*CHP* III, 118–119), neither are 'happy' since they are unable to keep their mind to the imaginative 'flight' (*CHP* III, 122–123) of doing so: their 'clay' sinks their 'spark immortal', and 'penn'd' in the 'fold' (*CHP* III, 652) of 'Man's dwellings'(*CHP* III, 127), they become 'Restless and worn, and stern and wearisome' (*CHP* III, 128).

It is with this sense of inevitability, the sense that consciousness will always fall away from the consolations offered to it in visionary moments and back into its accustomed solitude and alienation, unable to recall those visionary consolations, that the first two cantos of *Childe Harold* end: 'Then must I plunge again into the crowd ... ?' (*CHP* II, 909).

We began by arguing, with Brian Nellist, that cantos I and II of *Childe Harold's Pilgrimage* are constantly inventing themselves. We can now look back and offer a description of the 'finished product'. The cantos begin as a narrative, but one that is constantly fending off closure by reinventing itself. Experimentation with narrative then becomes an experimental move beyond narrative, as the cantos shift from a narrative to a lyric sequence, and from Harold to the narrator. As they do so, a melancholy gloom begins to pervade the whole poem, which shifts it away from its earlier burlesques and satires towards cynicism and pathos. In an effort to contain this gloom, Harold is re-employed, at the margin of the poem, as almost an emblem of it. The narrator is to some extent freed to explore other avenues: to articulate pleasure and joy, and to flirt with 'Fair Florence' (*CHP* II, 280). But a sense of inescapable solitude, alienation, and 'ruin' finally pulls the poem back to its mood of melancholy, while the series of deaths that were interpolated into the poem at the very end of its composition push this melancholic gloom into something more profound. Loaded down with grief, the cantos end on a note of unmitigated pathos, and the narrator, like Harold, ends up as a dark, marginal, brooding figure.[67]

---

[67] As *Childe Harold* I and II face up to 'tragic' losses, and as they focus on, and articulate, 'woe' and grief, we see the early stages, I think, of a larger movement than that from burlesque to pathos. For though *The Giaour* to some degree replicates the pathos with which *Childe Harold* I and II end, it also pushes beyond pathos and into the tragic. It dramatizes 'suffering and heroism', 'the shortness of heroic life', and 'the fierce sport of human hatreds', for example, and these are, we might say, some of the 'motifs and images

With this description of the first two cantos of *Childe Harold* in mind, I want now to turn to *The Giaour*. To what extent did *Childe Harold* I and II lead into, influence, or infiltrate Byron's composition of his first tale?

---

around which the sense of the tragic has crystallized during three thousand years of western poetry' (Steiner, *The Death of Tragedy*, pp. 2, 5).

CHAPTER TWO

'The Frame of Things Disjoint'

McGann states that *The Giaour* was 'born phoenix-like' out of two abortive attempts to write 'a poem of 6 Cantos as like the last 2' (that is, *Childe Harold* I and II) as possible.[1] On first reading *The Giaour* alongside *Childe Harold* I and II it is the striking difference between the two poems that we notice, but I want to focus here on some of the less immediately obvious likenesses.

Looking back briefly to *Childe Harold* I and II, it seems that Byron originally turned to the idea of a travel narrative because he saw in such a narrative a way of extending his poetic composition beyond the formal limits of song and satire. His stated aim was 'variety', 'all ... kinds of composition', and the result was a 'medley', 'a collection of lyrics'. But these lyrics, which were almost always located at a specific place, were tied together into a single composition by the framing idea of a journey.

As Brian Nellist suggests, Byron was still essentially a 'lyric poet' when he wrote *The Giaour*,[2] though a dramatic element also begins to emerge in Byron's use of monologues and dialogues. But if he was going to avoid producing another 'collection of songs like the *Hours of Idleness*', Byron needed a structure that would sustain and prolong the 'process of poetic invention' like the one supplied by his journey across Europe.[3] He turned to the adventure narrative. Here he found, on the one hand, a kind of invention that would generate episodes that could be lyricized and dramatized, and, on the other, a structure that could hold those episodes together as parts of something larger than themselves.

However, Byron was not only looking for a kind of writing that would extend the range of his lyricism beyond the limitations of song. He was also looking for a poetic form that 'left him free to introduce ... whatever sentiments or images his fancy, in its excursions, could collect'.[4] In other words, Byron carried forward, from *Childe Harold* I and II, his desire for a form that facilitated 'variety', that admitted 'all ... kinds of composition', that

---

[1] See *Works* III, p. 414. McGann is quoting Byron's letter to John Murray of 5 September 1812 (in *BLJ* II, p. 191). The title of this chapter is taken from *Macbeth*, III, ii, 18 (in *William Shakespeare: The Complete Works*, ed. by Wells, Taylor, Jowett, and Montgomery (Oxford: Clarendon Press, 1986). According to Jonathan Bate, *Macbeth* is Byron's 'favourite source' of Shakespearean quotations in his letters and journals. Bate suggests that 'Partly because of his own Scottish ancestry, Byron felt a special affinity with the world of *Macbeth*' (*Shakespeare and the English Romantic Imagination* [Oxford: Clarendon, 1986], pp. 227, 228).

[2] 'Lyric Presence', p. 46.

[3] Ibid.

[4] Thomas Moore, *Life of Lord Byron, with his Letters and Journals* (London: John Murray, 1830; repr., London: [n.pub.], 1854), vol. 2, pp. 190–191.

gave 'full scope to' his 'inclination' and left him free to be 'droll or pathetic, descriptive or sentimental, tender or satirical, as the humour' struck him.[5]

He opted for 'disjointed fragments' of narrative,[6] and his self-acknowledged model for this fragmentation is Samuel Rogers's 1812 poem, *The Voyage of Columbus*. In his Preface, Rogers makes claims for his fragmented narrative that are, in at least one important respect, similar to Beattie's claims, which Byron quotes in the Preface to *Childe Harold* I and II, for writing that utilizes the Spenserian stanza. Rogers says:

> The following Poem (or, to speak more properly, what remains of it) has here and there a lyrical turn of thought and expression. It is sudden in its transitions, and full of historical allusions; leaving much to be imagined by the reader.[7]

The idea of a poem in the form of the disjointed, fragmented, often lyrical remains of a larger poem offered Byron a freedom akin to that offered by the Spenserian stanza. It gave him a way of telling a story that brought with it a considerable degree of freedom from the obligations imposed by a straight-forward narrative. Its fragmentation, sudden transitions, and lyrical turns of thought and expression meant that he could move freely among the episodes of his narrative, as he had moved through the episodes of his journey, lyricizing, dramatizing, and commenting on them, as the 'humour' struck him.

Before Byron began writing *The Giaour*, then, he was, firstly, looking to a narrative structure to sustain and prolong his lyric invention by offering a series of episodes to be lyricized. Secondly, he had found, in Rogers's fragmented narrative form, a kind of writing that would, to some extent at least, leave him free to give 'full scope' to his 'inclination'. But since one of Byron's aims seems to have been to assure himself as much freedom and room for variety as possible, it is perhaps odd that he did not utilize the possibilities for such variety which a cast of characters could open up. For as Byron began to compose the poem, and work on the first episodes he chose to single out, he decided to focus on the consciousness of his narrator alone.

Perhaps Byron recalled the trouble he had with his first fictional and narrated character, Harold, at the beginning of *Childe Harold*? Harold had never become the vehicle for the 'variety' Byron was aiming for, becoming instead the projection of a particular kind of gloomy consciousness. And, of course, Harold was the prototype for a great many of Byron's later fictions. The narrator of *Childe Harold* I and II, on the other hand, provided Byron with a much better means of being 'droll ... pathetic ... descriptive ... sentimental'

---

[5]   As David Seed argues in '"The Platitude of Prose": Byron's Vampire Fragment in the context of his Verse Narratives' (in *Byron and the Limits of Fiction*), 'rapid shifts of pace and technique ... characterize' Byron's 'verse narratives' (p. 146). According to Seed, Byron's preference for verse over prose is due to the 'greater liberty offered by verse ... to shift the very register of his language, from, say, description to narrative or monologue' (p. 144).

[6]   *The Giaour*, Advertisement, 1. All quotations from *The Giaour* are taken from *Works* III. Line references will be given after each quotation in the text.

[7]   Preface to *The Voyage of Columbus*, in *Poems of Samuel Rogers* (London: [n.pub.], 1834), p. 217.

and so on. As *Childe Harold* I and II progressed, Byron increasingly transformed his poem into a lyrical dramatization of its narrator's consciousness.

In broad terms, this offers a template for future practice, and indeed, we can argue that it is a model which Byron seems to have drawn on in the early stages of *The Giaour*'s composition. Very early on in the first version of the poem,[8] narrative is 'dissolved into lyric modes',[9] and as lyric modes replace narrative modes, so the lyric subject, the poem's narrator, lays claim to our attention and engages our interest. Throughout the first half of Byron's first body of fragments, lyric modes dominate. We watch the narrator being drawn into events at their margin.

The first episode of his story that Byron chose to lyrically dramatize was the Giaour's flight from Hassan's anger. Oddly, Byron chose a moment of that escape that is, for the Giaour at least, of no real significance. It is only really significant to the fisherman who witnesses it. He recalls his memory of the Giaour's flight, and as he does so the poem 'melts into the fisherman's narrative'. This follows his introduction in lines 168–179 'as he rows with weary determination to Port Leone'.[10]

The fisherman's account of events is not as a narrative. Those events are recounted as a series of lyric rehearsals of his own immediate response to them as they happened. As the narrator of *Childe Harold* I and II stands outside the scenes he describes, but is to some extent drawn into them, so the narrator of *The Giaour* stands outside the events he recounts but is sucked into the narrative which structures them. And like the speakers of the 'dramatic monologues' of Browning and Tennyson, a form which *The Giaour* clearly prefigures, the fisherman is not only engaged in a present situation about which he is supplying us with information. He draws our attention to himself by responding to the sequence of events he initiates us into. Indeed, our attention is drawn to him because of the complex intensity of his response to the Giaour. He begins by loathing him, but is quickly moved to sympathize with his pain. A kind of revulsion rises up, however, pushing away the sympathy he briefly feels. As a result, the fisherman regains the detachment with which he first looked on the Giaour, but not before the reader has glimpsed this brief psychological drama:

> I know thee not, I loathe thy race,
> But in thy lineaments I trace
> What time shall strengthen, not efface;
> Though young and pale, that sallow front
> Is scath'd by fiery passion's brunt,
> Though bent on earth thine evil eye
> As meteor-like thou glidest by,

---

8   According to McGann, *MS.L.* is the 'original draft'. It contains lines '1–6, 168–99, 277–87, 352–87, 422–4, 426–72, 519–602, 604–619, 655–88, 723–32, 735–8, 787–831, 1319–34' (*Works* III, p. 406).

9   Nellist, 'Lyric Presence', p. 49.

10   Michael G. Sundell, 'The Development of *The Giaour*', in *Studies in English Literature 1500–1900* 9 (1969), p. 590.

Right well I view, and deem thee one
Whom Othman's sons should slay or shun. (191–199)

The fisherman's sympathy for the Giaour is brushed aside by the phrase 'thine
evil eye', but the detachment he achieves still has a hollow ring to it. This is
sounded by the word 'should', which could, for instance, have been 'do' or
'will', or even 'have'. The fisherman seems to be intrigued and sympathetic
against his better judgement, and his contradictory responses to the Giaour
recall the contradictory responses of *Childe Harold*'s narrator as he looks on at
events in Spain. The fisherman feels a sympathy, however, that he does not
want to admit, even to himself.

In this way, we find ourselves drawn into the emotional life of our
narrator, as we were in *Childe Harold* I and II. And like the speakers of later
dramatic monologues, the fisherman has inadvertently revealed rather more of
himself than he intended. By doing so, he becomes interesting in his own
right, as a centre of psychological conflict.

We might, of course, argue that Byron here is simply giving his narrative
an isolated 'lyrical turn', or agree with McGann's contention that the Giaour is
being 'dramatized ... through the responses he elicits from those who watch
him'.[11] These arguments would only hold, however, if the poem went on to
focus our attention exclusively on the Giaour, or if, rather than repeatedly
asserting the fisherman's presence and predicament, the poem confronted us
with a multiplicity of distinct speakers.

MS.M., Byron's first 'fair copy' of the poem, does neither of these
things.[12] It does, of course, continue to interest us in the Giaour but, as David
Seed points out, even in its completed form the poem whets 'the reader's
desire for information' about the Giaour and the events in which he figures,
only to actually withhold that information.[13] Thus, while McGann is absolutely
right to suggest that the poem offers a series of responses, these responses do
not so much dramatize the Giaour, as whet our curiosity about him. They do
so by dramatizing his impact on a watcher, or the impact of events in which the
Giaour is intimately concerned on a consciousness only marginally concerned
with them. As a result, not only is our curiosity about the Giaour aroused, a
curiosity that is consistently frustrated, but a secondary object of attention is
repeatedly thrust forward by the poem. As lyric modes and dramatic responses
push narrative to one side, so our attention is shifted from the object of that
narrative to the subject of the lyrical drama. We do not lose interest in the
Giaour, or the narrative that runs obscurely through the fragments, but become
additionally interested in the consciousness of the fisherman, who we watch
recounting and recalling events throughout *MS.M.*[14]

---

[11]   McGann, *Fiery Dust*, p. 150.

[12]   McGann, *Works* III, p. 406. McGann tells us that *MS.M.* is 'dated at beginning
1813, containing the epigraph, the dedication, and a brief version of the "Advertisement"', as
well as the following additions to *MS.L.*: '425, 473–89, 491–503' (*Works* III, p. 406).

[13]   David Seed, '"Disjointed Fragments": Concealment and Revelation in *The
Giaour*', in *Byron Journal* 18 (1990), p. 14.

[14]   We assume that it is the fisherman speaking throughout *MS.M.*, though there are
no explicit indications of who is speaking at any one time, or in any particular fragment.

However, I have suggested, despite the obvious differences between *Childe Harold*'s narrative and *The Giaour*'s, that in interesting us in the poem's narrator as well as the poem's narrative by lyrically dramatizing the consciousness of that narrator, Byron is repeating a strategy he first developed in cantos I and II of *Childe Harold*. This hypothesis seems sound, but let us hold off from concluding that it is right and seek further confirmation. If Byron was indeed using *Childe Harold* I and II as a model of procedure as he began the business of writing an adventure tale, we might expect to find other instances of a seemingly deliberate repetition of the practice of *Childe Harold* I and II in the early manuscript versions of *The Giaour*.

How far does the replication of Byron's practice in *Childe Harold* I and II extend into Byron's writing of *The Giaour*, then? Here it is helpful to remind ourselves of how Byron built *Childe Harold* I and II around his own 'Grand Tour'. He began with a fictional narrative that followed the route of his journey but which centred on a fictional character. That character was a projection of a particular kind of consciousness, one that remained immune to the scenes encountered on the journey, resisted any kind of 'broadening of the mind' that travel might lead to, and remained locked in misanthropic gloom.

Alongside this narrative, Byron ran a lyrical sequence that began by depicting a consciousness responding immediately and spontaneously to the images thrown up by his journey. It also dramatized that consciousness 'awaking to her woes' and finally ends in grief, as Byron extends his lyric sequence to incorporate the series of deaths he came home to.

Looking at *The Giaour* in its final form, there seems to be no narrator that corresponds to that of *Childe Harold* I and II. Indeed, no single dominant narrator seems to emerge at all.[15] There is a sort of Western *Citoyen du Monde* who laments the present state of Greece, but we do not hear of any personal loss, or see this speaker develop into a focus of attention in his own right. He is only one of a number of speakers, and is only present at the beginning of the poem. Among the other speakers in the poem, we have the Moslem fisherman and a monk, neither of which titles immediately suggest a relationship to the

---

There is a general critical consensus about this, however. McGann, for example, agrees with Karl Kroeber's suggestion that the fisherman speaks from line 180 to line 797 (*Romantic Narrative Art*, p. 140 and *Fiery Dust*, p. 143), while Sundell argues that the whole story 'appears to be told by a Moslem fisherman' ('The Development of *The Giaour*', p. 590). As a rule, we are forced to 'infer from the context' that the speaker 'is still the fisherman' (William Marshall, 'The Accretive Structure of *The Giaour*', in *Modern Language Notes* 76, 1961, p. 504), although the fragmented form of the poem encourages the reader to make as many connections as he or she can. *The Giaour*, in this sense, looks rather 'modern'. Wolfgang Iser says of modern poetry that it is 'often so fragmentary that one's attention is almost exclusively occupied with the search for connections between fragments' (*The Implied Reader: Patterns of Communication in Prose Fiction from Bunyan to Beckett*, trans. by Wilhelm Fink [Baltimore: Johns Hopkins University Press, 1974], p. 280). *The Giaour* invites this kind of attention too, indeed demands that we make 'connections between fragments', and 'fill in the gaps left by the text' (*The Implied Reader*, p. 280) as well as we can.

15   Though we do, as Kroeber argues, find ourselves 'puzzled more by the character and circumstances of the narrators than by the fatal order of events' (*Romantic Narrative Art*, p. 140).

narrator of *Childe Harold* I and II. Yet it is worth looking again at the fisherman. He is, as we have seen, lyrically rendered, and our attention is drawn to him almost as soon as *MS.M.* begins. The responses the poem dramatizes are not responses to a series of geographical locations, but to a series of events, yet the poem does dramatize those responses, giving the impression that we are watching as the fisherman recalls his own immediate and spontaneous reaction to events. And, though he is somewhat overshadowed in later versions of the poem, his presence does dominate the early manuscript versions. We watch as he slowly realizes that Leila has been murdered – indeed, that he has participated in that murder – and as he suffers and laments Leila's loss.

The narrator of *Childe Harold* I and II is Western, educated, and does not participate in any murders. Yet despite the obvious differences in character and history, Byron's development of the fisherman does seem to bear the mark, in its own fictionality, of his development of the narrator of *Childe Harold* I and II. He robs both of their detached role of observer, subjecting both to grief and loss, turning both into rather moving, grief-stricken mourners, and replicating in *The Giaour*, to some degree, the pathos of *Childe Harold* I and II. In *The Giaour*, we watch a fictional awaking on the part of the narrator that runs alongside the poem's narrative in the same way that in *Childe Harold* I and II we see an autobiographical 'awaking' projected into the poem as the experience of its narrator, alongside his telling of Harold's narrative.

This replication of *Childe Harold* I and II is primarily structural: even the details of the fisherman's 'woes' are very different from those of *Childe Harold* I and II's narrator. The fisherman has not only 'ignorantly participated in ... murder', as Michael Sundell puts it,[16] but he has participated particularly in the murder of Leila, a young woman whose beauty 'stood superior to them all' (499). It is her loss that most affects him.

Indeed, in almost every detail the two narrators are quite different. Even the fisherman's progress from ignorance to realization is a gradual one, and so to this extent unlike the sudden 'awaking' prompted by the deaths at the end of *Childe Harold* I and II. Yet both poems dramatize a consciousness awaking to the reality of death and loss.

The death which lies at the centre of *The Giaour* is introduced in a 'pointedly cryptic' manner, because of the fisherman's initial 'ignorance of why he is being asked to carry the emir and his "burthen", and the emir's obvious reluctance to spell out his purpose'.[17] Even as he begins to realize that this burden is human, the fisherman remains cryptic, because, it seems, he is awed by his discovery. It does, nevertheless, become obvious to him that the burden is human, and though he recalls his awe, he also recounts his own morbid fascination as it sinks below the water:

> Sullen it plunged, and slowly sank,
> The calm wave rippled to the bank;
> I watch'd it as it sank, methought
> Some motion from the current caught

16　'The Development of *The Giaour*', p. 590.
17　Seed, '"Disjointed Fragments"', p. 21.

Bestirr'd it more, – 'twas but the beam
That chequer'd o'er the living stream –
I gaz'd, till vanishing from view,
Like lessening pebble it withdrew;
Still less and less, a speck of white
That gemm'd the tide, then mock'd the sight;
And all its hidden secrets sleep,
Known but to Genii of the deep,
Which, trembling in their coral caves,
They dare not whisper to the waves. (374–387)

We can hear the fisherman's private knowledge in his choice of active verbs like 'withdrew', of personifying adjectives and adverbs like 'sullen', and in a number of other hints he deliberately lets slip, such as the idea that it might bestir, and the implicit contrast with the 'living stream'. At no point are we told that this is Leila, or that the fisherman has any inkling that it might be. Rather, we see the fisherman's morbid fascination as he watches and gazes at 'it' as it sinks. We see him trapped between, on the one hand, the urge to confess his own involvement in this act, and to share, even off-load on to his listeners, the horror of the experience, and on the other, an inability, bred perhaps by a sense of his own complicity in the deed, to articulate fully its horror. The fisherman seems stuck between a discomfort with the 'hidden' details, and a fear of disclosing details that now 'sleep'. He projects his quandary on to the Genii, who tremble and 'dare not' disclose their knowledge. As Seed suggests, the Genii are 'potential narrators awed into silence by the secret knowledge they possess'.[18] They are projections of the fisherman. Clearly, the fact that he is participating in a murder has unnerved the fisherman, but this is only part of his dilemma. Like the narrator of *Childe Harold* I and II, it is loss that the fisherman must finally confront. His sense of guilt is important but secondary, and is left largely implicit throughout.

Much more powerful is the growing suspicion that it was Leila in that sack. The fisherman recounts this suspicion from 'the inside', so to speak, and in the present tense. He begins haunted by the question of whether or not Leila still dwells in Hassan's Serai (445). Hassan's behaviour suggests not:

Not thus was Hassan wont to fly
When Leila dwelt in his Serai. (443–444)

'Strange rumours' (447) offer an explanation for this behaviour: Leila has 'flown her master's rage' with 'the faithless Giaour' (455–458). The fisherman's own experience belies this explanation:

But others say, that on that night,
By pale Phingari's trembling light,
The Giaour upon his jet black steed
Was seen – but seen alone to speed
With bloody spur along the shore,
Nor maid nor page behind him bore. (467–472)

---

18   Ibid.

Though hiding behind 'But others say', the fisherman clearly means himself here. What is most significant, though, is the tone of the last line of this quotation, which ends this particular fragment and so is allowed to hang in the air for a moment before we move on to the next. It is not a completed thought, but implies a completion. This makes the line suggestively melancholy because it manages to hint at, but hold back from actually articulating, the possibility that Leila, whose 'treachery' with the Giaour 'deserv'd a grave' (462), but who did not fly with the Giaour, might well have been the Emir's burden. This is not an unreasonable connection for us to make, because the desire innate in the reader of narratives to know what is going on drives us to be always making connections. Nor is it an unreasonable connection for the fisherman to make. He, too, is trying to read the situation correctly, and, in his note to the end of the poem, Byron claims that the 'circumstance to which the above story relates was not very uncommon in Turkey'. He goes on to relate the case of 'the twelve handsomest women in Yanina', who were 'seized, fastened up in sacks, and drowned in the lake'.[19] Yet the fisherman's mind is not numbed by the conventionality of Leila's punishment, nor consoled by the idea of her guilt. He is, rather, entirely taken up by the idea of her loss, which he laments with the eulogy beginning in line 473.

The lyricized histories of Byron's first two narrators both climax in grief. In the manuscript versions of *The Giaour*,[20] Byron's focus is on the quandary of his narrator right up to what is now line 504.[21] The fisherman is Leila's 'only constant mourner' (287) other than the Giaour, and through him Byron offers a pathetic portrait of powerful grief laced with guilt, isolation (he must hide what he knows while suffering universal ignorance), and anger. In this sense, the fisherman already looks a rather 'Byronic' figure, suffering a kind of guilty grief, and carrying a guilty secret.

Byron develops the fisherman, in other words, into something lesser in degree, but rather similar in kind, to his poem's central hero. Can we also argue that in doing so he is again reproducing the structure of *Childe Harold* I and II? At the end of the earlier poem, the narrator is forced by the losses and grief he suffers to become like Harold. The consciousness of Harold and his narrator come together. So too, it seems, do the Giaour and his narrator.

The fisherman begins the poem loathing the Giaour, yet when he sees the Giaour at the convent his attitude is very different:

> But once I saw that face – yet then
> It was so mark'd with inward pain
> I could not pass it by again;
> It breathes the same dark spirit now,
> As death were stamped upon his brow. (793–797)

---

[19] Byron's note to line 1334 (see *Works* III, pp. 422–423).

[20] *MS.L.* and *MS.M.* What I am saying here about the focus of the poem is also true of the 'Proof Edition' (see Table C, *Works* III, p. 411), of which fifteen copies 'were struck off for private circulation in late Mar. 1813' (*Works* III, p. 413).

[21] In *MS.M.* the fisherman's eulogy ends at this line.

This encounter closes *MS.M.*, where we only glimpse the aftermath of events, and there is significant evidence, though it is admittedly circumstantial, to suggest that, like the Giaour, the fisherman has been driven into a kind of exile.

In the early versions of the poem especially, what precisely has happened to the Giaour is only partly revealed: he has ended up at the monastery, living a sort of exile, haunted by the memory of Leila's loss and of his vengeance (822–832). The rest is pointedly closed off from view:

> ... lay me with the humblest dead,
> And save the cross above my head,
> Be neither name nor emblem spread
> By prying stranger to be read,
> Or stay the passing pilgrim's tread
> He pass'd – nor of his name and race
> Hath left a token or a trace,
> Save what the father must not say
> Who shrived him on his dying day. (1324–1332)

Byron seems intent on refusing to satisfy our curiosity about the Giaour in these early versions of the poem. He is hardly more explicit about the fisherman. We see him in a Christian land, mixing freely with those 'whom Othman's sons should slay and shun'. Is the fisherman in a kind of self-imposed exile? He mentions 'mine own land' (789), but the friar does not seem to recognize the fisherman as a Moslem: the friar mentions a 'Paynim land' (808) and the 'Othman race' (810), but makes no association between these and the man he is speaking to.

These, of course, are slight details, yet they do seem to hint at the idea that the fisherman is another 'gloomy wanderer', living a kind of exile. And they lead us to ask questions about the fisherman. If he is in exile, is it an exile imposed upon him by the painful and private memories we have been privy too? We know from the Giaour that memory can drive an individual into a tortured exclusion from life.

Despite the fact, then, that Byron withholds rather more information than he volunteers, we can suggest that some reproduction of the coming together of Harold and his narrator in mutual, or at least parallel, suffering is hinted at. That these hints come at the end of the manuscript versions of *The Giaour*, as the coming together of Harold and his narrator came at the end of *Childe Harold* II, suggests that the parallel they point to was much more important in the early stages of the poem's composition than in the later stages.

As the poem now stands, this 'coming together' happens in the middle of the poem and is overshadowed by the Giaour's monologue, but how we are to read the fact that in the early stages of *The Giaour*'s composition, it seems to reproduce features of *Childe Harold* I and II? Byron certainly carried forward the practice of lyrically dramatizing the poem's narrator, and of subjecting that narrator to the grief of loss in death. He may have gone further than this, as we have seen, and reproduced the psychological coming together of Harold and his narrator. But did Byron deliberately replicate features of *Childe Harold* I and II?

I would argue that he did, at least to some extent. In lyricizing his narrator, he does seem to be employing a strategy that had proved highly successful in *Childe Harold* I and II. But we can, I think, offer an alternative and better explanation of the other 'replications' of *Childe Harold* I and II that we find in *The Giaour*.

As Samuel Chew remarks, 'Byron, more than most poets, works again and again along the same grooves of thought',[22] and rather than argue that Byron modelled the fisherman's emotional progress through *The Giaour* on that of the narrator of *Childe Harold* I and II, we might argue that in both poems Byron is simply working along the same groove of thought. He is articulating, dramatizing, exploring 'grief'. Thus, both narrators follow parallel, but quite separate, and beyond some structural similarities quite unrelated, lines of development into this kind of suffering. We only have to think of Conrad, Azo, and Manfred to see that it is not only *Childe Harold* I and II and *The Giaour* that confront us with paralysed grief. Poem after poem returns to this thematic territory, and to this extent each of these poems replicates the others. Nevertheless, this replication is not the result of deliberately modelling one poem on another.

Similarly with the psychological coming together of Harold and his narrator, and then of the Giaour and his narrator: *The Giaour* may not replicate the earlier coming together of two distinct consciousnesses, so much as manifest Byron's growing fascination with the potent idea of exiles, escapees, and fugitives that carry with them into freedom, retreat, or hiding, a private 'Hell' (*CHP* I, 872) of painful recollection. The point here is that Harold and his narrator, and the Giaour and his, do not move towards each other, but all converge on and enter into, independently and to greatly differing degrees, the emotional territory of the exile or outcast.

The Giaour explicitly compares himself to Cain, the archetypal exile,[23] in lines 1057–1058, in which he claims that 'the curse and crime' of 'Cain', are 'written on my brow'. Harold is perhaps less obviously an exile in *Childe Harold* I and II. Indeed, it might be objected that Harold is a tourist in these cantos, yet, by replacing 'The Girl of Cadiz' with 'To Inez', Byron is clearly trying to turn Harold's tourism into a kind of self-imposed 'Exile' (*CHP* II, 857). And while 'To Inez' was 'probably not added to the canto until some time after 28 Mar. 1810',[24] the idea that Harold's tourism is also some kind of exile is, I think, repeatedly implied in the first two cantos, not least when Harold's gloom is described as 'Cain's unresting doom' (*CHP* I, 827). This phrase is found in the earliest manuscript.

Neither the narrator of *Childe Harold* I and II nor the fisherman, on the other hand, are explicitly compared to Cain. There is some evidence, as we have seen, to suggest that the fisherman does enter an exile parallel to that of the Giaour, but what about the narrator of *Childe Harold* I and II? This narrator

---

[22]   Samuel Chew, *The Dramas of Lord Byron: A Critical Study* (Gottingen: Vandenhoeck and Ruprecht, and Baltimore: Johns Hopkins University Press, 1915; repr., New York: Russell and Russell, 1964), p. 66.

[23]   See Genesis 4.14: 'Behold, thou hast driven me this day from the face of the earth; and from thy face shall I be hid; and I shall be fugitive and vagabond in the earth.'

[24]   McGann, *Works* II, p. 266.

is the least like an exile of all the figures we are discussing. Yet he, too, moves towards self-exclusion once he is isolated and set aside by grief. It is precisely when the narrator's voice sounds closest to that of Harold, in stanza 97 of canto II, that the narrator is on the verge of turning away from the 'crowd' and 'all that Peace disdains'(*CHP* II, 909–910), as Harold has already done.

Both narrators and both central characters seem to be developed into exiles, or towards becoming exiles. This, again, is not a matter of Byron consciously or deliberately replicating one figure in others, of modelling the Giaour on Harold say, but of a thematic repetition that naturally results from returning again and again to the same basic idea: the tortured exile.

The tendency to be drawn, as if passively, to certain images and thematic territories over and over again is a key feature of Byron's composition of poetry. It is not a tendency that is particular to Byron, but it is a marked feature of his work. It helps us to account for the replication of thematic features of *Childe Harold* I and II in *The Giaour* rather more than the idea that Byron deliberately used *Childe Harold* I and II as a model of procedure. It is a feature that is 'well illustrated by the recurrence of the Byronic hero-type'.[25]

Harold is the first distinctively Byronic hero-figure, the Giaour the second precisely because, while Harold exiles himself in rather aimless gloomy travelling, the tortured Giaour hides himself away in a convent. Both, for different reasons, and whether voluntarily or forced by circumstance, memory, or grief, exist in a kind of painful exile. Indeed, they announce the beginning of their (self-)banishment in a similar way. Their tones differ, of course, but, on the one hand, Harold proclaims 'And now I'm in the world alone' (*CHP* I, 182), and on the other, the Giaour declares 'And now I go – but go alone' (688).

In the local context of *Childe Harold* I and II and *The Giaour*, Byron's tendency to return to ideas and images explored in other poems is equally well illustrated by the recurrence of the Levant as a central focus. Both poems explore the whole business of the Levant at length and in depth, but in *Childe Harold* I and II Byron's fascination with the 'tortured exile' and with the Levant are both held in check by a host of other images, locations, histories, and events that demand inclusion in a poem that is faithful not only to immediate imaginative invention, but to the fact of travel and the spirit of moving on.

In *The Giaour*, Byron is free to focus his attention more exclusively, because he is free of the demands of a travelogue. Byron's interest in Greece, and his evolving vision of 'Cain's unresting doom', or the perpetually tormented exile/wanderer/outsider, become the driving concerns of the poem.

Some conception of Byron's personality, or of the bent of his imagination, helps us to explain this kind of continuity between *Childe Harold* I and II and *The Giaour*. Yet it is in its departures from *Childe Harold* I and II that *The Giaour* is, finally, a distinct and separate poem. Indeed, while the thematic objects of attention remain the same through a number of Byron's poems, in each poem they are reimagined and reimaged. This desire, instinct, or even compulsion, to explore again from a new vantage point, played as important a

---

25   Chew, *The Dramas of Lord Byron*, p. 66.

part in the genesis of Byron's poetry as his ongoing fascination with key ideas or 'grooves of thought'.

We should look at this will, or need, to reimage because it played a vital role in Byron's movement into new kinds of writing and new kinds of imagining. It manifests itself most obviously in, on the one hand, Byron's experimentation with form, which as well as carrying Byron into new 'grooves of thought', enabled him to redramatize and so re-evaluate present ones. On the other hand, it shows itself in Byron's recognition of the possibilities opened up for his own imaginings by new fictional contexts: that of the mysterious monk with a past, for example, or of a pirate, a prisoner, a mutineer, a latter-day Faust. Byron's fascination with suffering exiles transforms each of these figures into another such exile, but equally, every one of Byron's hero-figures adds a new twist to the suffering of all his predecessors, and every one allows us to look at exile and at grief from a new angle.

To focus our attention on this experimentation in the context of *The Giaour*, we need to concentrate on the ways in which *The Giaour* departs from the model and practice of *Childe Harold* I and II, especially when it is working in thematic territories that were also important to those cantos. To help us do so, let us focus our attention on two of the most obvious differences between *Childe Harold* I and II and *The Giaour* in Byron's approach to and treatment of the subjects that are central to both poems.

Firstly, Byron's projected view of the Levant in *The Giaour*, projected from the inside through the fictional figure of the fisherman, is very different from the view projected in *Childe Harold* I and II, which is the view of the tourist, the outsider, the *Citoyen Du Monde*. The second difference I want to focus on is that between the two eponymous (or nearly eponymous) exiles. In *Childe Harold* I and II, Byron attempts to project the idea of the 'Exile' (*CHP* I, 857) who suffers a private 'Hell' through the figure of Harold. He is not entirely successful, because Harold repeatedly teeters on the brink of becoming a parody of certain kinds of literary sentimentality. In *The Giaour*, on the other hand, Byron's Venetian hero is both a fiercely heroic figure and an absolutely convincing projection of personal suffering. His presentation contains no elements of humour, and his history in the poem approaches the authentically tragic in 'the very excess of his suffering' and 'the shortness of [his] heroic life'.[26]

We can give a surprisingly full account of how these developments came about because *The Giaour* did not come into being fully formed, but in stages that are well documented. To begin with, the poem shows the traces of two earlier false starts. The fragmented remains of these two false starts offer invaluable clues to Byron's processes of composition, and to how *The Giaour* in particular came about. In them we can trace a series of experimental shifts away from the practice of *Childe Harold* I and II that progressively and accumulatively made *The Giaour* possible.

The first of these two fragments, 'The Monk of Athos',[27] as McGann points out, 'resembles the opening and closing stanzas of *CHP* II as well as

---

26   Steiner, *The Death of Tragedy*, pp. 9, 5.

27   'Composed early in 1811 while B was staying at the Capuchin convent near Athens' (McGann *Works* I, p. 424). All quotations from 'The Monk of Athos' are taken

B's long prose note to *CHP* II dated from the Capuchin Convent, 23 Jan. 1811'.[28] The fragment is set in and around the Greek uprisings of 1770 and 1791.[29]

Byron's melancholy when in Greece and his ardent hopes for the future 'deliverance of continental Greece',[30] help to explain his interest in this historical setting. Yet this history only found its way into *Childe Harold's Pilgrimage* in a note. We can only guess as to why this is so, but it perhaps had something to do with the lyrical mode that came to dominate canto II. It seems, from what little we can gather from the 'Monk of Athos' fragment, that Byron thought 'those disastrous days' ('M of A', 14) warranted a narrative treatment. He certainly implies that 'The Monk of Athos' was going to be a narrative poem, documenting 'private woes' ('M of A', 39), and telling of 'fond domestic ties / Asunder torn by War's relentless Hand' ('M of A', 46–47). His stated aim in writing this narrative was

> To wake Remembrance to a theme so dear,
> And mourn in simple and incondite lays
> The fate of Greece in those disastrous days,
> When late, though sunk beneath a tyrant's might,
> She boldly ventured (Oh immortal praise)
> In arms to reassert her ancient light,
> And freedom's standard rear'd, and dared the unequal fight. ('M of A', 12–18)

Byron seems to be moving away from a lyric mode that is sustained and prolonged by 'images supplied by' a 'European journey',[31] towards a primarily narrative mode that is sustained by a lyric perspective (the poem aims to 'mourn' what it recalls). If this is indeed the case, then this is the first shift in Byron's practice, and a shift in which we see him moving towards his use of narrative in *The Giaour*.

As he pushes more decidedly than ever before into narrative, Byron carries forward with him his fascination with the idea of the exile, which he had first implied, then explicitly projected, through the figure of Harold. Like Harold, the hero of 'The Monk of Athos' was, it seems, going to be an 'Exile' ('M of A', 51), and was going to drag 'a weary load of Grief and Care / From clime to clime astray, forlorn, and reckless' ('M of A', 53–54).[32] However, even in

---

from *Works* I. Line references are given after each quotation in the text, and prefaced by the abbreviation 'M of A'.

[28] *Works* I, p. 424.

[29] The poem begins in 'the years immediately after 1774', when the Greeks were 'Forsaken by their Russian allies in their abortive effort for independence from the Turks' (McGann, *Works* I, p. 424).

[30] Byron's prose note to *Childe Harold* II, dated 23 January 1811 (*Works* II, p. 202).

[31] Nellist, 'Lyric Presence', p. 46.

[32] It is worth recalling Byron's letter of 5 September 1812 here, in which he asked Murray, 'What will you give *me* or *mine* for a poem of 6 Cantos (*when complete – no rhyme – no* recompense) as like the last 2 as I can make them? – I have some ideas which one day may be embodied & till winter I shall have much leisure' (*BLJ* II, p. 191). According to McGann, 'The Monk of Athos' and 'Il Diavolo Inamorato' are 'the ashes' (*Works* III, p. 414) of this poem of six cantos.

the nine stanzas that Byron wrote, it is clear that in significant ways the hero of 'The Monk of Athos' was going to differ considerably from Harold. He is no tourist, nor he is an observer of events. He is, rather, a victim of them.

In *Childe Harold* I and II, Harold's self-imposed exile only sometimes seems a manifestation of 'Cain's unresting doom' (*CHP* I, 827). At other times, it seems the result of satiation and boredom. But there is a moment at which Byron seems to be trying to show Harold in a tragic light and attempting to use the almost ludicrous, and certainly burlesquely sentimental, Harold to project an idea of suffering that is more than pathetic or sentimental. Harold is, it is briefly suggested, not simply the 'gloomy wander' (*CHP* II, 137), but haunted and terrorized by 'The blight of life – the demon, Thought' (*CHP* I, 860), which inflicts upon him its own special 'Hell'. By demonizing thought in this way, Byron appears to momentarily equate it with the kind of 'daemonic energies' which, as Steiner puts it, 'prey upon the soul' in Greek tragedy.[33]

However, the historical context in which 'The Monk of Athos' is set is enough to transform Byron's 'gloomy wanderer' into something more like the tragic heroes of drama than Harold ever became. Harold's melancholy isolation and self-imposed exile is transformed into the 'hopeless Exile's Anguish and Despair' ('M of A', 51) by 'War's relentless' tearing 'Asunder' of 'domestic ties'('M of A', 46–47). Here we trace a second shift that moves Byron away from *Childe Harold* I and II and towards *The Giaour*: a shift towards sites of greater 'tragic' potential.

This shift is accompanied, necessarily, by another. The hero of 'The Monk of Athos' is more wholeheartedly fictional than Harold, who comes out of a background like, and clearly based on, Byron's own. This shift away from self-projection is an important factor in the genesis of *The Giaour*. Both Harold and the narrator of *Childe Harold* I and II are, to some extent, projections of Byron, and while it is true that the later poem was suggested by an event in which Byron participated,[34] it is populated by an almost entirely fictional cast. The movement away from self-projection and into a more purely fictional kind of writing begins in 'The Monk of Athos'.

Already, then, we can say that the writing of *The Giaour* is coming into view in 'The Monk of Athos', and doing so in a number of specific ways. Firstly, in Byron's attempt to move away from the distinctive lyricism of *Childe Harold* II and back to narrative, which he had briefly experimented with at the beginning of *Childe Harold* I, but which he had left largely unexplored, despite maintaining a narrative of sorts throughout *Childe Harold* I and II. Neither 'The Monk of Athos' nor *The Giaour* actually break clear of lyric modes, but in them Byron is clearly moving away from the topographical, lyric mode of *Childe Harold* I and II and towards telling stories.

Secondly, we can trace the movement away from *Childe Harold* I and II and towards *The Giaour* in the shift into a quasi-tragic mode which pushes beyond the pathos and lyrically rendered melancholy that eventually take hold of *Childe Harold* I and II, and towards narrating 'catastrophic' events and their attendant 'Anguish and Despair'.

---

33   *The Death of Tragedy*, p. 7.
34   See Marchand, *Byron: A Biography*, pp. 257–258 and notes.

Finally, I have suggested that in 'The Monk of Athos' Byron is inventing a purely fictional hero for the first time. We might add that in Byron's exclusive geographical focus on the Levant, there is also the beginnings of a shift away from the travelogue mode of *Childe Harold* I and II, and towards a politicized and topographical kind of writing that is less interested, and so rather more limited, in geographical sweep. We have to be tentative here. Only the beginnings of such a shift are at work in 'The Monk of Athos', if at all. While the poem is set in the Levant, the 'Exile', it seems, was to wander from 'clime to clime'.

We can say with more confidence that in *The Giaour* Byron replicates the general approach to the Levant he attempted to adopt in 'The Monk of Athos'. In the earlier fragment, Byron approaches the whole business of Greece by focusing in on an imagined 'private woe'. Giving that woe centre stage is a way of mourning the 'disastrous days' and the 'fate' it images. In *The Giaour* Byron once again approaches the subject of the Levant, and once again gives centre stage to a 'private woe', but like 'The Monk of Athos', *The Giaour* is rooted in a concern for the 'fate of Greece'. It is a poem about a personal and private hell, suffered alone in exile, but it is simultaneously a 'polemic' that enters into and brings face to face 'the two great monotheistic codes, Christianity and Islam' that fought for 'personal control over the lives of men and women' in the Greece of the early nineteenth century.[35] *The Giaour* is built around these two centres, and it is in 'The Monk of Athos' that Byron first isolated them, and brought them into a powerful relation: the Greek context, it seems, was to give birth to the suffering.

We do not know why Byron gave up 'The Monk of Athos', but we can speculate. As we have seen, Byron seems to have envisaged 'The Monk of Athos' as a narrative, but the fragment drifts back very quickly to the lyric mode which dominates *Childe Harold* II. Is this why Byron abandoned the poem? That the poem does lose its narrative hold of its material and falls back into a lyric mode is especially true of stanzas 7, 8, and 9, but this struggle between lyric and narrative impulses is not limited to these stanzas or to 'The Monk of Athos'. We can certainly see lyric and narrative modes jostling each other in *The Giaour*.

Stanzas 7, 8, and 9 of 'The Monk of Athos' are worth looking at with reference to *The Giaour* for other reasons too. While they bring the 'Monk of Athos' fragment to a close, and carry forward Byron's obviously considerable interest in geographical location, they also offer a brief foretaste of *The Giaour*. The reader naturally surmises that in these stanzas Byron is homing in on one of the convents found in the 'shady groves' ('M of A', 64) of 'Majestic Athos' ('M of A', 60), in order to situate his monk there. If we assume for a moment that this monk is the hopeless exile of stanza 6, then he is rather obviously a

---

[35] Marilyn Butler, 'The Orientalism of Byron's *Giaour*', in *Byron and the Limits of Fiction*, p. 91. See also McGann's discussion of the poem in *The Beauty of Inflections*. McGann describes the poem as 'a political allegory', and argues that the 'subject of the poem, at the plot level, is the state of modern Greece around 1780. At the narrative level, the poem is a contemporary (1809–1813) meditation on the meaning of the European (and especially the English) understanding of the Levantine politics between 1780 and 1813' (p. 263).

prototype for the Giaour. Even if Byron had no such poem in mind as the one we are here constructing, he has brought together elements that he will carry forward. In *The Giaour*, the figure of a monk and the figure of an anguished exile are combined in the figure of the Giaour himself, who we find in a convent at the end of the poem.

Alongside definite shifts in practice, then, we need to notice this coming together of the imaginary world of *The Giaour*. It is a coming together to which 'Il Diavolo Inamorato',[36] the second of the fragments we are looking at, also contributes. According to a letter written to Thomas Moore in August 1813, 'Il Diavolo Inamorato' was going to involve

> a story, grafted on the amours of a Peri and a mortal – something like, only more *philanthropical* than, Cazotte's Diable Amoureux.[37]

This may explain why Byron takes as his starting point the memory of 'early youth' ('DI', 1), of 'pleasaunce' ('DI', 3), of 'jocund days' ('DI', 4), and 'the life of life' ('DI', 11) in love. The early stanzas all stress the pleasure of past days. Yet Byron's intention here, as far as we can infer it, seems to have been to follow that pleasure into pain. This is at least what he leads us to expect when he has the poem's speaker say that he wants to 'teach' the 'youthful' 'that naught on earth can long be true' ('DI', 12–13). In order to do so, the speaker presents us with a young hero, Honóre, very like Harold at the beginning of *Childe Harold* I:

> Light were the limbs and pure the freshening glow
> That marked the form and face of young Honóre,
> Lord of himself; – his every joy and woe
> Were his own seeking as from shore to shore
> He bent his course wherever fancy bore:
> All wealth could purchase, or that youth could win,
> Were his ere yet his summers passed a score,
> And uncontrolled by Sire or aught akin,
> What marvel such should be no foe to smiling Sin? ('DI', 19–27)

Byron's presentation of Honóre seems to demonstrate a lingering attachment to the details of Harold's early history, and, as a result, we do not find very much in his brief appearance in what remains of 'Il Diavolo Inamorato' that looks forward to the figure of the Giaour. However, Honóre seems to be part of the structure on to which Byron was going to graft his own story.[38] There is again no way of telling what Byron's 'story' might have been,

---

[36]   According to McGann, this poem survives only as a 'rough fragment, dated Aug. 1812' (*Works* III, p. 392). This fragment was first published by McGann in his short article 'Byron's First Tale: An Unpublished Fragment' in *Keats–Shelley Memorial Association Bulletin* 19 (1968). I have taken my quotations from *Works* III. Line references will be given after each quotation in the text, and prefaced by the abbreviation 'DI'.

[37]   Letter dated 28 August 1813 (*BLJ* III, p. 101).

[38]   'The fragmentary state of the MS. does not permit any real certainty about who was to be the paramour of Byron's Peri. An innocent youth named Honóre is introduced first,

though it is worth noting that the shift towards narrative that seemed to be implied in 'The Monk of Athos' is confirmed in 'Il Diavolo Inamorato'. But even without trying to guess at Byron's story, we can notice various elements of it which Byron had already assembled when he gave the poem up.

The first thing to notice is that the poem is set in Venice rather than Greece. Here Byron might simply be following Cazotte's lead, but the Venice of Byron's poem offers a parallel to Greece in that there, too, 'strangers rule' ('DI', 39). In this sense, Venice and Greece seem to have been almost interchangeable for Byron: the stanzas on Venice here were reworked, set in Constantinople, and became part of Byron's lament over the lethargy of Greece's patriotism at the end of canto II of *Childe Harold*.[39]

Byron carries forward from 'The Monk of Athos' the practice of approaching his historical context by focusing in on an individual caught up in it. Indeed, he claims that Venice's 'wrongs are foreign to my strain' ('DI', 41), but asks:

> But midst this throng in merry masquerade,
> Lurk there no hearts that throb to secret pain,
> Even through the closest searment half betrayed? ('DI', 64–66)

The rhetoric here is homing in on a single figure: the 'Man' ('DI', 73), but what 'secret pain' is this? The stanzas that follow the reworked version of this stanza in *Childe Harold* II may help us to form a guess. There the pain is explicitly a patriotic one: the pain of being bondsmen. Yet, if Byron did have rebellious and patriotic discontent in mind here, it was not long before a better idea occurred to him: 'long-desired – but still-deferred Revenge!'('DI', 81). Up to this point, the 'Man' looks rather like Harold. The fact that he 'stalked' ('DI', 77) and 'seemed foreign to this Revelry' ('DI', 79) obviously recalls Harold, but, in a more general sense, Harold and the 'Man' are both distinctive because they carry their history with them, and suffer the fate of having memory exclude them from the present that surrounds them.

The 'Man' seems to be another of Byron's exiles, then, and recalls Harold, but in line 81 he suddenly takes a very different narrative line from Harold.[40] Byron leaves Harold behind here, and takes another step towards the writing of *The Giaour*. He will carry the idea of revenge forward, and have the 'vengeful Giaour' (*The Giaour*, 680) kill Hassan before he exiles himself to the convent.

In 'Il Diavolo Inamorato' as in 'The Monk of Athos', Byron is exploring new realms of possibility that will develop his vision of the suffering exile away from the direction taken by Harold. He no longer looks to his own history to generate new possibilities. Rather, as McGann argues, Byron's 'mind turned away from the autobiographical form' in these poems. According to McGann, however, it was not until he wrote *The Giaour* that Byron 'refined

---

and his general resemblance to [Cazotte's] Alvare indicates that he might be the lucky man' (McGann, 'Byron's First Tale: An Unpublished Fragment', p. 19).

[39]   See *Childe Harold* II, stanzas 78–83.

[40]   Byron glanced at the idea of 'the memory of some deadly feud' (*CHP* I, 66) in canto I of *Childe Harold*, but turned away from it.

Byron the narrator out of existence',[41] while what remains of 'Il Diavolo Inamorato' betrays 'Byron's difficulty in getting himself as a poet out of the way long enough to tell the story that was on his mind'.[42]

In *The Giaour*, Byron has the fisherman narrate the poem. The fisherman is aggressively Moslem, so that his fictional consciousness allows no quarter for Byron's Western frame of mind. Byron's choice of a Moslem fisherman as his narrator, then, may well have its roots in precisely the difficulty McGann sees manifested in 'The Monk of Athos' and 'Il Diavolo Inamorato', and in the fact that this difficulty kept manifesting itself. The fisherman, we might suggest, solved a problem that Byron first discovered in these unfinished poems.[43]

In addition to developing Byron's 'exile' into an increasingly fictional figure and adding a revenge motif that Byron will carry forward into *The Giaour*, and despite the shift from Greece to Venice, 'Il Diavolo Inamorato' retains a trace of the setting of 'The Monk of Athos' by recalling Mount Athos in the final stanza. *The Giaour*, in its turn, retains a trace of the Venetian setting of 'Il Diavolo Inamorato': the Giaour is a 'young Venetian' (*The Giaour*, Advertisement, 7). Retaining background details, or any features of one poem that caught his imagination, and then detaching them from the contexts in which they arise and carrying them into new poems and new contexts, is a distinctive feature of Byron's composition of poetry. In the case of *The Giaour*, it is as if Byron accumulated ideas almost randomly, so that the fictional world of the poem formed itself out of the wreckage of other poetic projects. This habit of mind gave the Giaour his Venetian background, his 'long-desired – but still-deferred Revenge', and his convent retreat.

'The Monk of Athos' and 'Il Diavolo Inamorato' clearly give us a number of important clues not only to how *The Giaour* came about, but also to Byron's

---

[41] *Fiery Dust*, p. 141.

[42] Ibid. Byron also had trouble giving up the Spenserian stanza. Byron wrote to Lord Holland complaining that 'When I began "Ch[ild]e Harold" I had never tried Spenser's measure, & now I cannot scribble in any other' (letter of 26 [27] September 1812, in *BLJ* II, p. 210).

[43] In a cancelled Preface to cantos I and II of *Don Juan*, Byron lampoons Wordsworth's attempt in 'The Thorn' to invent a fictional character to displace 'himself' as the poem's speaker (see *Byron's Don Juan: A Variorum Edition*, volume II, ed. by Truman Guy Steffan and Willis W. Pratt [Austin: University of Texas Press, 1957], pp. 3–7). Despite this later satire, Byron's strategy in *The Giaour* is actually not unlike Wordsworth's in 'The Thorn'. Both poets create a fictional consciousness through which to project their poems that is pointedly unlike their own. Where Wordsworth displaces himself with the idea of a retired 'Captain of a small trading vessel, for example' (*The Poetical Works of William Wordsworth*, vol. II, ed. by E. de Selincourt [Oxford: Clarendon, 1944], p. 512), Byron does the same with his Moslem fisherman. He changes his mind, however, in the note at the end of the poem, claiming that the speaker of the poem is 'one of the coffee-house story-tellers who abound in the Levant' (*Works* III, p. 423). Byron is perilously close here to asking the same kind of 'exertion of Imagination' (*Don Juan: A Variorum Edition*, p. 4) of his readers that he mocks Wordsworth for asking of his. According to McGann, we are to read the poem throughout as this storyteller's, or 'ballad singer's' virtuoso 'performance', and see the fisherman simply as one of the 'roles' he adopts in the course of that performance (see *Fiery Dust*, pp. 141–148).

habits of mind as a poet.[44] These poems, like many others, show Byron's tendency to return to various key ideas or subjects, but they also demonstrate an experimental determination to be always modifying his approach to them, to rethink them and explore them from a new vantage point, to explore new ways of imagining. They also demonstrate a smaller habit of mind, namely, the picking up and keeping, magpie fashion, bits and pieces of detail, building up a context, history, and identity for a hero-figure that combines, as he evolves, elements drawn from a deliberately maintained plethora of literary precedents. This displays a loyalty to, and a trust in, what the imagination throws up, or latches on to, that remains a feature of Byron's poetry throughout his life. This deliberate repose in accidental fecundity and hoarded detail is a major source of new form in Byron's poetry.

This seems to be a good point for us to very briefly pause and review the progress we are following in broader terms. In trying to describe the way in which *The Giaour* came into being, we have been following Byron's continued progress away from his early self-projecting lyrics and from the satire he thought his 'forte'. We first notice this movement in cantos I and II of *Childe Harold*, in which Byron attempts to use a fictional narrative and his own journey to structure and sustain an extended experiment aimed at achieving 'variety'.

We know that Byron was keen to try and write a second travel narrative 'as like' *Childe Harold* I and II as possible, but soon found that he would have to give up the idea, at least temporarily. He 'must see the scenes before writing about them', as Gleckner puts it.[45] While in England, he turned instead to the 'adventure narrative', and more specifically to what we might call the 'revenge narrative', for a structure that would, on the one hand, facilitate his lyric impulse, and, on the other hand, continue to extend its range.[46]

Byron certainly found a kind of writing that suited him in the revenge narrative. All of the tales that Byron wrote between 1812 and 1816 are, like *The Giaour*, highly lyricized revenge narratives.[47] Each tale is driven to its

---

[44] 'Why Byron abandoned "Il Diavolo Inamorato" is perhaps suggested by some remarks on versification in his dedicatory epistle to *The Corsair*: "The stanza of Spenser is perhaps too slow and dignified for narrative; though, I confess, it is the measure most after my own heart"' (McGann, 'Byron's First Tale: An Unpublished Fragment', p. 19; see *Works* III [p. 149] for the *Corsair* quotation). McGann goes on to argue that what Byron 'means, of course, is that the Spenserians did not seem appropriate for the fast-paced adventure tales which he was then writing' (p. 19).

[45] *Ruins*, p. 95.

[46] Andrew Rutherford argues that 'in the tales themselves, he [Byron] plunges into fiction and invents melodramatic plots to replace the feeble narrative interest of his tour' (*Byron: A Critical Study* [Edinburgh and London: Oliver and Boyd, 1961], p. 38).

[47] Selim is driven by the desire to avenge his father in *The Bride of Abydos* II (202, 269). Conrad's piracy in *The Corsair* is his 'adder-like' vengeance on a world that has 'trampled' him (I, 399). The events of *Lara* are the result of Otho's thirst for 'vengeance' (II, 213). Alp, too, in *The Siege of Corinth*, battles to avenge himself on Minotti (275–280) and on his homeland generally (70–95), but the poem develops into a blood-drenched story of vengeance gone mad. As warriors are killed, 'Avengers over their bodies' (887) rise, and it is 'the thirst for vengeance' (944) that pushes events to their devastating climax. Finally, *Parisina* recounts the enactment of Azo's vengeance, though this personal revenge is to some

climax by the desire for vengeance, and, as Rutherford argues, the 'heroes are
... bent on vengeance, whether on individuals or social groups, nations or all
mankind'.[48] These tales, from *The Bride of Abydos* to *Parisina*, inherit a form
first discovered in *The Giaour* and occupy the thematic territory first marked
out there. In them Byron works out, and refines, the 'tragic vision' of human
suffering towards which 'The Monk of Athos' begins to move, and which *The
Giaour* begins to explore.[49] It is a vision that exerted a considerable influence
over Byron's subsequent relation to the whole business of writing. It exerted
such a powerful attraction for him that he had to fight his way clear of it. We
will be looking at some of his struggles to shake it off, and to push into new
territory, in subsequent chapters, so it will be helpful to have a clear sense of
the vision that so held Byron's imagination.

　　Byron was not primarily interested in revenge narratives *per se*. The
revenge narrative was a formal means to a thematic end. Byron's first interest
was in heightened emotions and extreme emotional states,[50] and his revenge
narratives are powerful in the first instance precisely because the events in them
drive the protagonists of each tale into such emotional extremes, and leave
emotional wrecks in their wake. *The Giaour*, for example, relentlessly pushes
its eponymous hero towards emotional and mental suffering and then holds
him there. As the first of Byron's tales, it sets a precedent for the others.
Certainly, each of Byron's early tales drives with the same determination to the
same extremity.

　　The result is a striking thematic consistency in these poems. In them all,
Byron seems fascinated by remorse and by extreme, desolating grief which
often combine to produce a 'Woe without name – or hope – or end' (*The
Giaour*, 276).[51] Initially, it is 'the heart ... left desolate' by the loss of the

---

extent hidden behind the guise of 'punishment'. Despite Azo's repeated insistence that
Hugo's death is a 'just decree' (576), it is at bottom the 'sentence of his ire' (143). All
quotations from Byron's tales are taken from *Works* III. References to canto (where
applicable) and line are given after each quotation in the text, and prefaced by the title of the
poem from which the quotation is taken.

[48]　Rutherford, *Byron*, p. 42. Rutherford claims that 'all' the heroes 'are bent on
vengeance' (p. 42), but this is not quite true of Lara. He is motivated, as Rutherford
concedes, by the need 'to protect himself' (p. 43) from vengeance rather than the desire to
avenge himself.

[49]　The vision of suffering offered by these tales is not 'tragic' in any strict
Aristotelian sense, but is built around, and deliberately employs, various tragic motifs: the
idea of 'descent from prosperity to suffering and chaos', heroism, hatred, jealousy, murder,
and, in the case of *The Siege of Corinth*, 'the fall of the City' (Steiner, *The Death of
Tragedy*, pp. 12, 9). The tales aim, we might say, at a Romantic version of the tragic which
combines elements taken from tragedy with moments of pathos and 'melodrama'.

[50]　As Rutherford points out, Byron also shares with Coleridge 'the characteristically
romantic interest in abnormal mental states' (*Byron*, p. 42).

[51]　The vision of suffering offered by these poems is, one could argue, made
'untragic' by Byron's fascination with remorse. For, as Steiner argues, 'By virtue of remorse,
the tragic sufferer is restored to a condition of grace' and in this sense, studies of remorse
'cannot be ultimately tragic' (*The Death of Tragedy*, pp. 129, 133). However, in Byron's
case, remorse does not necessarily lead away from tragic. In *Manfred*, for example, 'Byron
does reject the facile redemptive solution' opened up by remorse, and this is, I think, also

beloved that drives events towards revenge in these tales, as that heart 'Must fly at last for ease – to hate' (*The Giaour*, 943–944). Yet revenge finally leaves the desolated heart 'With nothing left to love or hate' (*The Giaour*, 988), and the result is

>   ... the dreary void –
> The leafless desart of the mind –
> The waste of feeling unemployed. (*The Giaour*, 958–960)

For the hero of these tales, once he finds himself in this final extremity, there is no possibility of new emotional or intellectual growth, and no possibility of moving forward by establishing new emotional connections: his mind is 'leafless' and his bosom 'vacant' (*The Giaour*, 939) once each emotional capacity has been blasted. Yet the hero can still feel the grief and remorse that have desolated his being. Whether Byron offers this as a cruel trick of memory, or assumes that the hero, even in absolute dislocation from the present, retains a vital connection with the emotional past that has brought him to this extremity, the hero soon comes to value the ability to remember, and in remembering feel, past pain: 'The vacant bosom's wilderness / Might thank the pang that made it less' (*The Giaour*, 939–940). The 'vacant bosom' can almost be grateful for that pain because it lifts, momentarily, the awful weight of 'dreary void', and gives the bosom, for a fleeting moment, the only sense of vitality that is available to it. When the Giaour finds himself thrown into vacancy he cleaves to the memory of his grief because he soon discovers that 'The keenest pangs ... / Are rapture to the dreary void' (*The Giaour*, 957–958).

In doing so, the Giaour can claim, in the face of his final desolation, that 'I have felt – and feel' (*The Giaour*, 1109), and this is his victory over the void. For the Giaour, pain is infinitely better than vacancy, which, of course, is a kind of death. It is better because, however painful, it is a form of life. As Peter B. Wilson argues, the Giaour 'seeks to escape a condition of total numbness ... by courting an intense suffering'.[52] The Giaour is denied 'Ambition, glory, love' (*Lara* I, 79) as Lara is, and is 'past all mirth or woe' (*Parisina*, 545) like Azo. He is denied all sources of feeling or animation, with 'nothing left to love or hate' (*The Giaour*, 988). His ability to relive that suffering by recollecting it and to suffer pangs of remorse for his past actions is his only escape, and the only proof now available to him of the fact of his own existence.[53]

In order to fight off the void, each hero must, like the Giaour, cling to their own grief and remorse. Yet for Byron grief and loss have the power to kill, as

---

true in his early verse narratives. As in Manfred, there is often 'a final arrogance' in the heroes of these narratives which gives them 'an element of real tragedy' (*The Death of Tragedy*, pp. 208, 132).

[52]   Peter B. Wilson, '"Galvanism upon Mutton": Byron's Conjuring Trick in *The Giaour*', in *Keats–Shelley Journal* 24 (1975), p. 120.

[53]   Writing to Annabella Milbanke, Byron famously insisted that 'The great object of life is Sensation – to feel that we exist – even though in pain'. The rest is the 'craving void' (letter of 6 September 1813, in *BLJ* III, p. 109).

instanced by the fate of Zuleika and Kaled. Guilt and remorse have the power
to overwhelm the consciousness of Parisina with despair (*Parisina* 345–355)
and, though we have to infer what is going on in the case of Lara, it seems
certain that it is some kind of encounter with his past that overwhelms Lara's
consciousness almost to the point of death:

> Cold as marble where his length was laid,
> Pale as the beam that o'er his features played,
> Was Lara stretch'd. (*Lara* I, 211–212)[54]

By courting intense suffering in order to restore some sense of vitality that
holds off the void, the hero is, we must not forget, intensely suffering. But he
also inviting, if not his own destruction, then certainly further emotional
devastations. The heroes of Byron's early tales, forced to feed off 'inward
starts of feeling' because each lacks 'the power to fill again / The desart gap
which made his pain' but 'would not yield' to that 'desart' gap, are then forced
to fight for their very lives by struggling to bear the emotional impact of
'thoughts ... / Too deeply rooted thence to vanish', even while feeding off
those thoughts (*Parisina*, 550–572). This last extremity drives the Giaour close
to madness, and forces Azo and Lara into a constant struggle to prevent the
suffering that keeps them alive from overwhelming them. Azo, for example, is
'past all mirth or woe', but alive, and alive only inasmuch as his vitality
manifests itself in 'sleepless nights and heavy days' during which he 'Intently
thought – intensely felt' (*Parisina*, 547–552). His vitality is reduced to 'those
waters of the heart' (*Parisina*, 562) that flow through memory, and while they
supply him with a kind of intensity that is 'cherished' (*Parisina*, 568), Azo is
forced, for survival's sake, into perpetually struggling to hold those waters in
'check' (*Parisina*, 543–567).[55]

This is the final extremity towards which all these tales push their
distinctively 'Byronic' heroes and heroines.[56] Indeed, this kind of suffering
always remained the fate of the main line of Byronic heroes, as 'The Dream',

---

[54] 'What or whom he sees in the midnight chamber that makes this ferociously
tough character faint is never disclosed' (Nellist, 'Lyric Presence', p. 61). The reader is left
with little doubt, though, that it is some manifestation, reminder, or recollection of Lara's
past. As Gleckner argues, Byron's 'point' in *Lara* is that 'the past ever lives in the present'
and that 'man is inescapably bound to his hell within' (*Ruins*, pp. 158–159). The problem is
that the 'mysteriousness of the hero's past, and the insistence on it as key to his identity,
assume the power of a riddle to which, however, we are given no solution' (Nellist, 'Lyric
Presence', p. 61). There is, of course, the question of whether or not *Lara* is a sequel to *The
Corsair*, but most critics who have addressed this question seem to dismiss Byron's hint that
it might be (see the Advertisement in *Works* III, p. 453). As Chew has pointed out, for
example, the 'links between the two poems' are actually 'few and tenuous' (*Childe Harold's
Pilgrimage and Other Romantic Poems* [New York: Doubleday, Doran, and Company,
1936], p. 245, n.).

[55] As is Lara, in whom the only signs of vitality have their roots in 'some deep
feeling' (I, 83) connected with 'buried ... thoughts that mortal lips must leave half told'
because they 'choak the feeble words that would unfold' (I, 285–288).

[56] This is clearly true in the cases of Kaled, Zuleika, and Parisina, for example, but
perhaps less obviously true in the case of Medora or Francesca.

Manfred, and *The Island* testify. But other heroes and other poems fight against this fate, and this brief account of it will provide us with an essential point of reference when we look at some of the later poems which rebel against the vision of extreme human suffering offered by this series of narratives.

The first poem to do so was canto III of *Childe Harold's Pilgrimage*. Here, Byron turned away from the Byronic hero, his revenge-narrative form, and the quasi-tragic idiom of that form. He set about exploring a very different kind of writing and began to explore a thematic territory which, in prospect, offered an answer to the dilemma of his tragic hero, and an entirely different 'vision of the human condition'.[57] In the next chapter we will be scrutinizing this attempt to push forward, once more, into something entirely new via thematic, formal, and idiomatic experimentation.

---

[57]   Gleckner, *Ruins*, p. 100.

CHAPTER THREE

'A Narrow Escape into Faith'

When Byron left England in April 1816, as McGann suggests, he was confronted with the problem of how to 'come to terms', both publicly and privately, 'with the collapse of his marriage and the public response to that event in England'.[1] When trying to 'decide what his public response should be' he had 'a model, or at least suggestions, in the character of his own heroes',[2] and canto III of *Childe Harold* suggests that the temptation to envisage himself as one of the heroes of his own tales was a strong one.

But the tragic and heroic ideals of those tales impose certain tragic absolutes. Most important is the absolute impossibility of moving beyond desolation. 'Tragedy', says Steiner, 'is irreparable',[3] and Byronic heroes do not recover from the shocks that desolate them.

Canto III of *Childe Harold* is a rejection of this tragic finality. It looks determinedly to the possibility of a redeeming return of vitality to the desolated subject. It especially looks to the revitalization and renewal that is held up by Wordsworth's poetry.[4] And the poem does move beyond the idea of irrevocable desolation. It discovers renewal and revitalization, and this achievement should command our attention for a range of reasons. For the purposes of this study, we will be looking at *Childe Harold* III's thematic advance on Byron's earlier verse narratives because in that advance we see Byron push past his own attraction to the emotional extremes of tragic experience, and into a new kind of poetic territory altogether.

Before we turn to the poem itself, however, and as a necessary preliminary to doing so, we must insist on the fact that *Childe Harold* III is not primarily a fictional work. The fictional Harold does play an important part in the canto, but he is not the centre around which it is built. In *Childe Harold* III, Byron discovers a path out of his 'tragic' discourse but it is not a fictional path, and though he is looking to celebrate 'an idealized art', he is wary of celebrating nothing more than 'a comforting fantasy' or a 'mere lie of fiction'.[5] He therefore 'comes forward in *propria persona*' to explore the possibility of renewal for himself and to test Wordsworth's consoling vision in his own

---

[1]   *Works* II, p. 300. The title of this chapter is taken from Christopher Fry, 'Comedy', in *Tulane Drama Review* 4:3 (March 1960), p. 77.

[2]   Rutherford, *Byron*, p. 48.

[3]   *The Death of Tragedy*, p. 8.

[4]   As Cooke argues, 'Byron ... experiments with [Wordsworthian naturalism] in his particular crisis' (*The Blind Man*, p. 47).

[5]   Bernard Beatty, *Byron's Don Juan* (London and Sydney: Croom Helm, 1985), pp. 224, 153.

person.[6] Byron speaks throughout the canto 'in his own person',[7] and his project is to record, in verse, his own experience as his own experience.[8]

Childe Harold III, then, demands to be read as a record of 'the "immediate, visible responses" of a human being'; as 'an expression of self'.[9] But how are we to read Byron's expression of self correctly, given the treacherous correspondence between a linguistic signifier and a non-linguistic signified? Doubts of this kind are reasonable, but I nevertheless hold on to the notion that any act of self-articulation communicates traces of its intended subject despite the play of self-referential differences it sets in motion. Furthermore, as Eric Griffiths argues, uncertainty about the accuracy of our interpretation of such acts should not lead to 'Abstract scepticism about the possibility of [a] correct critical description' of the presence (some) literature tries to convey. Such scepticism, for Griffiths, 'is possible but as empty as abstract epistemological scepticism', and while any account of a literary text may be

> thick with errors, ... its errors would be demonstrated by other, better instances of this kind of description, not by abandoning such descriptions altogether.[10]

We will proceed, then, in the hope that 'all one's descriptions or judgements are not wrong',[11] and that for the most part we accurately describe our object.

---

6   McGann, *Fiery Dust*, p. 134. See also Newey, 'Authoring the Self: *Childe Harold* III and IV', p. 152.

7   Rutherford, *Byron*, p. 49.

8   Much theoretical thinking over the last thirty years has, of course, argued against any association between a poem's speaker and its author. Most famously, Barthes asserted that 'language knows a "subject", not a "person", and this subject, empty outside of the very enunciation which defines it, suffices to make language "hold together"' ('The Death of the Author', in *Image-Music-Text*, trans. by Stephen Heath [Glasgow: Fontana, 1977], p. 145). Such apocalyptic visions of 'The Death of the Author' have been discredited by Jacques Derrida, among others, who argues that 'a written sign carries with it a force of breaking with its context, that is, the collectivity of presences which organize the moment of its inscription', but that 'the category of [authorial] intention will not disappear; it will have its place' ('Signature Event Context', in *Margins of Philosophy*, trans. by Alan Bass [Brighton: Harvester Press, 1982], pp. 317, 326). No explicit statement of an authorial intention that is trying to guide *Childe Harold* III's direction exists, but it is difficult to ignore the implicit aim to articulate the writing subject's experience of selfhood which does guide, even if it doesn't entirely control, that canto. This intention, despite the fact that it is never explicitly stated, should, I suggest, inform any reading of the poem.

9   McGann, *Fiery Dust*, p. 34, n. 4. We might note that by 1821, Byron's ideas about the nature of poetry had changed considerably (as they changed all his life): 'A man's poetry' he wrote in a letter to Thomas Moore dated 16 November 1821, 'is a distinct faculty, or soul, and has no more to do with the every-day individual than the Inspiration with the Pytheness when removed from her tripod' (*BLJ* IX, p. 64). After *Childe Harold's Pilgrimage*, Byron never wrote another long poem in the confessional mode of *Childe Harold* III, though *The Lament of Tasso* and *The Prophecy of Dante* are fictional versions of such confessionalism.

10   Eric Griffiths, *The Printed Voice of Victorian Poetry* (Oxford: Clarendon Press, 1989), p. 38.

11   Ibid.

Quite early on, the canto offers, as its ideal, an image of Wordsworthian communion with nature in which we glimpse 'Intimations of Immortality', but at the outset it has a long way to go before it arrives at any such communion. Yet Byron's determination to get clear of the memory of his own galling past and move forward is foregrounded in the first stanza, in which Byron creates the illusion of 'Awaking with a start' (*CHP* III, 5) from the recollection with which he opens the poem. He dramatizes himself turning his attention from 'Albion's lessening shores' (*CHP* III, 9) and all they contain: 'I depart' (*CHP* III, 7) he insists.

Byron's first strategy for sustaining this mental turning away is to turn self-imposed exile into adventure:

> Once more upon the waters! yet once more!
> And the waves bound beneath me as a steed
> That knows his rider. Welcome to their roar! (*CHP* III, 10–12)[12]

Byron's second, and complementary, tactic is to put aside himself and the present pain that recalls the past, and turn instead to Harold. Here the poem's advance is temporarily checked. As Byron pauses to become 'the reader of his preceding two cantos' and look again at Harold's history,[13] he tells us that he finds

> The furrows of long thought, and dried-up tears,
> Which, ebbing, leave a sterile track behind,
> O'er which all heavily the journeying years
> Plod the last sands of life,– where not a flower appears. (*CHP* III, 23–27)

It is no surprise to learn that Byron seems to have stopped writing for a while at this point.[14] Harold offers an image of 'journeying' very different from the one Byron offers in stanza 2.[15] Harold's history bears 'witness to past sorrows',[16] but also images a 'sterile' future, 'where not a flower appears', and Byron had imagined this final extremity over and over again in the verse narratives that preceded *Childe Harold* III. He clearly had no desire, now, to turn himself into one of his heroes, however, and when he picked up the poem again, he began by drawing a distinction between himself and Harold:

---

[12]   As Newey argues, Byron here depicts himself as an 'adventurer'. He 'revels in the pure "bounding" instant, embracing the excitement of being "all at sea"' ('Authoring the Self', p. 149). Cooke adds that an 'atmosphere of confidence as to the destination and exuberance over the new beginning is palpable in these lines' (*The Blind Man*, p. 45).

[13]   Michael O'Neill, *Romanticism and the Self-Conscious Poem* (Oxford: Clarendon Press, 1997), p. 115.

[14]   '*MSS. M* and *BM* together show that sts. 1–3 were written "at Sea", i.e. on 25 Apr.. B copied these three stanzas fair three days later, and for the rest of his trip from Belgium to Switzerland he apparently would write draft stanzas on whatever pieces of paper were to hand' (McGann, *Works* II, p. 298).

[15]   Byron's own sense of embarking on an adventure is itself vulnerable. It is undercut by the end of stanza 2 by 'a reverse configuration: Byron declares himself to be "as a weed" – insignificant, insentient, forever acted upon' (Newey, 'Authoring the Self', p. 149).

[16]   O'Neill, *Romanticism and the Self-Conscious Poem*, p. 115.

> Since my young days of passion – joy, or pain,
> Perchance my heart and harp have lost a string. (*CHP* III, 28–29)

Byron does not present himself as desolated in the way that Harold, the Giaour, and Azo are. Rather, he claims that his heart has lost 'a' string, and we might paraphrase Byron here by saying that he claims to have lost the capacity to feel one particular feeling, not all feeling. 'Perchance' even holds back from this degree of finality, retaining as it does some hope of total recovery.

Byron implies here that in his own case a fertile and vital future is possible. His strategy for moving forward to that future is to recover 'a sense of his own vitality' and a sense of self.[17] This will involve freeing the self and allowing it to flow into the kind of relations with the world that might win him such a future.[18]

In the first instance, however, both writing generally, and a new-minted Harold in particular, have their part to play in Byron's projected recovery of a sense of self. Byron tells us that he will 'bear' the 'theme' of Harold (*CHP* III, 21–22) with him 'as the rushing wind / Bears the cloud onwards' (*CHP* III, 22–23), that is, Harold will make manifest the existence of the poet, make that existence available for scrutiny, as moving cloud evidences wind.

Writing, on the other hand, is undertaken

> So that it wean me from the weary dream
> Of selfish grief or gladness – so it fling
> Forgetfulness around me. (*CHP* III, 33–35)[19]

---

[17] McGann, *Fiery Dust*, p. 114. According to de Man, 'True knowledge of a self is knowledge that understands the self as it really is. And since the self never exists in isolation, but always in relation to entities, since it is not a thing but the common centre of a system of relationships or intents, an authentic understanding of a self means first of all a description of the entities towards which it relates, and of the order of priority that exists among those entities' ('Time and History in Wordsworth', in *Romanticism and Contemporary Criticism: The Gauss Seminar and Other Papers*, ed. by E. S. Burt, Kevin Newmark, and Andrzej Warminski [Baltimore and London: Johns Hopkins University Press, 1993], p. 93). It is towards this kind of 'true knowledge' of the self that *Childe Harold* III is moving. It looks to a manifestation of the self in its relation to the natural world, and especially in the eager outwards straining intensity of a descriptive attention to nature that either aims at or is informed by a 'love' of 'Earth ... for its earthly sake' (*CHP* III, 672).

[18] In *Childe Harold* III, Byron seems to move towards 'a sort of Fichtean "interdetermination" whereby self is defined by', even brought into existence by, its 'response to the not-self' (Newey, 'Authoring the Self', p. 162, recalling Mark Kipperman, *Beyond Enchantment: German Idealism and English Romantic Poetry* [Philadelphia: University of Pennsylvania Press, 1986], p. 186).

[19] Julia Kristeva has argued that a writer 'must at one time or another have been in a situation of loss – of ties, of meaning – in order to write', but that 'the writer is able to describe her/his depression to us, and this is already a triumph over depression' ('A Question of Subjectivity – An Interview', in *Modern Literary Theory*, ed. by Philip Rice and Patricia Waugh [London: Edward Arnold, 1992], p. 133). *Childe Harold* III offers an interesting contradiction of this idea of triumph in description. Though intent on describing his immediate experience, Byron cannot 'embody and unbosom now / That which is most within me' (*CHP* III, 905–906), and so is denied the kind of triumph Kristeva describes. For Byron in *Childe Harold* III, attending to, and precisely describing, one kind of experience is a way of

The wish to forget the 'selfish' would seem to suggest a desire for escape from the self rather than a desire to recover it, but 'forgetfulness' is to be flung 'around me', not to be 'of me'. What is desired here is not, I suggest, an 'absence' of, or 'escape' from, self.[20] Rather, it is the self's entrapment in the perpetual oscillation between 'grief or gladness', generated by selfish ambition and heard especially in the word 'or', that Byron declares he wants to be weaned from. Here begins the poetic 'quest for self-identity'.[21] Writing might 'wean' the self, 'me', from its absorption in 'the weary dream', so that this 'me' can step forward and be known. A sense of self can, perhaps, be recovered and the self thus rediscovered can, potentially, be freed-up and allowed to assert itself and move forward.

With this aim in view, and appropriate means seemingly in place, the poem's central project appears set to begin at the end of stanza 4. Yet the poem falters as if unable to really get under way. In what reads like a dangerously vacant pause between stanzas 4 and 5, Byron's mind seems to have turned once more to the idea of one who has

> ... grown aged in this world of woe,
> In deeds, not years, piercing the depths of life,
> So that no wonder waits him; nor below
> Can love, or sorrow, fame, ambition, strife,
> Cut to his heart again with the keen knife
> Of silent, sharp endurance. (*CHP* III, 37–42)

We have already seen Byron draw a distinction between his own fate and the idea of final desolation. But it seems that his own fascination with this extremity threatened to keep drawing his imagination back to this, the figure that dominates so much of his work up to this point.[22] Clearly Byron needed to hold this fascination at bay, and we see him attemping to do so by resisting the temptation to be drawn on

> Why thought seeks refuge in lone caves, yet rife
> With airy images, and shapes which dwell
> Still unimpair'd, though old, in the soul's haunted cell. (*CHP* III, 43–45)

This is the 'refuge' from the void, in the 'lone caves' of memory, where 'old' images are 'unimpaired'. Byron resists the temptation to elaborate with

---

forgetting another. Writing is a way of forgetting his own depression rather than a means of describing it. To adopt the role of the poet is a 'diversionary tactic' (Gleckner, *Ruins*, p. 95).

[20] O'Neill, *Romanticism and the Self-Conscious Poem*, pp. 97, 103.

[21] Geoffrey Hartman, 'Romanticism and Anti-Self-Consciousness' in *Beyond Formalism: Literary Essays 1958–1970* (New Haven and London: Yale University Press, 1970), p. 308. Hartman argues that 'the Romantic "I" emerges nostalgically when certainty and simplicity of self are lost' (p. 304), and perhaps there is an element of nostalgia in Byron's sense of having a recoverable self. Byron's 'me' is certainly like other Romantic selves in as much as it is 'that self within the self which resembles Blake's "emanation" and Shelley's "epipsyche"' (Ibid.).

[22] Compare, for example, line 40 of *CHP* III with *The Giaour*, 988–989, and with *Lara* I, 79–81.

the phrase 'he can tell' (*CHP* III, 42), which immediately precedes this quotation. The implication is, of course, that 'he' who is 'grown aged in this world of woe' can tell, while Byron either cannot or will not. This helps the poem to briefly bypass a subject that is compelling, but it is still being pulled in by the temptation to answer its own implicit question: 'Why does thought take refuge?'. It soon does so, and a new vitality becomes immediately apparent – the very 'Vitality of poison' (*CHP* III, 299) described repeatedly in Byron's early tales. Suddenly, Byron slips into the voice of the hero-figure he has been trying to keep at arm's length:[23]

> 'Tis to create, and in creating live
> A being more intense, that we endow
> With form our fancy, gaining as we give
> The life we image, even as I do now.
> What am I? Nothing; but not so art thou,
> Soul of my thought! with whom I traverse earth,
> Invisible but gazing, as I glow
> Mixed with thy spirit, blended with thy birth,
> And feeling still with thee in my crush'd feeling's dearth. (*CHP* III, 46–54)

Almost like a vehement confession comes the claim that he, too, is after all desolated: 'What am I? Nothing ... in my crush'd feeling's dearth'. By stanza 6, Byron appears to have succumbed to his own fascination with the idea of a final desolation, and has slipped into the rhetoric used by and about the fictional Byronic heroes that suffer this final desolation. Byron begins to image himself, and, perhaps, imagine himself, bereft of any vitality and locked in a struggle to win what intensity he can by imagining or recalling 'A being more intense'. And by projecting himself as one of his own tragic heroes, Byron comes close to submitting to the notion that he cannot look to a future that will be any different from the present.

In stanza 7, Byron pulls in the reins and tries once more to distance his poem from his own compelling, but damning, idea of human desolation. The difficulty of doing so, however, moves forward with him. The 'me' of line 33, the self that can, potentially, be freed-up and allowed to assert its vitality, is not only tangled up in memory and 'the weary dream / Of selfish grief and gladness'. It must also continue to fight clear of 'the lure of false ultimates',[24] and more specifically, the notion, imported from fiction, that it is doomed to an inescapably tragic, or at the very best diversionary, existence.[25]

---

23   Rutherford argues that this 'fusion of the poet with the hero-type he had created is the central feature of *Childe Harold*, canto III' (*Byron*, p. 49). I would argue rather that one of the dangers Byron must fend off if his project in *Childe Harold* III is to be successful is such a slippage of self into fiction. Rutherford carries on to assert that Byron obliterates 'his earlier distinction between hero and narrator' (p. 49), but, as we shall see, it is precisely this distinction that Byron struggles to hold on to.

24   Hartman, 'Romanticism and Anti-Self-Consciousness', p. 307.

25   The danger of the writing subject slipping into his/her own fictions is well described by Karen Swann in her 'Literary Gentlemen and Lovely Ladies: The Debate on the Character of Christabel' in *English Literary History* 52:1 (Spring 1985): 'In moments of imaginative generosity, of voluntary relinquishments of self to fictions, writers and readers

Oddly, given this imperative, Byron does not return to his earlier distinction between his own fate and that of the desolated Byronic hero. He is, in the first instance, more ambitious than this. He puts aside the whole question of his own suffering, and turns instead to Harold as a fictional image of suffering itself, though Byron's suffering, of course, figures in this image. Rather than self-consciously pull back from the idea that he is, now, irrevocably desolated, Byron sets about countering the notion that the human spirit can be blasted to the point of vacancy and must fend off such vacancy in suffering, perpetually, the blast that devastated it. Harold, 'Proud though in desolation' (*CHP* III, 107), 'fain no more would feel' (*CHP* III, 67), but is saved from such vacancy by the invisible 'chain / Which gall'd for ever, fettering' (*CHP* III, 77–78) him to his own painful past. More importantly, however, it seems Harold is saved from vacancy by the natural and spontaneous return of sensations that for heroes like the Giaour and Conrad are dead:

> ... who can view the ripened rose, nor seek
> To wear it? who can curiously behold
> The smoothness and the sheen of beauty's cheek,
> Nor feel the heart can never all grow old?
> Who can contemplate Fame through clouds unfold
> The star which rises o'er her steep, nor climb? (*CHP* III, 91–96)

Desolation is redeemed by a spontaneous return of sensation and a renewed connectedness with the external world. Time has mysteriously effected the change in Harold: 'Time, who changes all, had altered him' (*CHP* III, 69). The idea that desolation can be redeemed by or in time has been provisionally projected into, in the figure of Harold, the fate of the irrevocably blasted Byronic hero. The result is, potentially, a total transformation, which is surprising to the reader of Byron's early verse narratives, even in prospect, for there time is the enemy because it will 'strengthen, not efface' (*The Giaour*, 193) what the heroes suffer.

The idea of such a possible transformation, however, almost immediately needs protection. What we might call Byron's hitherto 'tragic sense of life' re-surfaces,[26] suggesting the idea that Harold's fate describes a 'giddy circle' (*CHP* III, 98) that escapes, but then returns to, devastation. Harold, having 'quaff'd ... life's enchanted cup ... and ... found / The dregs were wormwood', 'fill'd again, / And from a purer fount' yet 'deem'd its spring perpetual ... in vain' (*CHP* III, 72–76). The devastated subject may look forward to renewal, but is doomed to future desolation.

Can renewal be held on to, and future desolation fended off? This question underpins the resistance we now see to Byron's usual, almost reflex equation of a return to 'life' with a return to the 'False' and 'hollow' 'Revel' and

---

flirt with the possibility of going too far – of losing their "Substance" to a "ghost", of "letting themselves slip" into delusions which could become difficult to escape, of acceding to "holds" they might "never ... wish to shake off"'(p. 416).

[26]   This often used phrase was originally the title of Miguel de Unamuno's famous work, *Del sentimiento tragico de la vida* (1912).

'Laughter' of urbane and urban society, where 'smiles form the channel of a future tear' (*CHP* II, 909–916). Instead of this, we are offered a very different model of what it might be to live in vital connectedness with the world. Here the world is not humanity, but nature, and Byron's new model, drawn most obviously from Wordsworth,[27] posits the idea of relationships which draw the 'heart', 'soul', and 'mind', but do not prove 'wormwood':[28]

> Where rose the mountains, there to him were friends;
> Where roll'd the ocean, thereon was his home;
> Where a blue sky, and a glowing clime, extends,
> He had the passion and the power to roam;
> The desert, forest, cavern, breaker's foam,
> Were unto him companionship. (*CHP* III, 109–114)

Byron here uses the figure of Harold to image what a 'redeemed' Byronic hero might look like. But more importantly in the context of *Childe Harold* III, Harold is here a projection of the kind of self Byron might become.[29] Byron has yet to explore how either he or the Byronic hero might actually become this newly imagined self, but Harold's notional experience projects the idea of a companionship with the natural world and a permanent 'passion and ... power' in that companionship that both fiction and fact can aim at. *Childe Harold* III, certainly, quests after this permanent renewal of 'passion and ... power'.

Yet behind the prospect of permanent revitalization is another, even more tantalizing prospect. Harold, or rather the model of existence he bodies forth (and Harold has progressed from being a typically Byronic figure to an even more recognizably Wordsworthian one here), posits, in addition to the possibility of permanent and sustainable renewal, the possibility of transcending 'earth-born jars' altogether:

> Like the Chaldean, he could watch the stars,
> Till he had peopled them with beings bright
> As their own beams; and earth, and earth-born jars,
> And human frailties, were forgotten quite. (*CHP* III, 118–121)

The idea of transcendence is heard in the word 'forgotten' here and in the later word 'flight' (*CHP* III, 122), and is to be found in what we might describe as a 'happy' (*CHP* III, 123) trance-like communion with the natural

---

27 'Wordsworth had subdued poetry to the theme of nature's role in the growth of the individual mind' (Hartman, 'Romanticism and Anti-Self-Consciousness', p. 308). 'Byron knew the *Lyrical Ballads*, and reviewed the *Poems in Two Volumes* (1807) for *Monthly Literary Recreations*. By 1815 he had read *The Excursion*, and he was acquainted with the collected poems published in the same year. In fact, Byron had probably kept a fairly close eye on Wordsworth' (Martin, *Byron: A Poet Before His Public*, p. 65).

28 Throughout Wordsworth's poetry, we find a 'pleasure at finding responses, satisfying possibilities of relationship even for someone who ... "stands alone"' (de Man, 'Time and History in Wordsworth', p. 77).

29 Harold describes possible 'future experience by means of the fiction of a past experience which is itself [it is hoped] anticipatory or prefigurative' (de Man, ibid., p. 82).

universe. Embedded in *Childe Harold* III's quest for 'passion and ... power' is a new and deep-rooted yearning for this transcendence.

Two prospects – permanent renewal, and the faint possibility of a permanent spiritual transcendence of the earthly – draw *Childe Harold* III on. The Spenserian stanza is put to something much closer to 'its original purpose' in this canto than in *Childe Harold* I and II, namely, to depict 'pilgrimage' and 'questing'.[30] The poem claims to record in language, firstly, a quest for self-renewal, revitalization, and intensity, and, secondly, a quest for transcendental trance-like communion with nature: stanzas 13 and 14 echo, and give their own voice to, the idealism of Wordsworth's poetry.

Byron's attitude to Wordsworth's poetry clearly changed dramatically between 1809 and 1816. Nevertheless, from the outset *Childe Harold* III is more openly aware than Wordsworth's poetry of what stands in the way of any human and 'earthly' quest for a permanent transcendence of the human and earthly. Compare the following lines of stanza 14 with a few lines from Wordsworth's 'Resolution and Independence':

> Could he [Harold] have kept his spirit to that flight
> He had been happy; but this clay will sink
> Its spark immortal, envying it the light
> To which it mounts, as if to break the link
> That keeps us from yon heaven which woos us to its brink. (*CHP* III, 122–126)

> ... the whole body of the Man did seem
> Like one whom I had met with in a dream;
> Or like a man from some far region sent,
> To give me human strength, by apt admonishment.
> ...
> My former thoughts returned: the fear that kills;
> And hope that is unwilling to be fed.[31]

---

[30]   Francis Berry, 'The Poet of *Childe Harold*', in *Byron: A Symposium*, ed. by John D. Jump (London and Basingstoke: Macmillan, 1975), p. 43. Berry argues that 'Byron ... re-tuned the Spenserian stanza to suit his own nature' (p. 42) but that the stanza's 'original purpose – pilgrimages, questing knights or apprentice knights – provided Byron with the bold "plan"' (pp. 42–43).

[31]   'Resolution and Independence', 109–114. Quotations from this poem are taken from *The Poetical Works of William Wordsworth*, vol. II, ed. by E. de Selincourt (Oxford: Clarendon, 1944). 'Resolution and Independence' was first published in *Poems* (1807), and so Byron certainly knew of it (see note 25). However, no clear parallel between *Childe Harold* III and 'The Leech Gatherer' has been suggested before to my knowledge. According to Thomas Moore, Wordsworth was certainly aware of the fact that his work had a strong influence on *Childe Harold* III, but he was in no doubt that 'Tintern Abbey' was 'the source of it all' (*Memoirs, Journal and Correspondence of Thomas Moore* (1853), quoted in *Byron: The Critical Heritage*, ed. by Andrew Rutherford [London: Routledge and Kegan Paul, 1970], p. 109, n.).

Byron here focuses our attention on something that Wordsworth's 'double operation' in 'Resolution and Independence' glimpses but passes over:[32] imaginative insight flies beyond the actual, to the 'brink of yon heaven', but its flight cannot be maintained. Consciousness is pulled back to the self. The 'spark immortal' sinks even as the subject perceives the possibility of 'some far region'.

In both poems, the subject's seemingly instinctive and certainly involuntary response to a flight of consciousness away from self is to self-consciously reflect on the fact of that flight: to 'fear' it is an illusion, let us say, while hoping it is not. The experience of spiritual 'flight' is interrupted and succumbs to (and is translated into) self-conscious reflection.

But Byron throws a spotlight on his enemy: self-conscious reflection. And he implies that, from the outset, any quest for a permanent transcendence of the threat of future pain must be, by necessity, a quest to overcome this 'enemy within'. Byron seems positioned somewhere between a forlorn yearning ('Could he have kept his spirit to that flight / He had been happy') for permanent transcendence and a resignation to its impossibility. Nevertheless, where *Childe Harold* I and II insisted on the impossibility of a permanent transcendence of 'earth-born jars', *Childe Harold* III is a quest poem and written in hope, regardless of how faint that hope may be.

As an account of a dual quest, firstly for a relation with the world that brings sustainable renewal and, secondly, after a spiritual transcendence of the world, we might expect *Childe Harold* III to be written in a narrative mode. But, as we have seen in the case of *Childe Harold* I and II, and again in the case of *The Giaour*, Byron seems to have been principally interested in narrative as a structure for lyrical output. In *Childe Harold* III, Byron once again fends off narrative modes. Indeed, he suddenly cuts across the narrative mode of stanza 16 – 'Self-exiled Harold wanders forth again' (*CHP* III, 136) – by reasserting the lyric travelogue mode of *Childe Harold* I and II: 'Stop! – for thy tread is on an Empire's dust!' (*CHP* III, 145). This effects a sudden shift from narrative to lyricism, and announces the poet's determination to keep the impulse to write narratives in check. A narrative quest structure still underlies the poem, however. Byron's insistence on lyricism should not obscure this fact, even though it enabled him to overlay a second structure (that of a travelogue) on to the first (that of an existential and spiritual quest) and so ensure that he could do more than write a quest poem. The poem could be, as and when he wanted it to be, a travelogue of any kind – topographical,[33]

---

32 O'Neill, *Romanticism and the Self-Conscious Poem*, p. 42. O'Neill uses the phrase 'double operation' to describe the way in which Wordsworth is 'moving "outside himself" while examining his imagination at work' in 'Resolution and Independence' (p. 42).

33 It is important to note that as it evolves, *Childe Harold* stays in touch with the topographical tradition out of which it was born while simultaneously transforming that tradition. McGann holds that '*CHP* is a highly moralized travelogue very much in the tradition of eighteenth-century topographical poem' but adds that 'B adopted only to translate radically the form which he borrowed' (*Works* II, pp. 270–271). Similarly, Diego Saglia points us to the fact that Byron's approach to place throughout *Childe Harold* is 'a complex evolution of 18th-century topographical poetry as it goes far beyond this genre's array of

satirical, historical, and so on – as well as the articulation (and, perhaps, the means of advancing) a quest for sustainable renewal in a relationship with nature.

Secondly, by writing a lyrical journey poem, Byron could structure his quest for renewed 'passion and ... power' in a relationship with nature, by using the act of writing such a poem to focus his attention on arrivals at, or approaches to, place. Each approach is announced and opens a distinct section of the poem: 'on the banks of thy majestic Rhine' (*CHP* III, 409); 'Lake Leman woos with me with its crystal face' (*CHP* III, 644); 'Now, where the swift Rhone cleaves his way' (*CHP* III, 878). Each of these announcements inaugurates an address or reverie designed to draw out a response on Byron's part, a response that will, or will not, manifest a return of 'passion and ... power'. Place, then, functions in a way similar to the 'theme' of Harold:

> And for these words, thus woven into song,
> It may be that they are a harmless wile,
> The colouring of the scenes which fleet along,
> Which I would seize, in passing, to beguile
> My breast, or that of others, for a while. (*CHP* III, 1040–1044)

Byron 'would seize' the 'scenes that fleet along' because, he claims, those scenes 'beguile' his 'breast', that is, divert its attention from memory and self-scrutiny. They do more, however. Places induce responses that, ideally, draw the self out into spontaneous and unselfconscious being, and here, at the end of the poem, Byron claims to have been seizing this spontaneity; articulating and so demonstrating it. It manifests itself, he implies, in the poem's 'colouring' of each scene.

The extra-textual aim insisted upon by the poem is, then, an unavoidably self-conscious one: to test whether or not the self does burst forth into renewed being in response to place, and to see whether or not the relationship such a response implies can be sustained. And, of course, self-consciousness is not the only obstacle to success that Byron carried forward with him: in *Childe Harold* III, we see him perpetually struggling to fend off (or keep at bay) memory, his own lingering attachment to the past, and his favourite, but damning, image of himself as the suffering Byronic hero. The whole poem presents us with an account of this struggle.

Or at least primarily. We should keep in mind that behind this immediate need we are given a second and surprising motivation for Byron's new-found desire to 'open himself up' to the influence of place. This is the hope that in a Wordsworthian communion with place, 'the contemplative Soul' might really advance 'to the country of everlasting life' and, more importantly, 'continue to explore those cheerful tracts' without being 'brought back ... to the land of transitory things' by self-consciousness.[34]

---

varied yet orderly arranged regional landscapes, picturesque ruins, decorative rural figures and so on' ('Spain and Byron's Construction of Place', in *The Byron Journal* 22 (1994), p. 40).

[34] Wordsworth, 'Essays Upon Epigraphs', in *The Prose Works of William Wordsworth*, vol. III, ed. by W. J. B. Owen and Jane Worthing Smyser (Oxford: Clarendon Press, 1974), p. 53. Hartman argues that the question of 'whether the mind can find an

Byron's first port of call, Waterloo, did not advance his existential and spiritual quest. Indeed, it seems to have reminded him of various cultural obligations that he felt as a poet, but which a private quest poem was not very likely to honour. For example, 'Stop! – for thy tread is on an Empire's dust' not only stops short a narrative beginning, but also answers a sudden sense of obligation to history, and a corresponding sense of the triviality of *Childe Harold* III's central enterprise in the face of such an event as Waterloo. Byron's self-imposed obligation here is to the preservation of the memory of past deeds, events, catastrophes, and achievements. The result is a prolonged contemplation of recent European history.[35]

Yet this contemplation leads the poem back to the reason for a quest like the one on which it is embarking, and the poem surmounts the threat posed to it by the idea of other kinds of poems. The idea of war leads to the idea of death, and death to loss, grief, and broken-hearted despair. Byron's musings arrive back at the fact of intense suffering and emotional desolation. 'To teach' those in such suffering 'Forgetfulness', he says, 'were mercy for their sake' (*CHP* III, 273–274).

This insight leads the poem back to its starting point,[36] but does not lead it back into its central quest. And there is a strange sense of relief when Byron turns to history and personal loss in stanza 30, and turns 'from all' Spring 'brought' to 'those she could not bring' (*CHP* III, 270). It is not until stanza 49 that Byron forcibly turns our attention back to nature: 'Away with these [speculations]! true Wisdom's world will be / Within its own creation, or in thine, / Maternal Nature!' (*CHP* III, 406–408).

My point here is that while Byron implicitly claims to want to turn to nature, he seems unable quite to do so, and reluctant to do so. When, in stanza 46, he turns to the nature of the Rhine valley, he depicts an idealized but explicitly fictional response. He makes no effort to claim this response as his own: 'There Harold gazes on a work divine' (*CHP* III, 410). The response Byron claims as his own is that response which is drawn not by nature, but by the 'chiefless castles' (*CHP* III, 413) that dot the landscape. Byron's attention, we are invited to presume, was drawn away from nature, even as his attention turned towards it, by images of 'Ruin' (*CHP* III, 414), and this highlights one of the obstacles to Byron's quest, namely, a consuming habit of mind which latches hold of everything that recalls, or can figure, 'a lofty mind / Worn, but

---

unselfconscious medium for itself or maintain something of the interacting unity of self and life, is the central concern of the Romantic poets' ('Romanticism and Anti-Self-Consciousness', p. 46).

35   As a consequence, the poem's mode becomes, for a time, that of 'public speech' rather than that of a confessional poem, or even a narrative one. As John Jump notes, in stanzas 21 to 27 (for example), 'Byron does not seem ... to be admitting us into his confidence; he seems to be addressing us collectively. He has something to say that he needs to communicate, and he is prepared to use all the methods of the orator, as well as those of the poet, in order to communicate it' (*Byron* [London: Routledge and Kegan Paul, 1971], p. 82).

36   'The notion that it would be merciful to teach these survivors "forgetfulness" (st. 31) recalls the poet's decision to resume composition in order to fling "forgetfulness" around himself' (O'Neill, *Romanticism and the Self-Conscious Poem*, p. 116).

unstooping' (*CHP* III, 415–416) and draws the mind back from the idea of growth to the idea of decay. But another, even more problematic, obstacle soon surfaces: a kind of apprehensive reluctance to forget the past. When Byron describes nature's power to wash history away (*CHP* III, 455), to cleanse the world of the past,[37] so to speak, the insight is immediately transferred to Harold, while the idea of 'the blackened memory's blighting dream' (*CHP* III, 458) and its invulnerability to the 'exulting' (*CHP* III, 442) power of the Rhine is inserted into the poem as Byron's own response

This 'anti-Wordsworthian thwarting of Nature by memory',[38] the reluctance to forget, seems partly due to a lingering attachment on Byron's part to his own history, and especially to his half-sister, Augusta.[39] He claims to speak from a 'spot ... to me so dear' that nevertheless does not absolutely absorb him. The banks of the Rhine '"want" one thing, "Thy gentle hand to clasp in mine!"',[40] and Byron cannot entirely 'dwell delighted here' (*CHP* III, 531) because he is haunted by the idea that he 'should see' the 'scene' with 'double joy wert *thou* with me!' (*CHP* III, 504–505).

The lingering attachment to Augusta, however, does not entirely explain Byron's seeming reluctance to detach himself from the past, and seek 'forgetfulness' in a communion with nature. We must not make too little of Byron's sense of duty to 'deeds which should not pass away / And names which must not wither, though the earth / Forgets' (*CHP* III, 635–637). There is a resentment against nature here: a resentment at the fact that the earth does forget, indeed, eventually washes the past clean away. This sense of duty and resentment must be overcome before Byron 'opens himself up' to nature.

Various other anxieties also help to create Byron's apparent reluctance to get on with his chosen existential quest. For him, 'the Alps' are 'The palaces of Nature' (*CHP* III, 590–591) and of 'All which expands the spirit, yet appals' (*CHP* III, 596). They demonstrate 'How earth may pierce to Heaven, yet leave vain man below' (*CHP* III, 598). The word 'appals', and the fear of being left 'below', suggest a basic anxiety that his quest for renewal and connectedness with nature will fail.[41] Byron cannot simply 'scan' these

---

[37]   'The course of the Rhine, almost made to fuse with the course of time, can wash away physical harm, or at least the evidence of it' (Cooke, *The Blind Man*, p. 50).

[38]   Ibid.

[39]   In his notes to the poem, McGann tells us that the 'one fond breast' (III, 476) to whom the lyric opening 'The castled crag of Drachenfels' (III, 496) is addressed is 'B's sister Augusta' (*Works* II, p. 304). In *Fiery Dust*, he informs his reader that 'In the Morgan Library MS of the lyric the lines are addressed by Byron to his sister' (p. 87). McGann also claims that Augusta's 'remembered presence passes in and out of the rest of the canto' (*Works* II, p. 304).

The lyric itself is deliberately and self-consciously sentimental, and while there is no reason to suppose his attachment to Augusta was not genuine and profound, we might want to argue that what is important here is not primarily Byron's reluctance to relinquish his emotional attachment to Augusta, but rather his reluctance to relinquish his sentimental attachment to the idea of thwarted emotional attachments.

[40]   Cooke, *The Blind Man*, p. 51, quoting *Childe Harold* III, 515.

[41]   As McGann argues, Byron's 'sense of his own littleness and insufficiency ("vain man") forces him ... to admit that his "aspirations to be great" (88) are "appalled" by the enormity of the venture (not to speak of the difficulties attendant upon such a quest ...)'

sublime and 'matchless heights', but must 'dare to scan' them (*CHP* III, 599). And a final, related anxiety also dogs the poem's progress. What if the sublimity that draws the canto on proves hollow? What if,

> Though high *above* the sun of glory glow,
> And far *beneath* the earth and ocean spread,
> *Round* ... are icy rocks, and loudly blow
> Contending tempests on ...[my]... naked head,
> And thus reward the toils which to those summits led. (*CHP* III, 401–405)

Perhaps the fear of such a reward helped hold Byron back from following the new 'Wordsworthian' Harold into a companionship with nature until he reached Lake Leman, but we can trace the continuing existence of all the obstacles we have touched on long after the poem's arrival there in stanza 68. But in stanza 68, Byron does turn to nature in its immediate relation to his own consciousness. Here a complex sequence of stanzas begins, and we will need to look at them closely. As soon as Byron's quest seems to get under way, it is once again under attack from memory, reflection, and self-conscious doubts:

> Lake Leman woos me with its crystal face,
> The mirror where the stars and mountains view
> The stillness of their aspect in each trace
> Its clear depth yields of their far height and hue:
> There is too much of man here, to look through
> With a fit mind the might which I behold;
> But soon in me shall Loneliness renew
> Thoughts hid, but not less cherish'd than of old,
> Ere mingling with the herd had penn'd me in their fold. (*CHP* III, 644–652)

While this stanza opens with the claim that 'Lake Leman woos' Byron's attention to nature in its immediacy, it rapidly loses touch with this claim. And yet, to feel the seduction of, let us say, 'beauty' is a vital response, and the return of such vitality is one object of *Childe Harold* III's quest. But here a 'tragic' sense of human isolation steps in between the self and the landscape that 'woos' that self. Byron projects himself as seduced into feeling, but also depicts the mutation of that feeling into one of exclusion: the stars and mountains view themselves in the lake, while the lake yields the stars and mountains to their view. Byron is moved, but present feeling is polluted by past feeling, so that he is moved only as far as to see a relationship he can have no part in, and this throws him back into a self-conscious sense of failure. The landscape becomes a mirror image of Byron's 'tragic' sense of himself as isolated and ultimately excluded from any vital connection with the world. An outwardly turned consciousness is suddenly turned inward once more, and self-consciousness produces the insistence on the first-person in phrases like 'I behold', 'in me', 'penn'd me'.

(*Fiery Dust*, p. 115). For McGann, this note of 'foreboding' enters the poem very early on. He argues that 'we are led to doubt the ultimate success of the poet's own mission' as early as stanza 14 (p. 84).

Despite this failure, the poem stays faithful to the initial, spontaneous response that opens the stanza. Resigned to failure now, Byron holds on to the hope of success 'soon'. The problem, according to Byron, is that 'there is too much of man here' for him to enter 'with a fit mind' any communion with external 'being'. Perhaps, but this is not the primary obstacle that must be overcome if the poem's quest is indeed to be successful 'soon'. As we have seen, self-conscious reflection pulls the fancy back from its 'flight', perception and insight back from their object. We now see that it stands in the way of fancy, perception, and insight almost from the outset: it bends consciousness back upon itself even as consciousness is moving away. Self-consciousness is an even more pressing threat than it seemed in prospect. Here the mind's habit of reflecting on the self and on experience is countered by wilfully imagining future experience, but it remains a severe problem. And the poem rushes headlong into more trouble almost immediately.

Since Byron's poem seems to be aiming at a Wordsworthian communion with nature, we might expect it to move towards an imagined 'solitude'. Byron pre-empts even the possibility of such a solitude here, by looking instead to the prospect of 'Loneliness'. Not only is present feeling polluted by past experience, but the future is also polluted by the past: the prospect of solitude becomes the prospect of loneliness because of a yearning for something or someone absent or lost. The feeling of loss rules out, by pre-empting, the 'stillness' of communion, in which one's being is still and might, bereft of distraction, respond to what is immediate.

Self-consciousness and recollection take possession of the present moment and, more dangerously, threaten to always take possession of every future moment. Yet the poem's quest does not collapse under this threat. Rather, Byron responds deftly to this slippage backwards towards the past with a contingency measure that at least protects his quest for now. Images of those very 'cherished' thoughts Byron is trying to push beyond – thoughts of his recent past – suggest themselves as we read 'But soon shall Loneliness renew / Thoughts hid'. We are conscious throughout the poem of Byron holding back thoughts of his recent past, but we are aware of them bubbling below the surface of the poem nonetheless. Byron seems to look to future pain in recollecting, and we are encouraged to respond with sympathy by the touch of pathos here. The confidence with which the stanza began seems entirely lost. But Byron's deftness appears in his quick recovery of that confidence. The comma and 'but' that follow 'Thoughts hid' mark the tonal shift, but, rather than pull the poem back from thoughts of the past, Byron uses the momentum of recollecting to push back through the recent past to thoughts that were 'cherished' before 'the herd had penn'd me in their fold'.

There is no way of knowing for sure what these thoughts are,[42] and, in any case, we do not need to know. What we do need to notice, however, is

---

[42] Byron might be evoking 'the young poet who wrote "Lachin Y. Gair" and "A Fragment"' (McGann, *Fiery Dust*, p. 114) here and thinking of an earlier dream of communion with nature, a dream to which he is now returning. Cooke argues strongly that the canto 'directs itself toward *recovering*, not discovering, an extra mundane view', and points us to the fact that Byron 'embodied' a 'faith' in 'transcendentalism ... in important lyrics before 1816' (*The Blind Man*, p. 40). He lists a number of these lyrics (p. 40), but

Byron's diversionary tactic. This tactic saves the present moment from being swamped by painful recollection by giving it over to recollections of a different kind. This is, of course, a temporary measure and the damage has been done: the internal struggle here dramatized is entirely divorced from the now lost sense of being wooed by the lake.

Though pulled back from any spiritual withdrawal from the world, Byron can still contemplate the idea of such a withdrawal. In order to fix his sights, this is what he now does:

> To fly from, need not to be to hate, mankind;
> All are not fit with them to stir and toil. (*CHP* III, 653–654)

The tone here is detached, the voice calm. The speaker is contemplating his own withdrawal, but without knowing what the withdrawal will lead to he is immediately susceptible to the draw of that world he does know, 'mankind'. There seems no point of stillness, and no invulnerable mental activity, that the poem can rest in.

The pull of mankind appears most strongly in stanza 70. The only things that counter it here are the desire to recover the connection with the landscape captured but then lost in stanza 68, and the hope of finding in that recovery not a sense of exclusion, but of inclusion. For a while, desire and hope hold, and Byron turns our attention back to the 'Earth' in stanza 71. To once more focus the poem on nature, he slips into a purely descriptive, topographical mode. Yet this mode itself slips into something more obviously and vulnerably rhetorical, that is, into a rhetorical celebration of an absorption into the natural world which Byron has yet to achieve.[43] His vision of this absorption relies on the assumption that it will be the opposite of 'the crushing crowd' (*CHP* III, 679) of 'human cities' (*CHP* III, 683). But evoking such a diametric opposition involves recalling that crowd and those cities. Thus, even while Byron is asserting the Wordsworthian ideal of communion with nature, the 'torture' (*CHP* III, 683) of human cities comes ever more into view. This seems to have drawn on and drawn in Byron's own recollection of that torture: as the sequence of stanzas (*CHP* III, sts 69–76) progresses, the rhetorical expansiveness of assertions like 'I live not in myself, but I become / Portion of that around me' (*CHP* III, 680–681) looks increasingly like a gesture to hold in check a seemingly inevitable movement of mind back to the idea of torture.

---

claims that Byron's 'most accomplished transcendental piece' is 'To Edward Noel Long, Esq.' (p. 57).

[43] As Cooke points out, the 'professions of positive faith in or identification with Nature' that occur at this point are not 'quite plausible' (*The Blind Man*, p. 52), but Cooke also argues that 'Byron seems to be asking for reassurance, to be trying to reason himself into transcendentalism' (p. 53). Martin, on the other hand, suggests that Byron is here 'on a literary sortie' (*Byron: A Poet Before His Public*, p. 70), and while Byron is certainly drawing on a Wordsworthian model, he is declaiming a version of Wordsworth's idealism precisely to force his attention to focus on it. He is not, I suggest, declaiming 'as an inevitable consequence of an inability to understand poetry as anything other than a form of declamation' or in an 'attempt to stake a claim for himself in an area of poetry which he had ignored previously' (Martin, *Byron: a Poet Before his Public*, pp. 70, 79).

And, eventually, Byron seems to have lost his conviction that he can fly from mankind:

> Are not the mountains, waves, and skies, a part
> Of me and of my soul, as I of them? (*CHP* III, 707–708)

The rhetorical question here articulates a doubt that haunts the whole sequence of stanzas from 69 to 75. The list of line 707 gives the question a frantic edge, and though the phrase 'as I of them' sounds confident here, it appears less so in its original form, which has 'and' instead of 'as' and so makes the phrase part of the question.[44] The doubt that absorption into the natural world is possible,[45] coupled with the recollection of human cities, ensures that alongside the poem's movement towards the model of Wordsworth's poetry, there runs a specifically Byronic counterpoint, always ready to repossess the poem and its speaker:

> But there are wanderers o'er Eternity
> Whose bark drives on and on, and anchored ne'er shall be. (*CHP* III, 669–670)

Here again is the Byronic hero of the earlier verse narratives, and the Harold of *Childe Harold* I and II. It is also a speculative image of the speaking 'I', and one that threatens to take possession of it. This image of Byron's 'being' must be held at bay for another to be explored, though the temptation to make himself into another Byronic hero still seems as strong as it did at the beginning of the poem. The Corsair challenges the Wanderer for Byron's poetry once again, or rather Byronic myth challenges Wordsworthian doctrine, threatening to transform the communion the latter advocates into another form of futility.

The rhetorical questioning and the doubt that lies beneath it hold the poem back and prevent the idea of communion with nature eclipsing the prospect of unanchored wandering. Doubt eats away at idealism:

> Is it not better thus our lives to wear,
> Than join the crushing crowd, doom'd to inflict or bear? (*CHP* III, 678–679)

Cleaving to a love of nature, or what Byron calls elsewhere a 'feeling for nature',[46] and attempting to commune with nature, belong to the verb 'wear'

---

[44]   See the MS. variants listed at the bottom of page 104 of *Works* II, and McGann's commentary on the poem. 'As' appears in *MS.M.*, 'B's first draft' (McGann, *Works* II, p. 297).

[45]   In this we seem to trace a fundamental ambivalence in Byron's attitude to his Wordsworthian model. The same ambivalent attitude to Wordsworth can often be heard elsewhere. See, for example, *Medwin's Conversations of Lord Byron*, ed. by Ernest J. Lovell (Princeton: Princeton University Press, 1966). Medwin's Byron claims that Wordsworth 'now and then expressed ideas worth imitating' and that he 'had once a feeling for Nature' (p. 194), but recalls that Shelley 'used to dose me with Wordsworth physic even to nausea' in Switzerland in 1816, and asserts that 'since he [Wordsworth] is turned tax-gatherer, [he] is only fit to rhyme about asses and waggoners' (p. 194).

[46]   Ibid., p. 194.

here. They cover up an existential nakedness and vulnerability with a cosmetic security that hides it from view.

But this is only the first episode in the quest to find a renewal of sensation in a relationship with nature. It begins with such a renewal, but that renewal proves unsustainable: it comes under attack from self-conscious reflection. In order to hold this at bay, Byron embarks on a series of deflective and diversionary tactics that only just hold the poem on course. Once it is back on course it must then hold that course and this, too, proves problematic. Attacks here come from doubt, and in the wake of doubt the idea of failure; of ending up like the Giaour or Conrad. Doubt introduces a critical detachment from the model of Wordsworth which *Childe Harold* III has been emulating, so that the poem begins to veer between emulation and criticism as Byron struggles to keep it on track.

But the poem does pull out of this crisis. Byron turns to the figure of Rousseau, and not simply as a useful, if temporary, distraction. He projects on to Rousseau his own devotion to images of 'affliction' (*CHP* III, 726) and 'woe' (*CHP* III, 727) in an attempt to externalize and transcend that devotion. To put it another way, in stanzas 76–81 we see Byron attempting to externalize and transcend his own attachment to 'self-torturing' (*CHP* III, 725) fictions.[47]

Firstly, Byron stresses the 'ideal' (*CHP* III, 740) rather than 'living' (*CHP* III, 738) nature of the image to which Rousseau was so attached. This stress on the fictional, non-actual status of Rousseau's object of adoration clearly reflects back on Byron's own 'ideal' fiction of heroic, 'tragic' suffering. Having reminded himself of the fictional essence of his own 'ideal', Byron begins to distance himself from that 'ideal' by focusing instead on the attachment to it, which, he implies, is perhaps no more than a habit of mind learnt from Rousseau. Finally, he projects this attachment to idealized fictions into the history of Rousseau as a cause of his madness. As a result, Rousseau's fate stands as a warning.[48]

This strategy is successful. It allows the poem to pull out once more from the image of suffering and final desolation which had returned to hover over it. By stanza 85, the poem seems securely back on track, as it turns once more to Lake Leman. Byron opens the stanza by wilfully, and somewhat self-consciously, redirecting our attention to Leman, but he also suggests that he is once more feeling a pull on his consciousness, and a response from within himself:

---

[47]   As Newey points out, the figures of Napoleon and Rousseau, as they appear in the poem, 'are the products of a mature "ego" in the act of exteriorizing and transcending the darker possibilities of imaginative existence'. They are, he adds, 'an *ideé fixé* and a denial of its tyranny, a recurrent surfacing and censoring of psychological danger' ('Authoring the Self', p. 157).

[48]   In *Childe Harold* III, Rousseau, like Napoleon, is one of those '*exempla*, examples of fateful human propensities' that O'Neill describes as not simply of immediate use to Byron, but also as figures 'that take on a generalized moral force' (O'Neill, *Romanticism and the Self-Conscious Poem*, p.110). What stands as a warning for Byron is also offered as a warning to his readers.

> Clear, placid Leman! thy contrasted lake,
> With the wild world I dwelt in, is a thing
> Which warns me, with its stillness, to forsake
> Earth's troubled waters for a purer spring.
> This quiet sail is as a noiseless wing
> To waft me from distraction; once I loved
> Torn ocean's roar, but thy soft murmuring
> Sounds sweet as if a sister's voice reproved,
> That I with stern delights should e'er have been so moved. (*CHP* III, 797–805)

As Newey stresses, the 'activity of the mind is inscribed at every point' in this stanza.[49] Like the speaker of Wordsworth's 'Resolution and Independence', Byron reads and interprets what he intuitively senses as a communication directed at him, a 'leading from above' ('Resolution and Independence', 51): the lake 'warns' him 'with its stillness'. We could even add Wordsworth's word 'sent' ('Resolution and Independence', 111) at the end of the fifth line here and seem to be only making more explicit what is already implied.

It is helpful, once again, to recall Wordsworth's poem in more detail because a comparison between the procedures of these two poems as they arrive at two very similar thresholds will throw better light on Byron's practice than a close scrutiny of his stanza in isolation.

Wordsworth's speaker can only hold on to the experience of communion or visionary perception that visits him in the poem for as long as it takes to read and interpret it. The interpretation then becomes more important than the experience itself: the speaker does not look to a perpetuation of the experience, but seems content to be consoled by the idea that some benevolent, and presumably divine, presence may have made itself known to him and led him through his present dilemma.

The Wordsworth of the poem is left with a reading of what has happened to him that feels like knowledge. Yet, because it is a reading it very soon becomes vulnerable to endless rereadings. The poem's interpretation of what has happened begins as the consequence, but becomes the prey, of self-conscious reflection. Doubt and fear generate a tangle of endlessly reflexive rereadings so that the experience itself is eventually lost entirely.

Childe Harold III suggests that Byron was not looking for anything that he could take away from the present moment. We might say, rather, that he was looking for a new kind of present moment; not looking for a consoling idea, but for the return of spontaneous sensation and of intense feeling.[50] As a result, we see Byron holding on to the immediate experience of a felt connection longer than the speaker of 'Resolution and Independence' does. To

---

[49] 'Authoring the Self', p. 159. As Newey argues, this mental activity is seen 'in the opening imperative (nature *ordered*), in "contrasted" (nature *situated* in relation to the quest for sanctuary from previous turmoil), in "warns" (nature *read* as a signpost towards a purer state of being), in the sibilant consonants and hushed vowels which *compose* nature's voice as a "soft murmuring", and in the concluding ... psychological leap determined by sexual, or desexualized, impulse' (p. 159).

[50] As O'Neill insists, 'Byron is intent ... on writing "for the moment", on "intensity"' (*Romanticism and the Self-Conscious Poem*, p. 111).

feel the 'stillness' of the lake, and to feel warned by it, is much more important than any interpretation of the stillness which suggests itself: the sense of being warned that Byron lyrically dramatizes here is a vital reaction to the stillness, whatever the lake might mean by that stillness.[51] And though mental activity cannot be switched off, the subject can pay scant heed to it as it transforms sensation into the kind of figurative language (the metaphorical connection between the sound of the lake and 'a sister's voice', for example, achieved via the intermediary personification of 'soft murmurings') which Byron employs to make his literary text. In doing so he does not privilege language or thought over sensation. They are simply all he has with which to make his poem. And mental activity progressively becomes less and less important in the face of an experience which the stanza barely conveys but which it points us towards. The poem at this point almost becomes a repository for a mental activity which reads, orders, situates, and describes the scene, but which Byron pushes to one side as part of the 'distraction' from which the stillness of the scene 'wafts' him. Articulation is losing touch with sensation, we might say, and as the poem progresses from here we must be careful to fix our attention on those traces of sensation that do find their way into the poem.

This is certainly possible since Byron has not disappeared entirely behind his own words. The next four stanzas lyrically dramatize a struggle to hold on to the sensation of 'stillness' and to let go of the 'mental process' that reads that sensation. This brings the poem a little closer to the experience that informs it. On the one hand, Byron presents himself revelling in the sensual details of the stillness which surrounds him: the 'hush' (*CHP* III, 806), the 'margin and mountains ... distinctly seen' (*CHP* III, 808), the 'living fragrance from the shore' (*CHP* III, 811), the 'light drip of the suspended oar' (*CHP* III, 813) 'on the ear' (*CHP* III, 812). On the other hand, thought remains a dangerous distraction from what is immediate, especially imaginative thought. To imagine what is immediate is not necessarily to feel what is immediate, and the Byron we see here is alive to this danger. In stanza 87, it seems that the activity of his own imagination once more draws his attention: 'There seems a floating whisper on the hill' (*CHP* III, 819). He checks that activity immediately: 'But that is fancy' (*CHP* III, 820).

In this way the poem holds on to its connection with the stillness of the landscape until stanza 89. Here the sequence climaxes, and culminates 'in a sense of universal harmony'[52] as we see Byron sink 'with delightful inebriety into the immensity of that beautiful system' that surrounds him:[53]

> All heaven and earth are still – though not in sleep,
> But breathless, as we grow when feeling most;
> And silent, as we stand in thoughts too deep;
> All heaven and earth are still: From the high host

---

[51] According to McGann, 'the stillness of the lake is not an invitation to seek rest and peace, but Nature's announcement of the wild storm whose "wondrous" (92) strength will shortly break out over the lake and mountains' (*Fiery Dust*, p. 88).

[52] Newey, 'Authoring the Self', p. 159.

[53] Jean-Jacques Rousseau, *Reveries du promeneur solitare* (1782), quoted by Newey ('Authoring the Self', p. 159) and Martin (*Byron: A Poet Before His Public*, p. 226).

> Of stars, to the lull'd lake and mountain-coast,
> All is concentred in a life intense,
> Where not a beam, nor air, nor leaf is lost,
> But hath a part of being, and a sense
> Of that which is of all Creator and defence. (*CHP* III, 833–842)

This stanza lyrically dramatizes a complete absorption into the life of 'All heaven and earth', and the stanza's present tense attempts to replicate that absorption in its immediacy. In its description of the 'stillness' we glimpse an intensity. But, more importantly, we see a seemingly spontaneous response to that intensity.

In this stanza, 'All is concentred in' intense stillness, nothing is lost – including the speaker. Though an observer of 'heaven and earth', he is simultaneously part of the 'All of earth', and part of the larger 'All' of 'heaven and earth' in a sense that he was not in the Rhine valley. On Lake Leman, he is plugged into the 'life intense' he senses precisely because he does sense it, and is 'part of [the] being' he observes because he, like everything around him, is still but infused with a foreboding of the coming storm.

Here is the longed-for feeling of inclusion, of integration, of being 'a part' (*CHP* III, 707), a 'Portion of that around me' (*CHP* III, 680). It is a feeling that seems to lie beyond the reach of speech – Byron's sense of inclusion is only ever implied. But his 'testing of [the] redemptive possibilities' proposed by the Wordsworthian vision of communion with nature has discovered its own moment of redemption.[54] In stanza 89, Byron's poem lyrically captures its author's renewed sense of a vital connectedness with the world, of a 'passion and ... power' he shares and partakes in.

There is something more here, too. Byron seems to have achieved what we might call a 'narrow escape into faith'. The whole stanza has a prayer-like quality, which climaxes in Byron's claim to feel 'a sense' of something which he is prepared to believe is a sense of 'that which is of all Creator and defence'. The stanza moves towards this sense of divinity from the outset, opening with an immediate expansion in the self's relation to the stillness around it: 'All heaven' is still as well as 'All ... earth'. Here Byron describes the beginning of some kind of 'flight' beyond the 'earthly', perhaps a flight of 'fancy' but perhaps a flight of spirit – we are certainly meant to read it as something distinct from the 'fancy' that hears a whisper on the hill.

Be it the consciousness, fancy, or spirit that is expanding here, it is an expansion that is made possible by an absence of self-consciousness. The word 'I' is conspicuously absent from the stanza, and its absence attempts to articulate the fact that the self and 'earth-born jars' are 'forgotten quite' in this moment of communion. The poem here has a real 'purchase on areas of unself-conscious feeling' as it lyrically dramatizes Byron's response to the 'All' around him,[55] a response momentarily free of any self-reference, any action of mind that seeks to understand what the self is experiencing and what the experience means for the subject. Thought is not inert, but instead of being a

---

54   Newey, 'Authoring the Self', p. 160.
55   Ibid.

distraction, it is part of the general movement towards a beyond. Thought stands in, but does not reflect on, indeed is silenced by, 'thoughts too deep'.

We notice, of course, that Byron does finally interpret what he senses, giving it the gloss of 'that which is of all Creator'. Nevertheless, the feeling remains bigger than any shapeable idea. 'That which is' pre-emptively prevents 'Creator' having any kind of graspable meaning, and insists instead on what is felt to be something mysterious, beyond interpretation or knowing. Byron struggles to hold on to the bigger intuition before settling for a notion of a creator that will retain a trace of, but inevitably fall short of, what was originally felt as an indescribable presence. Sensation is valued more highly than intellectual comfort, and for a moment Byron simply revels in the 'sense' of 'that which is'.

Stanza 89 lyrically dramatizes Byron's moment of triumph, in which, the stanza powerfully suggests, he did not feel himself to be the excluded 'tragic' figure, severed from life, that he feared himself to be. He lyrically recounts his own discovery of the kind of 'passion and ... power' which the fictional Harold found in his 'companionship' with nature, and of the forgetfulness Harold found in the transcendence of 'that flight' described in stanza 14. He also lyrically dramatizes the discovery of an unlooked-for sense of divine presence which leaves him with a new and tentative 'faith'.[56]

Yet the Harold of stanza 14 proves truly proleptic, and if Byron was indeed hoping to find a permanent communion with nature, or a permanent transcendence in forgetfulness, he rediscovers, instead, its impossibility. Here we might agree with Michael Cooke, who argues that nature in *Childe Harold* III offers 'relief' that is only 'periodical'.[57] Could Byron 'have kept his spirit to that flight / He had been happy', but, like Harold, he finds instead that this 'flight' cannot be sustained. The poem

> stresses the irreducible power of our earthly nature, a temporal and spatial reality which will, when challenged or ignored, intensify its weight.[58]

In stanza 89, one feature of our 'temporal ... reality' in particular, the 'chain' that clings 'invisibly' but which fetters us to our past and especially, for Byron, to past suffering, asserts itself in the word 'defence', in which we catch an echo of such suffering. The memory of that suffering latches hold of Byron's sense of divine presence and projects into it a self-referential meaning that is smaller than 'the feeling infinite' (*CHP* III, 842) hinted at by Byron's use of 'that which is'. The recollection of suffering suddenly projects what it

---

[56]   As Newey argues, stanzas 89 and 90 are 'a lot more impressive than several critics have been willing to allow, including Michael Cooke, who refers to Byron's "transcendental manqué" and Philip W. Martin who (much less interestingly) downgrades Byron at every opportunity to the level of an inept pickpurse of conventional Romantic ideas. We have only to compare ... [stanzas 89 and 90] with something from Rousseau's *Reveries* ... to appreciate how vividly Byron realizes the experiential content and gains of solitary contemplation' ('Authoring the Self', pp. 159–160).

[57]   *The Blind Man*, p. 43.

[58]   Newey, 'Authoring the Self', p. 153.

yearns for into the intimation of infinite otherness, so that painful memory cuts the self off from the thing towards which it wants to move.

The moment of self-forgetfulness and intimate communion with nature is already ending in stanza 89, and as the poem moves on we see Byron's new 'relation to Nature' fall 'subject to so many adversities as to be lost'.[59] Byron discovers what he already knew, namely, that the self 'cannot be truly lost this side of the ultimate dissolution' of death.[60] Even as stanza 90 opens, we notice the shift of tense as Byron reflects back on stanza 89 from somewhere outside the experience it recounts.

However, we should also notice the word 'solitude' (*CHP* III, 843). Loneliness and the lingering attachment it manifests have been surpassed by something better. These two details – the shift of tense, and Byron's use, now, of the word 'solitude' – point us to the two traits of consciousness that take over the poem at this point, and which inform its progress from here on. Firstly, a falling away from unselfconscious communion with nature and a return to self-consciousness. As we shall see, self-projection replaces communion in the storm sequence coming up. Secondly, however, there is the desire to redescribe and especially to reaffirm the experience and implications of Byron's brief communion with nature. This develops into a desire to celebrate the natural universe and its influence on the human consciousness.

In the stanzas which follow stanza 90, the slippage back to the self and to the past gains the upper hand. The self 'has proven more tenacious than its saviors' and has called Byron away from his communion with the lake.[61] But a further distraction now comes into view:

> The sky is changed! – and such a change! Oh night,
> And storm, and darkness, ye are wondrous strong,
> Yet lovely in your strength ...
>
> ... every mountain now hath found a tongue,
> And Jura answers, though her misty shroud,
> Back to the joyous Alps, who call to her aloud! (*CHP* III, 860–868)

The threat of violence in the storm is akin to that threatened by 'Torn Ocean's roar', and the anticipation of the storm here is reminiscent of the anticipation in stanza 2. The 'stillness' of Lake Leman has already warned against this love of what is 'troubled', but in the storm sequence that love powerfully resurfaces and draws the poem back to distraction. Almost immediately Byron begins to resemble his own 'tragic' heroes once more. And a figurative correspondence between the external 'tempest' and his own internal tempest brings his briefly forgotten suffering back into view. Self intervenes between the self and the storm, and when Byron peoples the landscape, projecting fictional voices on to it and imaging those voices engaged in a cosmic conversation, he quickly recognizes that it is a 'conversation' from which he is excluded.

---

[59]   Cooke, *The Blind Man*, p. 40.
[60]   Newey, 'Authoring the Self', p. 161.
[61]   Cooke, *The Blind Man*, p. 59.

The poem is suddenly and perilously close to where it began: with separation. Byron's response is to project into the storm's violence an innate understanding of human 'desolation':

> ... of all the band
> The brightest through these parted hills hath fork'd
> His lightnings, – as if he did understand,
> That in such gaps as desolation work'd,
> There the hot shaft should blast whatever therein lurk'd. (*CHP* III, 891–895)

In the phrase 'as if' we are forced to notice the mental activity that is inscribed in Byron's description of the storm. Yet here, the mental activity involved in describing is not pushed to the margin by a felt (even if imagined) connection with what is being described. Byron does not 'syphon off' mental activity from a self engaged in something else but, rather, articulates a self wholly absorbed in that activity. And while 'as if' knows its own vulnerability as a fictional projection, Byron wilfully ignores that vulnerability, insisting on the notion of a kinship between the destructive forces of nature and the self-destructive forces of the human subject. Mental projections of notional kinship and innate understanding now swamp Byron's apostrophe to the storm:

> ... the far roll
> Of your departing voices, is the knoll
> Of what in me is sleepless, – if I rest. (*CHP* III, 899–901)

Byron wilfully humanizes the storm and wilfully projects, along with this 'humanity', a recognition of himself, so that the fictional voices which he projects on to the storm end by articulating the suffering 'that time cannot abate'. The 'roll' of voices is occasioned by the 'knoll' of 'what in me is sleepless', so that Byron's own painful memory is inserted into the landscape over which the storm passes. Recognition of that memory is projected into the storm's noise. Nature, by this fiction, is a cosmic acknowledgement of suffering humanity.[62]

Yet this is manifestly a 'comforting fantasy', a 'mere lie of fiction', in a way that the sense of inclusion that is dramatized in stanza 89 is not. And the storm itself robs Byron of his fantasy by 'departing' and moving beyond his reach or power to follow:

> But where of ye, oh tempests! is the goal?
> Are ye like those within the human breast?
> Or do ye find, at length, like eagles, some high nest? (*CHP* III, 902–904)

---

[62] I am assuming here that by 'knoll' Byron means something like 'A small hill or eminence of more or less rounded form: a hillock, a mound' (*OED*). This is the word's more common usage. 'Knoll' can also be used as a synonym for 'knell' (*OED*), however, so that the poet might actually be imagining that he hears, in the storm's 'departing roll', 'a sound announcing' the 'death ... or passing away'(*OED*) of 'what in me is sleepless'. In either case, my main point is the same. Wilful self-delusion has replaced the brief but intense 'stirring' of the 'feeling infinite' (*CHP* III, 842).

This rhetorical question articulates Byron's loss of his 'comforting fantasy'. What finally undermines that fantasy is the idea that the storm finds 'some high rest', a rest denied 'the human breast', and the storm sequence ends in crushing doubt, in a sense of having been duped by the desire for cosmic sympathy, and in a confrontation, once again, with separation and exclusion.

This is clearly a dangerous point of rest for a poem struggling to push beyond Byron's earlier 'tragic vision'. Reminded of his own suffering, Byron slips back towards the notion of heroic fortitude as the last resort, towards the image of himself as able to 'Bear, know, feel, and yet breathe' (*CHP* III, 910) and nothing more. Overwhelmed by the prospect of a cosmic indifference to human suffering, and severed from any communion with the 'life' of 'being', the poem is once again swamped by the isolating memory of past pain, and the idea of inescapable suffering.

This return to pain forces a concession. Byron's looked-for transcendence has not proved permanent, and 'That which is most within me' (*CHP* III, 906), he says, cannot be unbosomed (*CHP* III, 905).[63] Yet this does not lead to a final submission to the tragic absolutes with which the poem began, and the 'keynote of the ... canto' should not 'be described as negative'.[64] Despite the fact that the 'self' has proved 'tenacious', the poem is not a failure.

In the first place, Byron insists that the will can still intervene between the subject and suffering. What is 'most within me' can remain 'unheard' (*CHP* III, 912), can become 'a most voiceless thought' (*CHP* III, 913), sheathed 'as a sword' (*CHP* III, 912). The will can achieve, in other words, 'a holding operation'.[65] But, I suggest, the poem's *'telos'* is not 'of standing alone and standing fast'.[66] As we read forward, we re-encounter the impulse to celebrate:

> The morn is up again, the dewy morn,
> With breath all incense, and with cheek all bloom,
> Laughing the clouds away with playful scorn,
> And living as if earth contained no tomb,
> And glowing into day: we may resume
> The march of our existence: and thus I,
> Still on thy shores, fair Leman! may find room
> And food for meditation, nor pass by
> Much, that may give us pause, if pondered fittingly. (*CHP* 111, 914–922)

The phrase 'dewy morn' recalls the mention of 'dews' in stanza 87, in which 'the starlight dews / All silently their tears of love instil' (*CHP* III, 821). And when 'morn is up again', Byron claims, that 'love' is still written on the landscape and has not been obliterated by the violence of the storm. We should also hear another echo, in the phrase 'cheek all bloom'. There is a hint here of

---

63   At the outset of *Childe Harold* III, 'Byron wants (that is, lacks *and* desires) somewhere to steer, a locus of higher truth and a state of higher being', but in coming to recognize that 'the self can never fully be embodied or fully lost ("unbosomed")', Byron discovers that 'incompleteness, the wanting that is both aspiration and not having, is the inescapable condition of being' (Newey, 'Authoring the Self', pp. 151–152, 163).

64   Cooke, *The Blind Man*, p. 44.

65   Newey, 'Authoring the Self', p. 164.

66   Ibid.

that earlier phrase, 'the sheen of beauty's cheek' in stanza 11, where it is the response which 'beauty's cheek' elicits that is important ('who can ... behold ... beauty's cheek, / Nor feel the heart can never all grow old?').

Stanza 98 articulates precisely such a response. It registers nature's continuity alongside the tenacity of the self and, most importantly, nature's perpetual ability to woo the consciousness despite the distractions that pull consciousness away again. Nature 'woos' us back, the stanza implies, to the 'brink' of 'yon heaven' (*CHP* III, 126).

A sense of playful well-being resurfaces here that we have not noted before, but that can first be heard in stanza 90 when Byron claims that the 'beauty' which surrounds him 'would disarm / The spectre Death, had he substantial power to harm' (*CHP* III, 849–850). This playful denial of death shows *Childe Harold* III already moving towards the pastoral vision of stanzas 99–103, in which 'the fact of death is muffled' by the fecund 'opulence' and 'romantic radiance' of the 'pastoral environment'.[67] Here an overpowering sense of natural beauty momentarily 'deprives' death of its 'factuality',[68] and in stanza 90, in a moment of playful exuberance that is infused with the joy of the 'feeling infinite' (*CHP* III, 842) and of 'Eternal harmony' (*CHP* III, 847), death becomes almost unimaginable.

We should perhaps have noticed that Byron addresses the 'Most glorious night' of the storm playfully: 'let me be / A sharer in thy fierce and far delight' (*CHP* III, 869–871). This sense of play gets lost in the recollection of his own inner 'tempest', but Byron's description of morning is infused with a renewed sense of playfulness which laughs away the storm and the shift of mood it produced 'with playful scorn'. We are describing an absolute about-face here: a transformation of the poem and of the consciousness it purports to communicate. Originally chained to a 'tragic sense of life' which it was desperate to escape, the poem is now rooted in a sense of playful well-being that is not seriously shaken, and is certainly not irrevocably pushed beyond reach, by what seems in retrospect to have been no more than a brief excursion back in the direction of the tragic.

But what kinds of poetry does this about-face make possible? In the first instance, a nostalgic yearning for the communion now lost gives way to a new pastoral idiom. And as the poem progresses, any sense of inescapable woe is overwhelmed by a sense of inescapable fecundity and natural opulence:

> A populous solitude of bees and birds,
> And fairy-form'd and many-coloured things,
> Who ...
> ... innocently open their glad wings,
> Fearless and full of life: the gush of springs,
> And fall of lofty fountains, and the bend

---

[67] Thomas McFarland, *Shakespeare's Pastoral Comedies* (Chapel Hill: University of North Carolina Press, 1971), p. 33. The phrase 'romantic radiance' is not McFarland's, but comes from W. Moelwyn Marchant, *Comedy* (London: Methuen, 1972), p. 21.

[68] Erwin Panofsky, 'Et in Arcadia Ego: Poussin and the Elegiac Tradition', in *Meaning and the Visual Arts: Papers in and on Art History* (New York: Doubleday, 1955), p. 301.

Of stirring branches, and the bud which brings
The swiftest thought of beauty. (*CHP* III, 950–957)

Byron's vision of Clarens is not simply a pastoral idyll, however, or
rather, it is not precisely a pastoral idyll. It has none of the languor of the
pastoral tradition that is most strongly recognized among the Romantics by
Keats. Byron's idyllic scene is, on the contrary, infused with an energy that
emanates from, and manifests a delight in, the natural universe, and as we read
we witness a movement beyond the pastoral and towards something closer to a
comic vista.

Comedy, for Christopher Fry, 'believes in a universal cause for delight',[69]
and towards the end of *Childe Harold* III, Byron seems to share this belief. A
new-found love of nature informs his description of everything that surrounds
him, and the figure of 'Love' (*CHP* III, 929, 933, 941, 958) which appears in
the Clarens sequence is an allegorical figure for that love.

But Byron's sense of 'a universal cause for delight' is rooted in more than
a new love of nature. For a while at least, Clarens appears to have encouraged
in him a belief in a universal capacity to love: he not only suggests that Clarens
has renewed and revitalized his own capacity to love, but also claims that it
would awaken or revitalize the same capacity in anyone.[70] And in the human
capacity to love, Byron here sees a vital connection between man and the
universe. For in the Clarens sequence, 'Love' is an allegorical projection of
internal feeling which reads that feeling into the scene which inspires it. The
poet, in other words, is imagined as partaking in, as being part of, a 'love'
which radiates out from the landscape. The feeling itself thus becomes a
benediction, a 'boundless blessing' (*CHP* III, 966), felt as a response but
actually infused inwards from outside. The figure of 'Love' is, in this way, an
allegorical figure for a kind of communion, and a celebration of a felt and
essential integration, of a sense of inclusion and connectedness:

> ... the feeling with which all around Clarens ... is invested, is of a still
> higher and more comprehensive order than the mere sympathy with
> individual passion; it is a sense of the existence of love in its most
> extended and sublime capacity, and our own participation of its good and of
> its glory: it is the great principle of the universe, which is there more
> condensed, but not less manifested; and of which, though knowing
> ourselves a part, we lose our individuality, and mingle in the beauty of the
> whole.[71]

This is clearly an unstable and vulnerable vision of man's connection with
the universe. Indeed, as Cooke argues, the 'sense' here described 'is not
translated in *Childe Harold* III without corruption'.[72] Byron may well have
known this, and added this note because he felt the poem needed propping up,
so to speak. Yet the note is also there to insist upon this vision of man's

---

[69]   'Comedy', p. 77.
[70]   'He who hath loved not', for example, 'here would learn that lore', while 'he who
knows / That tender mystery, will love the more' (*CHP* III, 959–961).
[71]   Byron's note to line 927 (*Works* II, p. 312).
[72]   *The Blind Man*, p. 54.

participation in the whole. It is a vulnerable vision, but one offered with conviction in the face of the corrupting suspicion which Cooke describes: that Love has been banished to Clarens by 'vain men's woes' (*CHP* III, 962) and is in decline.[73] This suspicion may well have crept into Byron's 'sense' of 'love' as 'the great principle of the universe' when he attempted to translate that 'sense' into verse, and with it, the notion of inescapable woe may have also reasserted itself. But the vision is offered as a sustainable vision despite these intrusions, and Byron does not dismiss it as a 'fancy'. Rather, he holds on to it as a 'truth' intuitively felt, and his endorsement and celebration of it mark out a new capacity to trust intuition; a capacity which increasingly gives Byron's lyric poem over to a comedic rather than a tragic impulse.

> The difference between tragedy and comedy is the difference between experience and intuition. In experience we strive against every condition of our animal life: against death, against the frustration of ambition, against the instability of human love. In the intuition we trust the arduous eccentricities we're born to ... .[74]

'In ... intuition we trust', and, while writing *Childe Harold* III, Byron seems to have come to trust intuition. This trust, or faith, in an intuitive sense of universal integration makes stanzas 99 to 103 possible despite the corruption that begins to eat away at them, and such faith, for Fry, lies at the very heart of comedy: 'Comedy is an escape, not from truth but from despair: a narrow escape into faith'.[75] *Childe Harold* III is comedic (but not comic or, in the strictest sense, comedy) not because it escapes the 'truth' of human suffering. It does not, as we have seen.[76] It does, however, escape the despair towards which it is repeatedly drawn. In *Childe Harold* III, we might say, 'Despair a smilingness assume[s]'(*CHP* III, 140).

It does so by trusting in the intuition that senses a connection with, or inclusion in, 'the universe'. Here we fall back on another, perhaps more conventional, idea of what comedy is, or does. Philip Edwards, writing about Shakespearean comedy, makes the point that comedy delights in 'the movement of the characters from separation to union, from discord to harmony, from severance to integration'.[77] *Childe Harold* III discovers a lyric version of this comic delight, as it celebrates an individual movement from the fact of separation to the intuition of integration.

The key note of the canto is, then, I suggest, affirmative and celebratory. The poem is, finally, comedic because it shares with comedy the movement 'from shadow to starlight' and from 'fearful doubt' towards 'the joy and

---

[73] 'The glorified picture of Clarens is tinged with pessimism, with the usual Byron "sense" that Love has been "driven" or banished to a hinterland, and has no place in the world (with this further inference, it seems, that since Love must either "advance or die", decay or grow, it is now decaying and dying)' (ibid.).

[74] Fry, 'Comedy', p. 78.

[75] Ibid., p. 77.

[76] As Cooke points out, even the farewell stanzas with which the canto ends 'announce a state of loss and abandonment' (*The Blind Man*, p. 55).

[77] *Shakespeare: A Writer's Progress* (Oxford and New York: Oxford University Press, 1986), p. 86.

certitude of grace'.[78] It does not arrive at certitude, and does not fight clear of 'fearful doubt'. But as 'Dante observed, in his letter to Can Grande, ... tragedy and comedy move in precisely contrary directions', and it is the direction in which *Childe Harold* III heads that is important here.[79] Tragedy moves in the direction of 'descent – from prosperity to suffering',[80] and there are plenty of moments of descent into suffering in *Childe Harold* III. However, these descents are overwhelmed by a larger and opposite movement of ascent: from images of 'wanderers o'er Eternity' (*CHP* III, 669), of absolute exclusion, to an intuitive and buoying 'sense' of universal integration.

This is enough to carry Byron to the end of the canto, where he looks out on a future redeemed by the proven capacity to still feel, and made enticing by the prospect of being 'permitted' to 'survey' (*CHP* III, 1018–1019), intuitively, something more of that heaven towards which nature 'woos us'. At the end of *Childe Harold* III, Byron no longer appears prey to the fear that he is another of his own heroes, doomed to vacancy or pain.

Yet Byron has a tendency to universalize his experience in *Childe Harold* III, and we might wonder how far he can legitimately do so. He has, we might say, got through 'his particular crisis', but has he discovered something about himself or about 'the human condition'? He has certainly subordinated his own impulse to imagine himself into his own 'tragic vision' to a new-found comedic impulse to delight in the redeeming consolations of the universe. Yet Byron has a choice: he is not a victim of the absolute emotional desolation he describes at the beginning of the canto.

The speaker of *The Prisoner of Chillon*, on the other hand, is. In this, his next major work, Byron attempts to achieve a second, and this time fictional, subordination of a tragic descent into darkness, loss, and grief to a larger movement of ascent, to light, to love, even towards a communion with nature. Ultimately, the prisoner is restored to the world, and to the 'life' and the 'light' he is so long excluded from: he is set free.

This structural framework is perhaps the most obvious trace of Byron's attempt to sustain his movement towards comedy in a fictional poem. Equally important is his ongoing reconsideration of Wordsworth's idealistic poetic vision, and his own modified version of that vision. In *The Prisoner of Chillon*, reintegration and the idea of nature drawing from the subject a renewed capacity to respond to the world and engage with it must face out the extremities of Byron's 'tragic vision'. Is the renewal described in *Childe Harold* III universally available, and can the victim of absolute emotional desolation be redeemed by an intuitive sense of being part of something larger than self? If events can desolate the human capacity to feel, then can the victim of such events be renewed, or infused with a joy that intimates Paradise? Or must we say that 'Byronic tragedy' damns the human soul beyond the consolations and resolutions glimpsed and offered by comedy?

These questions inform the composition of *The Prisoner of Chillon*, 'The Dream', and *Manfred*, and the next two chapters will accordingly focus on these poems. As we shall see, Byron's early move towards the comedic in

---

78   Steiner, *The Death of Tragedy*, pp. 11–12.
79   Ibid., p. 11.
80   Ibid., p. 12, recalling Aristotle's *Poetics*.

Childe Harold III begins to falter (if not quite peter out) in the face of his devotion to images and fictions of extreme, even absolute, human ruin.

CHAPTER FOUR

'Tears, and Tortures, and the Touch of Joy'

According to McGann,

> The Prisoner is B's version of the story of the imprisonment of François
> Bonivard (b.1493) in Chillon Castle between 1530 and 1536.[1]

This assertion encourages the reader to approach *The Prisoner of Chillon* via the history of Bonivard,[2] and it will be helpful to us to look briefly at the connection between this historical figure and the speaker of Byron's poem before we move our main argument forward. To what extent is 'the best of Byron's verse Tales' an attempt at a poetic historical biography?[3]

We might be forgiven for failing to notice any connection at all between Bonivard and Byron's prisoner on first reading the poem. The poem's speaker never names himself and no reference to Bonivard is made in the text. Contemporary readers, however, would perhaps have made the connection more readily. Byron's narrative was published in a volume called *The Prisoner of Chillon and Other Poems*, where it was immediately preceded by 'Sonnet on Chillon', in which we read:

> Chillon! thy prison is a holy place,
>   And thy sad floor an altar – for 'twas trod,
> Until his very steps have left a trace
>   Worn, as if thy cold pavement were a sod,
> By Bonnivard.[4]

The placing of this sonnet encourages us to read it as 'a prelude to "The Prisoner of Chillon"' and has meant,[5] as McGann points out, that 'readers have sometimes been mislead to think that the Promethean defiance of the sonnet carries over into the tale'.[6] The temptation to carry forward the name 'Bonnivard' is as strong as the temptation to read this 'Promethean defiance' into *The Prisoner of Chillon*. Even McGann, having noted that the relationship

---

[1]   *Works* IV, p. 449. The title of this chapter is from 'The Dream' (*Works* IV), 6.
[2]   Byron spells Bonivard 'Bonnivard', but, according to E. H. Coleridge, 'there is no contemporary authority' for this spelling (*The Complete Poetical Works*, vol. IV, ed. by Ernest Hartley Coleridge [London: John Murray, 1905], p. 2). Accordingly, I have followed the practice of McGann (in his notes in *Works* IV), Coleridge and Rutherford (in *Byron*), and spelt the name with one 'n'. Quotations retain their original spelling.
[3]   Rutherford, *Byron*, p. 66.
[4]   'Sonnet on Chillon' (*Works* IV), 9–13.
[5]   Cooke, *The Blind Man*, p. 87.
[6]   *Fiery Dust*, p. 167.

between the sonnet and the narrative is more problematic than it might at first appear, carries the name forward into his discussion of the narrative in *Fiery Dust*.[7] To do so is to read the poem in the same way we read, say, Browning's 'Andrea del Sarto', that is, as a monologue which imaginatively dramatizes the psychological plight of an historical figure.[8]

It is now thought, however, that the sonnet was probably written after the narrative.[9] Should we, then, read a knowledge of Bonivard's history into Byron's composition of *The Prisoner of Chillon*, or is the mention of 'Bonnivard' in the sonnet a retrospective attempt to associate Byron's narrative with Bonivard's story? Here a note added to *The Prisoner of Chillon* might help:

> When the foregoing poem was composed I was not sufficiently aware of the history of Bonnivard, or I should have endeavoured to dignify the subject by an attempt to celebrate his courage and virtues.[10]

The 'history of Bonnivard', and especially 'his courage and virtues', are clearly not identical with the poem's 'subject'. In fact, the poem may not start 'from the story he [Byron] heard told of Bonivard' at all, and might not attempt a 'vivid imaginative reconstruction' of Bonivard's imprisonment.[11]

It is, of course, likely that Byron knew something of Bonivard before he began the poem, but I cannot help suspecting that he did not. Certainly, on the evidence available, we might legitimately wonder if Byron had even heard of Bonivard until after the poem was written.[12] Can we be sure that *The Prisoner*

---

[7]   Martin (in *Byron: A Poet Before His Public*), Cooke (in *The Blind Man*) and Jump (in *Byron*), to name but three of many, also carry the name forward into their discussion of *The Prisoner*.

[8]   Indeed, M. K. Joseph describes *The Prisoner* as a 'dramatic monologue rather than a tale' (*Byron the Poet* [London: Victor Gollancz, 1964], p. 40), while Richard Holmes asserts that in it, Byron is 'emphatically casting himself into Bonivard's predicament' (*Shelley: The Pursuit* [London: Weidenfeld and Nicolson, 1974], p. 336).

[9]   '*MS.M.* ... shows that B probably composed his 'Sonnet on Chillon' ... after Claire [Clairmont] had completed copying *[The] Prisoner*' (McGann, *Works* IV, p. 449).

[10]   *Works* IV, p. 453. Coleridge makes this note the poem's Advertisement in his *Poetical Works of Lord Byron* (see vol. IV, pp. 2, 9–11).

[11]   Rutherford, *Byron*, p. 67. Bonivard's history was certainly not the only story of imprisonment that influenced Byron. According to Shelley, Byron had 'deeply studied' the 'death of Ugolino, and perhaps but for it would never have written *The Prisoner of Chillon*' (Thomas Medwin, *Life of Percy Bysshe Shelley* [Oxford: (n.pub.), 1913], p. 249, quoted in Martin, *Byron: A Poet Before His Public*, p. 95). Shelley is referring to the famous Ugolino episode in book xxxiii of Dante's *Inferno*, and Byron's prisoner clearly, and in quite specific ways, 'turns into another Ugolino: his confession "Among the stones I stood a stone" [for example] echoes *Inferno* xxxiii. 49' (Ralph Pite, *The Circle of our Vision: Dante's Presence in English Romantic Poetry* [Oxford: Clarendon Press, 1994], p. 210).

[12]   Bonivard is not mentioned in Byron's letters of the time and, as Gleckner has pointed out, Byron 'consistently refers to the poem as the "Castle of Chillon"'(*Ruins*, p. 191). See for example: Byron's letter of 20 July 1816, in which he tells Douglas Kinnaird that he has written 'a (not long) poem on the Castle of Chillon' (*BLJ* V, p. 83); Byron's letter of 29 July 1816 to Samuel Rogers in which he mentions his 'story on the "Chateau de Chillon"' (*BLJ* V, p. 87); his letter to John Murray of 20 August 1816, in which he talks of

of Chillon is 'Byron's version of the story of the imprisonment of ... Bonivard ... in Chillon between 1530 and 1536'? If it is not, then where should we begin an account of the poem?

Robert Gleckner offers a possible route towards a reading of the poem that avoids the problematic area of what Byron might or might not have known about Bonivard. He suggests that Byron's 'focus' is not the prisoner, but 'the prison', and that Byron is interested in 'the idea of imprisonment'. For Gleckner, Byron makes the prisoner 'a paradigm of the eternal human condition' which chronicles 'the decay of the human mind in the dungeon of its being'.[13]

To begin with, Gleckner's stress on place is, I think, helpful. Indeed, the prison itself has a specific geographical location. Lake Leman is named first in line 107. Here we see a line of continuity that runs back to *Childe Harold* III, and can begin to see where Byron might have actually started from. In *Childe Harold* III, Byron claims to sense in his response to the lake the possibility of 'forgetfulness' and spiritual 'flight' (*CHP* III, 35, 122), and the canto, as we have seen, progresses by repeatedly directing its attention towards a communion with the lake. It does so in order to quest into the possibilities such a communion might open up to the 'fit mind' (*CHP* III, 649).

In *Childe Harold* III, Byron describes feeling the pull of the lake on his consciousness three times – it 'woos' him (*CHP* III, 644), 'warns' him (*CHP* III, 799), and wafts him (*CHP* III, 802) – and lyrically dramatizes himself coming closer to the eventual discovery of a 'life intense' (*CHP* III, 838) surrounding and including both the lake and himself. The prisoner's history repeats this kind of patterning. The prisoner feels the lake 'by Chillon's walls' (107), feels 'the winter's spray' (119), and sees the 'wide long lake' (335).[14] *The Prisoner of Chillon* repeats and re-examines, in a fictional mode, the series of responses to Lake Leman which runs through *Childe Harold* III.

We are coming at the poem, then, from two directions. On the one hand, we are focusing in on the poem's emphasis on a landscape to which a self might respond, and, on the other, we are bringing into view the poem's creation of a self that will respond to that landscape. Let us focus, for now, on that self. The prisoner is not simply to be identified with the historical Bonivard. We can trace a precedent for the ways in which the prisoner differs from Byron's earlier heroes in the consciousness depicted in *Childe Harold* III. To put it another way, the prisoner is a reworking of Byron's own experience as it is represented in *Childe Harold* III.

The opening of *The Prisoner of Chillon* seems to suggest that this is not, in fact, the case:

---

having sent 'The Manuscript (containing the third canto of Childe Harold – the Castle of Chillon &c. &c. ...)' with Shelley to England (*BLJ* V, p. 90). Finally, neither Byron nor Shelley mention Bonivard when writing about their visit to Chillon.

[13]   *Ruins*, p. 191.

[14]   All quotations from *The Prisoner of Chillon* are taken from *Works* IV. Line references will be given after each quotation in the text.

... mine has been the fate of those
To whom the goodly earth and air
Are bann'd, and barr'd – forbidden fare. (8–10)

The 'food for meditation' (*CHP* III, 921) granted to the self in *Childe Harold* III is, it seems, denied the prisoner. But actually, both poems begin from a position of imprisonment and exclusion: in *Childe Harold* III, Byron tells us that he comes from being 'penn'd ... in their fold' by 'the herd' (*CHP* III, 652). Similarly, both speakers begin excluded because both are initially 'penn'd' in a particularly self-conscious relation to the world about them. Byron's first response to Lake Leman in *Childe Harold* III, for example, is highly self-reflexive; a glossing of otherness with self-referential meaning. Once the prisoner's narrative gets under way in section 3,[15] we quickly see that he, too, is distracted from confronting otherness by self-reflexivity and self-projection. Lake Leman, he says, 'enthrals' the 'battlement' of 'Chillon', making 'A double dungeon wall and wave' (110–113). The prisoner imagines a universe centred on and set against himself. By projecting a self-referential meaning out on to the lake, he precludes any kind of discovery of otherness. In *Childe Harold* III, it is only after he has depicted himself responding to the lake as 'a thing' (*CHP* III, 798) that Byron goes on to dramatize the movement of his consciousness outwards towards discovery. Until then, he emphasizes a sense of exclusion and imprisonment, and foregrounds a habit of response that is, like the prisoner's, self-reflexive and self-projecting.

In this sense, then, *The Prisoner of Chillon* begins at very much the same point as *Childe Harold* III does. And the correspondence gets stronger as the poem progresses. The prisoner, for example, says:

And I have felt the winter's spray
And through the bars when winds were high
And wanton in the happy sky;
  And when the very rock hath rock'd,
  And I have felt it shake, unshock'd,
Because I could have smiled to see
The death that would have set me free. (119–125)

The prisoner confronts the storm with the expectation of something quite specific. His attention is distracted away from the 'life intense' that we glimpse in 'spray', 'high', and in the playful 'wanton', and focused instead on the prospect of death. We find a clear precedent for this in *Childe Harold* III when Byron describes a draw on his consciousness coming from the lake, but loses touch with this felt connection by assuming that it will lead to something specific and predictable:

But soon in me shall Loneliness renew
Thoughts hid, but no less cherish'd than of old. (*CHP* III, 650–651)

---

[15]   'In the third stanza', or as I am calling it, the third section, 'the speaker, essentially repeating what he has already revealed, becomes, for the first time, narrative rather than descriptive' (Marshall, *Structure*, pp. 84–85).

The speaker of each poem is confronted with Lake Leman. Both seem to glimpse something powerful there, but are, at least initially, unable to attend to it. They distract themselves with projected expectations and self-referential interpretations of the world around them.

Let us suggest a hypothesis on the basis of this correspondence. If *The Prisoner of Chillon* replicates, to some degree, the structure of *Childe Harold* III and describes a similar consciousness, and if *Childe Harold* III dramatizes the movement of one of these consciousnesses away from its initial condition to another (from suffering, say, to comic integration via a kind of pastoral communion), then *The Prisoner of Chillon* may do the same. Byron's tendency to work along 'the same grooves of thought' makes it entirely possible, and section 8 seems to offer further evidence that supports this hypothesis:

> The last – the sole – the dearest link
> Between me and the eternal brink,
> Which bound me to my failing race,
> Was broken in this fatal place. (215–218)

The Prisoner appears here to be reworking ideas it inherits from *Childe Harold* III. Firstly, the prisoner echoes stanza 14, where 'link' and 'brink' are also rhymed, and in which it is said that the 'spirit' strains to break 'the link / That keeps us from yon heaven which woos us to its brink' (*CHP* III, 125–126). The prisoner acknowledges both this 'brink' and 'the link / That keeps us from' it: the kind of link, to the 'Earth's troubled waters' (*CHP* III, 800) let us say, that Lake Leman 'warns' the poet to 'forsake' in *Childe Harold* III (*CHP* III, 799). *Childe Harold* III has Byron learning to forsake the distractions of the self and its love of 'Earth's troubled waters', and as a result becoming absorbed by the 'life intense' he becomes aware of. And the prisoner is placed on an equivalent threshold: forced to quit his connections with mankind, and stand on the 'brink' of something bigger.

The prisoner, then, may well be moving towards the revivifying discovery of an 'infinite' and 'Eternal' 'being' of which he is 'part' (*CHP* III, 842–847, 840). Here we arrive at section 10 of *The Prisoner*, and a further point of correspondence between it and *Childe Harold* III:

> A light broke in upon my brain, –
>   It was the carol of a bird;
> It ceased, and then it came again
>   The sweetest song ear ever heard,
> And mine was thankful till my eyes
> Ran over with the glad surprise,
> And they that moment could not see
> I was the mate of misery. (251–258)

The prisoner here discovers a capacity to respond spontaneously very like that described in the sequence of *Childe Harold* III following stanza 65 – even after his profound and prolonged isolation, and despite his devastating grief, he also seems able to transcend the 'tragic' absolutes of Byron's earlier verse narratives. There is humility in the word 'thankful' and this echoes Byron's sense of being 'permitted' (*CHP* III, 1019) insight. But there is also an intense joy in the 'glad surprise'.[16] Finally, as a recounting of an experience this is self-conscious, but the moment as experienced is, like the momentary sense of inclusion in a 'life intense' lyrically rendered in *Childe Harold* III, one of supreme distraction from the self, of 'forgetfulness' and escape from desolation. Two things are important here, however. Firstly, that *The Prisoner* describes such a moment of escape, but secondly, that *The Prisoner*, like *Childe Harold* III, goes on to show its speaker losing touch with that moment. At this point in the poem, McGann focuses on the bird's departure, which, the prisoner tells us, leaves him 'doubly lone'(292).[17] Gleckner, too, seems to assume that the bird's departure is what is important when he says that the bird is made to visit only to restore the prisoner's sanity to

> the point at which blessed nothingness and vacancy of darkness yield to a renewed clarity of perception and a consequent doubled sense of imprisonment and death.[18]

Is it the bird's departure that is important here?[19] I suggest that the prisoner's movement back towards desolated loneliness begins long before the bird flies off. For the prisoner, the bird's song 'said a thousand things' (269), and 'seem'd to say them all for me' (270). This leads directly to the idea that the bird is 'a visitant' (284) 'in winged guise' (283), and we witness an act of mind very like Harold's in stanza 14 of *Childe Harold* III:

> ... he could watch the stars
> Till he had peopled them with beings bright
> As their own beams. (*CHP* III, 118–120)

The prisoner pre-empts or obscures the bird's 'otherness' as Harold obscures the stars with imaginative projections. Firstly, he ignores the bird in its immediate 'being', reading it as both something more and something less: a 'guise' adopted by something other than itself. Secondly, he 'peoples' that guise with an imagined 'visitant from Paradise'. The bird itself, the 'thing', becomes relatively unimportant in relation to the interpretation the prisoner latches on to it, in a way that is very like our other example of this shift from sensation to reflection, Wordsworth's 'Resolution and Independence'. There,

---

[16]   For Rutherford, the prisoner's 'reactions are described with genuine insight – first the impulse of joy, then a fresh realization of his wretchedness, and then delight on seeing the bird itself' (*Byron*, p. 72).

[17]   See *Fiery Dust*, p. 171.

[18]   *Ruins*, p. 197.

[19]   For Martin, it is not the bird's departure but its symbolical significance that is important. He argues that 'Byron follows Sterne in his use of the symbol of the bird as a means of presenting his prisoner as a victim' (*Byron: A Poet Before His Public*, p. 91). According to Martin, 'Sterne carefully guides his reader [in *A Sentimental Journey Through France and Italy*] into the prison by initially concentrating on the caged bird: Byron points his reader towards the natural pleasures from which Bonnivard is excluded by having a bird perch on top of his prison' (p. 93). Clearly there is a parallel here, but it is less clear, to my mind, that Byron 'is depending heavily on Sterne's basic formula' (p. 93).

as we have noted, consciousness transforms 'the Man' into 'a man ... from some far region sent / To give me human strength'. Like *Childe Harold* III, *The Prisoner of Chillon* explores the psychological territory marked out in verse by Wordsworth.[20] The prisoner 'reads' the bird, and in so doing retreats from the direct experience of something other than self, and back towards self-conscious reflection. Like Wordsworth's reading of the old man, the prisoner's 'reading' of the bird falls prey to rereadings, as the bird's 'meaning' is detached from the prisoner's experience of its presence. As fear and doubt reassert themselves in 'Resolution and Independence', so the memory of tragic loss asserts itself in *The Prisoner*. No longer engaged by what is immediately present, the mind falls back upon the self and, inevitably, to the grief that possesses it. The idea of the 'visitant from Paradise' falls victim to the idea of 'My brother's soul' (288).[21]

This brings one hopeful moment but is, of course, a delusion, and when the bird departs the prisoner must confront, once again, the loss of his brother. The bird's visit does not so much renew the prisoner's sanity in order to renew his perception of imprisonment, as demonstrate for the reader the psychological prison he is trapped in. His mind begins to move back towards his own tragedy long before the bird leaves him 'lone' once more.

The prisoner, drawn to the outer edge of his own 'tragic' consciousness, does not escape, because he is, finally, distracted from 'the brink' of something new by his own habitual tendency to interpret what he encounters in self-referential terms. This, in turn, leads back to the recollection of his own suffering.

Nevertheless, it is the recognition of this self-conscious habit of mind that marks the real beginning of *Childe Harold* III's quest for renewal and revitalization. The prisoner is granted a brief moment in which he forgets himself and his plight and enters a felt relationship with 'otherness'. Does the prisoner now know that he is not necessarily excluded from the life of 'being' by the walls of his prison but by his own habitual acts of expectation, self-projection, and self-referential interpretation: acts that distract his consciousness from that life? If so, does the prisoner follow Byron's example and use that knowledge to fix his enemy in his sights, so to speak, and struggle to overcome his tendency to distract himself back to himself?

The poem's answer to these questions seems, ultimately, to be 'no', but section 12 suggests that the prisoner is certainly moving in this direction, though not as knowingly or deliberately as Byron does in *Childe Harold* III. He no longer looks out to the lake yearning for escape or death. He makes 'a footing in the wall' (318), but 'not therefrom to escape' (319). Rather, he does so in answer to a growing response to the pull of the same landscape that Byron tells us 'woos' him in *Childe Harold* III:

---

[20]   Edwin M. Everett adds that 'though Byron was indebted to Wordsworth, he owed to Coleridge a debt not so frequently remarked' ('Byron's Lakist Interlude', in *Studies In Philology* 55 [1958], p. 64). For Everett's 'comparative analysis of "The Ancient Mariner" and "The Prisoner of Chillon"'(p. 64), see pp. 71–75.

[21]   This argument, for obvious reasons, touches only very briefly on the prisoner's brothers. For further discussion see Martin (*Byron: A Poet Before His Public*, p. 94) and Marshall (*Structure*, pp. 85–89).

> But I was curious to ascend
> To my barr'd windows, and to bend
> Once more upon the mountains high,
> The quiet of a loving eye. (328–331)

The prisoner is here simply 'curious' to 'bend ... a loving eye'. His mood is one of 'quiet' reverie and his act one of 'loving' reverence. This sudden welling up of love is important, since it is finally towards a vision of 'love' as the 'principle' that unifies the universe that *Childe Harold* III moves. Is the prisoner on the verge of discovering this consoling vision too?[22] By 'loving' he is, perhaps, at this very moment, mingling 'in the beauty' of 'a comprehensive order', the principle of which is 'love'. In *Childe Harold* III, this 'love', felt as a response, is seen as a sign of man's integration into the universe,[23] and is a springboard into something very like the territory of comedy.

The prisoner now looks out on 'otherness' undistracted by his own plight and discovers a continuity which he has become divorced from, but to which he might return. The world, he notes, is 'not changed' (333). The prisoner revels in the perceived details which, like 'the bud which brings / The swiftest thought of beauty' (*CHP* III, 956–957) in *Childe Harold* III, draw him forward into a kind of joyful delight: the lake is 'wide long', the Rhone 'blue' and in 'fullest flow', the torrents 'leap and gush' (335–336). Revelling in details, delighting in the nature that surrounds him, the prisoner is about to move into a moment of joyful absorption and forgetfulness like that rendered by stanza 89 of *Childe Harold* III. And yet he does not move forward into any such experience. He is once again distracted back to the self. Increasingly his description of the island is haunted by self-reference and a consciousness of the prison from which it is viewed: it is 'Scarce broader than my dungeon floor' (345). As the dungeon intrudes, so does the prisoner's lonely life of grief within it. We make an immediate connection between the three trees and his three dead brothers, for example, and notice that the phrases that range over the landscape; 'o'er it', 'by it', 'on it' (347–349) are all haunted by an implicit 'but not here'. In the end, the prisoner turns away from the fish that swam 'by the castle walls' and seem 'joyous each and all', excluding himself from that joy by allotting it only to 'They' (351–352).

At this moment of possibility, the prisoner's 'Consciousness' remembers 'her woes' (*CHP* I, 941), and, as a result, the prisoner remains a one of Byron's 'tragic sufferers'. But at what point, precisely, does the prisoner's mind turn back to his plight – and why?

I suggest this turning is obscured behind the phrase 'And then' (356). The simple word 'And', used in conjunction with 'then' or used on its own, is of considerable structural importance in *The Prisoner*, and the fact of its repeated

---

22   Certainly, 'by bending "once more upon the mountains high / The quiet of a loving eye"', the prisoner 'might be recognized as [momentarily] achieving the equivalent of the Ancient Mariner's salvation, or the "sensation sweet" and "tranquil restoration" that sustains Wordsworth's "hours of weariness" in "Tintern Abbey"' (Martin, *Byron: A Poet Before His Public*, pp. 88–89).

23   See *Childe Harold* III, stanzas 99 to 104, and Byron's note to *CHP* III, line 927 (in *Works* II, pp. 311–313).

use is itself a signifier. It starts to appear regularly and intrusively almost as soon as the prisoner begins to recount his descent back into 'misery' (see lines 356, 358, 375, 376, 382).

The phrase 'And then' does not make its first appearance in line 356: it appears in line 341. But in line 356, the prisoner uses the phrase because he decides that he will, rather than narrate how and why his consciousness pulls back from absorption to the self, simply narrate the fact of that retreat. Something pivotal is lost to the reader as a result of this decision, and obscured behind the prisoner's simple connective. This is the repeated impact of the prisoner's use of 'and': something is lost, hidden, or rushed over. In line 356, we are rushed forward from one moment to a new and distinct moment, in which, we are told, 'new tears came' (356) and the prisoner 'felt troubled' (357). We might suggest that the prisoner is troubled because suddenly recollecting his isolation, but such a progression is not made explicit in the poem.[24] In fact no causal progression is either implied or explicitly stated.[25] The prisoner baldly states 'I felt troubled' and offers no further information. He simply moves on to what happened next, 'when I did descend again' (359), adding this action on to what precedes it with nothing more revealing than the word 'And' (359).

'And' and 'And then' are employed deliberately in order to leave obscure, to pass over. And of the losses of vital information which this obscuration leads to, one loss stands out: the moment or sequence of moments during which the prisoner is looking out of the window, feeling troubled, and in which he decides to climb down. What is here obscured from view is why the prisoner turns back to his misery. We have a selection of separate moments whose connection, and the progress of consciousness between them, are obscured. This makes the end of the poem difficult to read because the story it tells is partly missing. All we have to go on, if we have anything at all, is the prisoner's assertion, offered long after his release, that he 'learn'd to love despair' (374).

At the pivotal moment, was the prisoner's love of nature blighted by a sudden onrush of despair? Or denied a home in the natural universe, has the prisoner gradually settled for the home he has, even though it is an enforced and painful one? Either might be the case, but the line does not actually tell us. It does not, for example, say 'I had learn'd to love despair'. If it did it would quickly help us to explain what happened to the prisoner in his dungeon. As it stands, however, it offers no reference back to section 13 or to the prisoner's descent from the window, but seems rather to describe a kind of perverse nostalgia for his prison which developed after his release. The claim to have

---

[24] Indeed, as Cooke suggests, we might infer that the prisoner is simply 'spent ... from the very effort of climbing, of aspiration' (*The Blind Man*, p. 88).

[25] Marshall argues that what the prisoner is recalling 'is a simple psychological reaction, exhaustion following emotional intensity and depression coming in the wake of exhaustion' (*Structure*, p. 94). Marshall goes on to suggest that the prisoner's 'depression could be derived from his philosophical awareness of his inability to attain full consummation in his love for Nature's elements' (pp. 94–95), but the problem is that we do not actually know what his 'depression is derived from', or even if it is 'depression'. We can do no more than guess at what is going on.

learned to love despair is, in fact, divided from the moment we are looking at by 'months, or years, or days' (366), and the fact that the prisoner 'learned to love despair' might as easily be a consequence of his descending from the window as the cause of his doing so.

The prisoner's assertion does not help us to reconstruct the moment that is missing from the poem, then. But *Childe Harold* III does help us here. For if we cannot finally reconstruct that missing moment, we can, at least, by looking back to *Childe Harold* III, partly explain why Byron makes the prisoner obscure his own descent back to darkness, loss, and grief. We can recall parallel acts of repression in stanzas 8 and 98, for instance. In each case, Byron is brought to the brink of self-articulation and to the brink of articulating a particular kind of experience: the 'whirling gulf of phantasy and flame' (*CHP* III, 58) he is so determined to detach himself from.

The act of putting this 'gulf' into words draws the consciousness to it and into it; it enforces recollection. And the articulation itself, as if inevitably, develops a quasi-tragic idiom in Byron's verse. In *Childe Harold* III, as we have seen, Byron is trying to push beyond his own quasi-tragic imaginings, and into something new. In *The Prisoner of Chillon* he is trying to do something very similar in fiction: trying to push a tragically blasted fictional consciousness beyond its own tragedy. *Childe Harold* III is successful because, in part, Byron can hide his own pain behind a 'silent seal', 'sheathing it as a sword' (*CHP* III, 65, 913). His acts of repression and refusals to articulate the recollection of his own pain facilitate his movement beyond such recollection. In this way, those acts of repression and refusal are prototypes for the prisoner's refusal to articulate the movement of his own consciousness away from communion with nature and back towards Byronic tragedy.

For the prisoner represses the memory of his descent by taking refuge in a particular kind of narrative structuring of the events he is recounting: a narrative structuring made up only of 'hinge-points'.[26] His narrative establishes and foregrounds a sequential relationship between events with the phrase 'And then' and the simple conjunction 'And'. These connectives set up a structure within which causal relationships between the events that form the sequence might have been made explicit by shifting into various other modes of discourse – confession, explication, interpretation, or digression, for example. Yet, at many of the key points in his retelling of his story, the prisoner uses only these connectives, which we might call the language of a purely sequential structuring, repressing any impulse towards other kinds of language. He refuses to slip into any kind of talk that might seek to explain why the sequence is as it is. To do so would necessitate self-scrutiny and remembering, in detail, what is painful. To take refuge in non-explicatory language is to take refuge from remembering.

The prisoner represses the memory of his own descent back to pathos and tragedy,[27] then, and as he does so we witness the surfacing of a direct line of

---

[26] Barthes, 'Introduction to the Structural Analysis of Narratives', p. 93.

[27] Peter J. Manning perhaps has this act of repression in mind when he describes the 'self-control Bonnivard achieves'. For Manning, this self-control 'enables' the prisoner 'to relate his misfortunes as none of Byron's earlier protagonists can. The moving restraint of his narrative counteracts in the reader's estimation his immobility and tacit admission of

development that runs not only from *Childe Harold* III to *The Prisoner*, but from *The Prisoner* to *Beppo*. On the one hand, the prisoner's repression of his own suffering is a distinct echo of *Childe Harold* III's comic impulse: it seems to hold on to a faint hope of a redeemable present and/or future, and certainly demonstrates a refusal to turn back, now, to the recollection of an irredeemable past. On the other hand, in the later comic work, Byron writes:

> To turn, – and to return; – the devil take it!
>   This story slips for ever through my fingers,
> Because, just as the stanza likes to make it,
>   It needs must be – and so it rather lingers;
> This form of verse began, I can't well break it,
>   But must keep time and tune like public speakers.[28]

In *Beppo*, the link between speech and self-articulation is entirely broken, as form itself dictates what is said. Digressions from the narrative of *Beppo* are possible in a way that they are not for the prisoner without a certain attendant danger. They are possible in *Beppo* because they are generated not by a desire to explain, but by 'time' (metre) and 'tune' (for example, rhyme). But the comic invention that informs these digressions is itself made possible by a putting to one side of self akin to that of the prisoner's. To put it another way, the kind of repression of the self depicted in *The Prisoner* plays a vital role in the birth of Byronic comedy.

As a result, the generic status of *The Prisoner of Chillon* is not quite clear. It certainly is not 'comic'. It ends with the prisoner's freedom, and this suggests a comedic structure: a 'happy ending' for the main protagonist.[29] But this freedom is won 'with a sigh' (394), as the prisoner remains enthralled by despair, grief, and loneliness.

Byron's attempt to interpolate the renewal discovered in *Childe Harold* III into the experience of a fictional and entirely devastated consciousness proved, for now, unsuccessful: the tragic polarity still holds on to the Byronic hero. Yet the project to push beyond his 'tragic vision' in a fictional work does not succumb entirely to the power of that vision. For if *The Prisoner* is not a comic poem, then it is not wholeheartedly 'tragic' either, even in the loose sense in which we are using the word. The prisoner is sad rather than stricken beyond all hope, and when the end of his tale is compared to the end of *The Giaour*, say, or *Lara*, it is obvious that while *The Prisoner* does not arrive at the renewal, reintegration, and recovery of a true comedy ending, it does not belong so entirely to a 'tragic sense of life' as these earlier poems do. *The*

---

defeat' (*Byron and His Fictions* [Detroit: Wayne State University Press, 1978], p. 89). Similarly, Marshall seems to touch on the prisoner's linguistic self-obscuration when he argues that in the prisoner's story 'silence is to become an outward sign of his ordeal' (*Structure*, p. 85).

[28]   *Beppo* (in *Works* IV), 497–502.

[29]   According to Frye, 'the theme of ... the comic is the integration of society, which usually takes the form of incorporating a central character into it' (*Anatomy of Criticism*, p. 43). At the end of the poem, the Prisoner is at least 'restored' to society, even if not entirely (re)incorporated into it.

Prisoner holds out the hope of a happy ending, as if it is a comedy that is not yet finished.

The possibility of such a happy future is glimpsed, I think, in the prisoner's repression, now, in his retelling of his story, of painful moments in his past. His refusal to look back in this instance is an advance, in the direction of comedy, on his earlier inability to do anything but 'descend again' to his own desolation and grief. The possibility of comedy, we can argue, asserts itself in the free space won by the repression of pain, and the prisoner's act of repression certainly looks forward to one kind of comedy: the speaker of *Beppo* is a 'broken Dandy' (410), but refuses to elaborate. Rather, he throws his energy into a kind of poetic discourse, close to conversation perhaps, that denies such elaboration. The self as an object of poetic attention is, in a sense, exiled from the poem. As a result, the speaker's talk is rooted in the immediacy of its own articulation. It delights in its own invention and belongs, for this reason among others, to the world of comic literature.

The Prisoner of Chillon, then, is pushing towards comedy but does not quite break free from the absolutes of Byron's earlier tales. 'The Dream', a poem that first appeared with *The Prisoner* in *The Prisoner of Chillon and Other Poems*, also pushes to the 'brink' of comedy but, like *The Prisoner*, sinks back, as if inevitably, into or towards the tragic. However, while *The Prisoner* obscures its descent into desolation and pain, 'The Dream' dramatizes such a descent, indeed it does so a number of times, as if Byron is trying to ascertain what it is that makes his tragic hero a prisoner of his fate. In 'The Dream' Byron can be seen to move away from the influence of Wordsworth once more, and his poetry begins to detach itself from the insights and impulses of *Childe Harold* III.[30]

We can trace these developments quite precisely, but in doing so we enter a relatively untrodden area of study. 'The Dream' is an often overlooked poem,[31] and even a general sense of how the poem has been received must be gleaned from comments made, more often than not, in passing.[32] However, it is worth pausing briefly to look at some of the things criticism has to say about the poem.

To begin with, McGann's notes in *Works* IV do offer a direct critical response to 'The Dream', but it is a disappointing one. The notes begin by saying that 'The dream device does little to veil the autobiographical character of the poem', and McGann insists on this 'autobiographical character' as far as

---

[30] 'The Dream' was 'written in July 1816', and so, perhaps, immediately after the 'original draft' of *The Prisoner* was finished 'on 2 July' (McGann, *Works* IV, pp. 455, 448–449). Certainly, Byron seems to have written 'The Dream' while making additions to *The Prisoner* (see McGann, *Works* IV, pp. 448–450, 455) .

[31] This has not always been the case, it seems. In 1915, Chew wrote that 'The Dream' was then 'the most famous of all Byron's shorter pieces' (*The Dramas of Lord Byron*, p. 69).

[32] Two exceptions to this general habit of neglect should be noted from the outset: Robert Gleckner (in *Ruins*), who I will be referring to throughout my discussion of the poem, and Samuel Chew (in *The Dramas of Lord Byron*), who discusses the poem at some length, though primarily in relation to *Manfred*.

to date the dream the poem claims to record 'between August and November 1803'.[33] This, then, is McGann's critical view of the poem:

> It narrates B's early passion for Mary Chaworth and is set in the environs of her home at Annesley Park and Hall.[34]

Gleckner, on the other hand, who is one of the few critics to include even a brief reading of the poem in a book-length study of Byron's verse, dismisses this biographical context as 'totally irrelevant', suggesting, rather, that the poem 'reflects' the 'unrelieved gloom' of earlier poems, 'as well as Byron's interest in the interanimation and confusion of dream and reality'.[35] Gleckner's account of the poem offers interesting insights into its position on various lines of continuity that run through Byron's poetry. His second point suggests a foreshadowing of *Manfred* in 'The Dream',[36] as his first suggests a more wholehearted return to the emphases and concerns of Byron's earlier tragic tales than we see in *The Prisoner of Chillon*. It is in the context of Byron's shifting poetic interests, and of our guiding concern with his movement between distinct kinds of writing, that I want to look at 'The Dream', rather than as thinly veiled autobiography.

Indeed, 'The Dream' is interesting for the light it sheds on the shifting focus of Byron's energies in 1816. We trace in the poem a resurgent interest in intense suffering, but the poem does not begin by setting off in the direction of tragedy and pathos. It traverses a difficult and blurred generic territory: repeatedly holding out the possibility of a 'happy ending', overwhelming that possibility with devastating twists of fate or consciousness, but never entirely relaxing into either a comic or a tragic mode. To put this another way, the poem repeatedly heads in the direction of tragedy and pathos, but it always has some hold on various comic impulses. 'The Dream' has its life, for the most part, somewhere between comedy and Byronic tragedy.

In order to get the grips with the poem, then, we need to map out this 'somewhere' in a little more detail. Here the poem's title and its dream-frame

---

[33]   *Works* IV, p. 455.

[34]   Ibid. McGann, of course, is not the only critic to stress the 'autobiographical character' of 'The Dream'. Chew argues, for example, that the 'autobiographical references in *The Dream* are indisputable in their cogency' (*The Dramas of Lord Byron*, p. 72 and n.), while Joseph claims that in this poem, Byron is 'using the dissolving scenes of the dream to describe various episodes of his past life' (*Byron the Poet*, p. 80).

[35]   *Ruins*, p. 200. Perhaps 'totally irrelevant' is a little too strong here. As M. Byron Raïzis points out, 'Real events from Byron's life are traced with 'photographic realism' ... while others are ... thinly disguised' in the poem. Yet, as Raïzis continues, 'there are ... fictions and omissions in it, too, or at least some deliberate deviations from biographical truth'. Raïzis's main point in this context is, I think, a fair one. He argues that 'Byron manipulates his data with artistic licence', so that 'Reality has been filtered through the transforming prism of imagination' by the time it enters 'The Dream' (see 'Byron's Promethean Rebellion in 1816: Fictionality and Self-Projection in His Poetry that Year', in *The Byron Journal* 19 [1991], pp. 44–45).

[36]   See *Manfred* I, i, 190–261 (in *Works* IV), where Manfred is in a faint and we do not know for sure whether or not he is dreaming what we hear in his overwrought state, or if we are seeing something actually there that Manfred does not see.

help us. 'The Dream' evokes a particular poetic tradition, the dream vision, and as Northrop Frye points out, the dream vision is a 'typical episodic theme' of romance. It is, he argues:

> best described as the theme of the boundary of consciousness, the sense of the poetic mind as passing from one world to another, or as simultaneously aware of both.[37]

The words 'twofold' and 'boundary' in lines 1 and 2 of 'The Dream' obviously point to a consciousness 'simultaneously aware' of two worlds. This, the title, the frame, and the lyric presence of a dreamer all suggest the genre of romance, and this suggestion is especially borne out by the poem, as we shall see, when the dream itself begins in the second section of the poem. And though we can only say that 'The Dream' is virtually a romance, since it is not a narrative exactly, by doing so we can see the poem as another manifestation of Byron's interest in romance conventions.[38] Equally, by describing the poem as in some sense belonging to the realm of romance, we can situate the poem in some kind of meaningful relation to the tragic and the comic. In his circular description of generic distinctions, Frye positions romance as follows:

> Tragedy and comedy contrast rather than blend, and so do romance and irony, the champions respectively of the ideal and the actual. On the other hand, comedy blends insensibly into satire at the one extreme and into romance at the other; romance may be comic or tragic; tragedy extends from high romance to bitter and ironic realism.[39]

Though Frye is open to criticism for being excessively schematic, this particular scheme offers a good perspective from which to view 'The Dream'. It allows us to suggest that Byron is using romance as a middle ground, a space, or more properly an idiomatic range, between comedy and tragedy, in which to move from one to the other and to explore such movements and the points of possible connection or conflict they manifest. Comic and tragic impulses fight over possession of the poem throughout, and Byron is seeking out an unprecedented kind of fluidity and freedom, rather than closure and finality.

Let us turn to the poem, then, and begin to trace its oscillation between tragic and comic possibilities. Its dream narrative begins in the 'middle ground' between tragedy and comedy, as we are calling romance. Section 2 opens with 'two beings in the hues of youth' (27),[40] who appear as archetypal lovers who

---

[37] *Anatomy of Criticism*, p. 57.

[38] Other manifestations of this interest that can be mentioned briefly include the fact that *Childe Harold's Pilgrimage* is subtitled 'A Romaunt' and *The Prisoner* is subtitled 'A Fable'.

[39] *Anatomy of Criticism*, p. 162.

[40] All quotations from 'The Dream' are taken from *Works* IV. Line references will be given after each quotation in the text.

have yet to be drawn into a plot, be it tragic, comic, or otherwise.[41] Rather, they occupy a lyrical antechamber to plot that draws on the pastoral and Arcadian: they stand on a 'Green' (29) and 'gentle hill' (28), looking out on 'the wave / Of woods and cornfields' (33).[42] The landscape is inhabited and created by man – it is a garden for his 'sport' (38) – and so the idealized 'maiden' and 'youth' (39) inhabit a world of created order and play: that of a romance, we might say, tending towards comedy.[43]

So we begin in a lyrical antechamber, where we are encouraged to see the two young people as lovers and to assume that they will stand at the centre of the poem. Only in line 63 do we realize that this is not in fact the case:

> Her sighs were not for him; to her he was
> Even as a brother – but no more; 'twas much,
> For brotherless she was, save in the name
> Her infant friendship had bestowed on him;
>   ... It was a name
> Which pleased him, and yet pleased him not – and why?
> Time taught him a deep answer. (63–70)

We find suddenly that we have been misled by the poem's opening, and must rearrange our understanding of the situation we are viewing and our expectations of what is likely to come. An unexpected figure comes into view with the knowledge that 'her sighs were not for him', and this new character begins to push the youth, who now appears to be an 'unrequited lover', towards the tragic margins of romance. Already the poem is moving off from the idyllic. A possible future shift towards tragic closure inches into view as a tragic fate for the youth is hinted at in the last line of this quotation. But if Byron is already setting off in the direction of tragedy, he has also opened up other possibilities. A happy destiny for the maiden seems to be taking shape in the lines that follow: she looks forward to a marriage, that is, to the kind of ending that belongs to comedy. If the poem is looking to leave the world of romance, it has espied not one, but two exits, both of which it approaches simultaneously.

Wherever the poem is about to head, it has pulled the carpet from beneath the reader's feet. Now it appears that the youth has knowingly accompanied the maiden to the hill to look for the approach of her lover, and has always, and again knowingly, been marginal to a central situation that is slowly coming into focus. We do not know quite what to expect of him now. Is he to become an unrequited lover, or an heroic 'protecting brother' who will selflessly play a part in bringing about the young woman's happiness?

---

[41] Gleckner describes these 'lovers' as 'the "Boy" and "Maid" of eternal spring and love and peace' (*Ruins*, p. 201).

[42] For Gleckner, this opening vision is 'Byron's favourite Edenic scene' (ibid.).

[43] Byron, it seems, drew quite specifically on Annesley Hall and park for the details of his dreamscape: 'The hill is Howatt Hill, situated about half a mile from Annesley Hall, on which was a circle of trees. John Musters, Mary's later husband, cut them down after reading this poem. They were later replanted (see Marchand I. 77–78)' (McGann, *Works* IV, p. 455). See also 'Fragment: Written Shortly After the Marriage of Miss Chaworth' (in *Works* I, p. 2), which opens 'Hills of Annesley, bleak and barren'.

An answer seems already implicit, though no more than that. The poem has allowed the youth to occupy a centrality before moving him to the margin. It foregrounds, and is clearly interested in, this marginalization. And it stays with the marginalized youth rather than following the 'happy couple'. As it does so, the poem's tone begins to change. It shifts, we might suggest, away from 'romantic comedy' towards 'tragic romance'.[44] The change is explicitly signalled: 'A change came o'er the spirit of my dream' (75) says the dreamer. This announcement opens sections 3 (75), 4 (105), 5 (126), 6 (144), 7 (167), and 8 (184) and at each usage takes on a new kind of power. Essentially, it marks out the stages of a definite shift towards the tragic, or, as Gleckner puts it, 'with each successive change eternity fades into time, vision into the light of common day, day in darkness'.[45] As this progress gains momentum, the illusion of intimacy fades into the fact of exclusion:

> There was an ancient mansion, and before
> Its walls there was a steed caparisoned:
> Within an antique Oratory stood
> The Boy of whom I spake; – he was alone. (76–79)

The poem focuses in on the youth's isolation. It also removes him from any restorative influence pastoral 'Nature' might exert. Very quickly, we realize that what the poem is actually isolating is a moment of intense suffering:

> ... then he lean'd
> His bow'd head on his hands, and shook as 'twere
> With a convulsion – then arose again,
> And with his teeth and quivering hands did tear
> What he had written, but he shed no tears.
> And he did calm himself, and fix his brow
> Into a kind of quiet. (82–88)

Torture bursts forth and momentarily carries the youth out of the world of romance altogether. Byron's instinct is to have the youth repress this outburst, calming himself back into a public role. This effort has a twofold aim. Firstly, it is an attempt to protect the maiden's idyllic contentment, and safeguard the new comic possibilities it has opened up. Secondly, it is an attempt to prevent the retreat of the idyllic world away from the youth who is, at present, marginally included in it – a retreat that would inevitably follow any declaration of this pain and its cause. Can suffering keep a hold on the consolations it is offered or can the lover be happy as the brother, and thereby escape a tragic fate and win absorption into the comic festivity of a wedding? It seems not. The youth manages only 'a kind of quiet', and it remains an effort to keep at bay forces that are hostile to the world of 'comic romance'. Such an effort must now be maintained, but it excludes him from any kind of contentment or even resignation. And his presence is unsettling, even corrupting, for it is

---

44   These terms, while appropriate, are necessarily loose and flexible. The territory in which we find ourselves in 'The Dream' is extremely difficult to map out.
45   *Ruins*, p. 201.

hostile to the very thing he wishes to keep within his reach. The knowledge that he is suffering, we can speculate, might easily eat away at the maid's happiness. The tearing of the letter even manifests a violent impulse as it articulates a private pain. At the back of our minds we sense a slight threat of violence hanging over the maiden's and her lover's future, and the suffering we glimpse here intrudes between us and the maiden's happiness.

For now, the youth does manage to contain his suffering. He is, nevertheless, forced to withdraw from the romantic comedy that absorbs the maiden. He succeeds, again for now, in leaving it intact, and his withdrawal does protect the comic possibilities the poem has glimpsed. Yet it does so at a profound expense to him, as we see in their final meeting:

> ... as he paused,
> The Lady of his love re-entered there,
> She was serene and smiling then, and yet
> She knew she was by him beloved, – she knew,
> For quickly comes such knowledge, that his heart
> Was darken'd by her shadow, and she saw
> That he was wretched, but she saw not all. (88–94)

As 'the Lady of his love' she is part of his narrative, but she has just left a very different kind of narrative and retains the signs of it: she is 'serene and smiling'. The two narratives meet, but do not mingle: she sees that he is wretched, but 'saw not all'. The fact of her partial knowledge plays a part in his torture but, perhaps most devastatingly, he is confronted with her story, in which he can be only marginal and excluded from its serenity. He is forever denied the kind of smile she inadvertently brings with her.

It is the recognition of the price of inclusion, at the margin, in her narrative that causes him to withdraw from it and into his own. Something of this recognition can be heard in the resentment that charges 'she knew' and 'she saw'. The torture of remaining silent is part of the price he pays for his 'self-less' act.

The poem dramatizes the splintering of a single situation into multiple narratives: into narratives that belong to very different literary discourses, but which here inform the same moment. They run alongside each other, but remain distinct. Byron wants to keep hold of both and so has the youth rise under the pressure of the incompatibility of his being and hers, and, as the newly elevated hero of a 'tragic romance', leave her world of 'romantic comedy'. Byron also makes sure that until he does, he adheres strictly to a conventional romance code of behaviour: his taking her hand in lines 95–96 is both courteous and almost chivalric, and shows Byron's determination that he will leave her romance without sullying it. Thus the youth leaves 'with slow steps' (99), but his courtesy ensures that they part with 'mutual smiles' (101).

In both *Childe Harold* III and *The Prisoner*, the possibility of comedy seems to rest for Byron upon an act of repression. Here, an act of repression attempts to safeguard future festivity. But in 'The Dream', at the moment a comedic world is vouchsafed, Byron no longer seems interested in what is won. Rather, his attention seems compelled by the fact that the 'romantic comedy' the youth's self-repression protects cannot reach out and absorb him.

In *Childe Harold* III, where a tragic sense of self is also held in check and exiled from the poem, this act of exile helps Byron to win a new idiom for his poetry. In 'The Dream', on the other hand, it is an exiled subject that commands Byron's interest: he follows the self that is exiled rather than the romance that is safeguarded. 'The Dream' dramatizes the gulf between Byron's tragic subject and comedy from its vantage point in the 'middle ground' of romance. However, it is compelled by exclusion: not as a means to happiness, but as its price. Byron's imagination is turning away from the idea of 'redemptive possibilities' and back towards the idea of the irredeemable.

Yet is the youth's fate absolutely irredeemable? Some hope that it is not seems still to inform the poem's progress. In section 4, the exiled subject seems to have been restored to 'Nature', as the poem gathers the youth into a new pastoral idyll, and an existence of repose in, and integration into, a natural 'home' (108). As I suggested earlier, the poem repeatedly heads in the direction of the tragic, but does not come to rest there. Interested as it is in fluidity and movement between genres, the poem struggles to hold, or win back, the 'middle ground' between tragedy and comedy, even while moving, as if inexorably, in the direction of tragedy. Consequently, the poem is deflected into a pastoral idiom here because, while the pastoral often deals with unsuccessful love, it is not a tragic mode. An excursion into the pastoral might safeguard the poem, for a while, from the 'tragic' mode of discourse which threatens to envelope it. Indeed, such an excursion might help to guide the youth's story back towards, even into, the realm of romance.[46] Can the youth be steered back into the 'middle ground' of romance? Can he escape the threat posed by tragedy? And can he now move towards some kind of comic or comedic redemption after all?[47] Such questions naturally suggest themselves as we read section 4, and seem to draw Byron's composition of the poem forward:

> ... in the wilds
> Of fiery climes he made himself a home,
> And his Soul drank ... sunbeams...
> There was a mass of many images
> Crowded like waves upon me, but he was
> A part of all; and in the last he lay
> Reposing from the noon-tide sultriness. (106–114)

Here, as in *The Prisoner*, we find Byron reworking and reassessing the ideas of *Childe Harold* III. It seems that the youth of 'The Dream' has achieved a kind of relation to 'Nature' similar to that briefly enjoyed by Harold in *Childe Harold* III. As Harold's spirit took flight towards the stars, the youth's 'Soul

---

[46] As Curran points out, the pastoral 'naturally assimilates itself to larger forms'. More specifically, 'Its inherent animism and closeness to folk traditions make it particularly congenial to romance' (Curran, *Poetic Form and British Romanticism*, p. 86).

[47] Certainly, the poem's shift into a pastoral mode might encourage us to think that the poem is heading towards some kind of 'romantic comedy'. According to Frye, the 'pastoral' is the 'chief vehicle' of 'romantic comedy' in its more 'idyllic' modes (*Anatomy of Criticism*, p. 43).

drank ... sunbeams'. Has the youth, like Harold, discovered 'forgetfulness'? Significant details here suggest not. The verb 'drank', for example, is very different from *Childe Harold* III's word 'flight'. *Childe Harold* III reaches out after a 'life intense' that is 'concentred' somewhere other than the self. Its speaker discovers his own part in 'being', and a 'sense / Of that which is of all Creator and Defence', by reaching out after it. The youth of 'The Dream', on the other hand, simply absorbs. He takes in rather than seeks after. His relation to otherness is self-'concentred' and self-reflexive: the very kind of relation that in *Childe Harold* III prevents forgetfulness. Further, if we are to read 'sunbeams' as in any sense an equivalent to Harold's starbeams, then it is significant that at noon-tide the youth is found 'Reposing from' them. The youth's languor and disengagement are a long way from Harold's intense connection.

The youth's languid detachment is also haunted by an earlier and distinct echo of Byron's early tales:

> ... he had ceased
> To live within himself; she was his life,
> The ocean to the river of his thoughts,
> Which terminated all. (55–59)

Unlike the poet of *Childe Harold* III, who claims that he 'live[s] not in' himself but 'become[s] / Portion of that around me' (*CHP* III, 680–681), the youth, like the Giaour or Lara, is at this point divorced from immediate presence because his consciousness is devoted to an absent loved one. In previous tales this detachment is final, but are we to read this finality into 'The Dream'? If so, the youth's languor is not peace, but a kind of void. If it is filled by anything, then it is filled with memory. Indeed, liquid imagery links the youth's absorption ('drank') of 'sunbeams' with 'the river of his thoughts', which, we are here told, all terminate in 'the Lady of his love'. Does his 'Soul' drink sunbeams only so that they can pass through his being and flow, with the flow of his thoughts, to her: absorbing a kind of animation from nature that he lacks, but only so that animation can be channelled into recollecting? If we are to give the phrase 'she was his life' the kind of finality it would carry in one of Byron's earlier narratives, then we would have to assert that in some profound way the youth exists only in his (mental) relation to the maiden, and that he is closed off from the restorative powers of 'Nature'.

It looks as though the Byronic tragic hero has rewritten *Childe Harold* III's relation to nature and ousted Wordsworth from Byron's poetry altogether. Certainly, in section 4 of 'The Dream', Byron reapproaches the idea of *Childe Harold* III's climax, as he did in *The Prisoner*, and rethinks the notion of a redeeming communion with nature. And in 'The Dream', nature does not revive or revitalize. There is no 'passion and ... power' (*CHP* III, 112) in the youth's repose – and there is, for him, no 'sense / Of that which is of all Creator and defence'. He knows that 'God' is 'to be seen in Heaven' (125), but not that he is to be felt on Earth.

'The Dream' has not come to rest in the idea of a restorative and redemptive communion with nature. Section 4 is more like a pastoral interlude. But perhaps the significance of such an interlude is not to be sought in narrative terms at all, but in terms of the poem's tone and its play among genres. The poem might not have discovered a redemption for its central character, but it does seem to have wrenched itself away from its determined shift towards the tragic, if only into a kind of pastoral indeterminacy. A better word might be 'neutrality', because the poem achieves a distance from its tragic idiom in a neutral repose. In doing so, as we shall see, it finds itself free to move from the pastoral towards the prospect of festivity in another wedding. To put this another way, the poem has shifted the youth, via the pastoral languor of section 4, away from the pull of tragedy and towards a festive reintegration into society. The question that concerns us here, then, is whether or not Byron has managed to bridge the gulf between the tragic and the comic so that the poem can move into a comic mode, or does this gulf reassert itself and drag the poem back towards tragedy?

When the youth reappears in section 4, two details are immediately striking. The first is the word 'return'd' (145), the second is the tag 'Wanderer' (145). 'Return'd' initially reawakens a quest motif latent in his departure, though we know that he 'ne'er repassed' the 'hoary threshold' (104) of his home again. Where is he 'return'd' to?

His return is to society: he is, it seems, going to marry. He is once more brought to the verge of redemption, here in an integration into another comic narrative, typically marked by a marriage ceremony. It seems, for a moment, that Byron has indeed managed to bridge the gulf between the tragic and the comic and that the poem can now move into a comic mode. And yet certain absolutes have become fixed for Byron even in the process of seeking out a fluidity that eats away at the very idea of absolutes. The poem holds out the promise, once again, of a 'happy ending', and to do so briefly represses the youth's suffering. 'The Dream' is, nevertheless, set once more to dramatize Byron's powerful attraction to the tragic. At the very last moment, as the youth 'stood / Even at the altar',

> ... o'er his brow there came
> The selfsame aspect, and the quivering shock
> That in the antique Oratory shook
> His bosom in its solitude, and then –
> As in that hour – a moment o'er his face
> The tablet of unutterable thoughts
> Was traced, – and then it faded as it came. (148–155)

If we recall that 'solitude' in the 'Oratory', a 'quivering shock' immediately follows the youth's writing of a note which, we presume, was to be a lover's plea or confession. Whatever shocks him makes him tear up the note and determine to remain silent and conceal what he can of his torture from the maiden. The 'quivering shock', we are forced to infer, is one of truly tragic recognition: it registers the youth's moment of 'anagnorisis', in which the fact that he is doomed to be unrequited hits him with its full force for the first time.[48]

---

[48]   'Anagnorisis' (recognition) is, of course, Aristotle's term (see *Poetics*). Byron does not use the word but, as Beatty suggests, 'Byron is ... concerned with that instantaneous

A second moment of recognition overwhelms him here, as memory asserts itself once more. The earlier moment is precisely repeated, has 'the selfsame aspect', and this repetition closes off, finally, the possibility of any kind of redemption for the youth. Tragedy jumps up to claim him, even altering his features and reshaping them in its own image. Memory traps him in unequivocal isolation:

> ... he could see
> Not that which was, nor that which should have been –
> But the old mansion ...
>   ... and the place
> The day, the hour, the sunshine, and the shade,
> All things pertaining to that place and hour,
> And her who was his destiny, came back
> And thrust themselves between him and the light. (158–165)

Byron has not discovered the fluidity between comedy and tragedy he is looking for. Rather, he has been drawn back to what holds his tragic subject off from redemption, be it comic or otherwise. Redemption, even the prospect of a paradise, is glimpsed in the word 'light', but memory is here finally inescapable, and this inescapability is fixed as an absolute which prohibits, absolutely, any movement of a Byronic fictional self from tragedy to comedy, from tragedy to redemption.

We might, from this vantage point, look back to the prisoner's descent from the window, and suggest that while *The Prisoner of Chillon* baffles any attempt to explicate that descent, it may obscure nothing more than the tenacious hold of painful memory. There too, memory may have 'thrust' itself 'between him and the light'.

In the case of the youth in 'The Dream', he has become an almost archetypal 'Wanderer': the tag sticks.[49] He has, furthermore, become 'a mark / For blight and desolation' (187–188), and is forced to resort to that 'Vitality of poison' (*CHP* III, 299) that reanimates the heroes of the earlier tales only to destroy them: 'He fed on poisons, and they had no power, / But were a kind of nutriment' (192–193). Byron does, then, at the end of 'The Dream', return to the hero of his earlier tales, who re-emerges with new force, immune to the 'redemptive possibilities' Byron had tried to open up to him.

Yet even at the end, perhaps the poem does not utterly rule out the one remaining possibility for a redemptive and comedic outcome: a reunion between the youth and the maiden. This seems rather unlikely, but it is possible that there is the faint suggestion, in the maiden's ensuing madness at the end of the poem, that she has come to recognize that she in fact does love

---

point of recognition'. This, he says, is 'Byron's peculiar territory' ('Fiction's Limit and Eden's Door' in *Byron and the Limits of Fiction*, pp. 11, 10). For a full discussion of the concept of 'recognition' see Terence Cave, *Recognition: A Study In Poetics* (Oxford: Clarendon Press, 1988).

[49]   Chew and Joseph both adopt the word when referring to the youth (see *The Dramas of Lord Byron*, pp. 69, 70, and *Byron the Poet*, p. 80).

him.[50] The poem could have conceivably moved from such a recognition to a happy reunion, and, though it does not move off in this direction, if it does indeed refuse to entirely resign itself to the impossibility of a reunion, the poem faintly but definitely foreshadows Manfred's 'reunion' with Astarte.[51]

There, of course, reunion itself becomes a further torture, but *Manfred* is not altogether a tragedy.[52] In it, the Byronic hero is allowed his own kind of victory. If 'The Dream' does end in deliberate incompleteness, it, too, looks to the possibility of clawing something back from suffering. But it is Byron's first drama that explores the possibilities for 'victory' that are open to the Byron's tragic subject.

---

[50]   Ultimately, however, 'the *cause* of the Lady's grief and madness is left unrevealed' (Chew, *The Dramas of Lord Byron*, p. 71).

[51]   The youth of 'The Dream' is 'a forerunner of Manfred' (Joseph, *Byron the Poet*, p. 80) in a number of ways. For a comparison of the two figures, see Chew (*The Dramas of Lord Byron*, pp. 67–73). For Chew, 'so far as it goes, the parallel is exact' (p. 71), and he argues that the poems were not only 'nearly coincident in time and place of composition', but that they were also 'the products of much the same mood and environment' (p. 69).

[52]   As Martyn Corbett points out, *Manfred* is 'not in any formal sense a tragedy' (*Byron and Tragedy* [Basingstoke: Macmillan, 1988], p. 25), though Steiner has suggested that there is a 'final arrogance' and 'grim justice' in Manfred's dying speeches which give 'to the close of *Manfred* an element of real tragedy' (*The Death of Tragedy*, p. 132).

CHAPTER FIVE

'To Increase our Power Increasing Thine'

We have followed Byron's exploration of Wordsworth's preoccupation with nature to the point at which he began to pull away from Wordsworth altogether.[1] In *Manfred*, Byron's 'Lakist Interlude' finally comes to a close.[2] The Wordsworthianism of *Childe Harold* III does creep into *Manfred*, but, as Corbett has it, *Manfred* is a 'tragic reversal of Wordsworth',[3] and in it we see Byron finally and decisively 'rejecting the Wordsworthian and Shelleyian notions of *Childe Harold*, Canto III'.[4] The play dramatizes the final passing away of Byron's interest in Wordsworth's poetry as a possible model for his own.

Childe Harold's Pilgrimage did not lead Byron into the writing of *Manfred*, then, nor, I suggest, did it play an important role in its genesis.[5] *Childe Harold* III did exert some influence on *Manfred*'s composition,[6] but that influence is

---

[1]   The title of this chapter is taken from *Manfred*, Act II, scene iv, 25–26. All quotations from *Manfred* are taken from *Works* IV. Act, scene, and line references will be given after each quotation in the text.

[2]   The composition of *Manfred* followed soon after 'The Dream'. 'The Dream' 'was composed in July 1816, probably towards the end of the month' (Chew, *The Dramas of Lord Byron*, p. 69), while 'Byron began writing *Manfred* well before late September 1816'. Indeed, 'remarks' made by Byron himself suggest that he in fact 'began the play in August' (McGann, *Works* IV, p. 463).

[3]   *Byron and Tragedy*, p. 28.

[4]   Rutherford, *Byron*, p. 81.

[5]   We should note here that Gleckner makes almost the opposite claim, arguing that 'thematically *Manfred* owes much to *Childe Harold* III' (*Ruins*, p. 257–258). Distinct lines of thematic continuity do exist, but *Manfred* advances the themes it inherits from *Childe Harold* III in ways which owe little to *Childe Harold* III's handling of them. Take, for example, the theme of 'forgetfulness' that runs through both works. Manfred carries forward the quest for 'forgetfulness' inaugurated in stanza 4 of *Childe Harold* III (see, for example, *Manfred* I, i, 135–144 and II, ii, 145–147). However, while in *Childe Harold* III the interest in forgetfulness is focused mainly on 'its two components of stern self-repression and desire to return to an earlier, untroubled stage of existence', in *Manfred* that interest broadens to explore the relationship between these two 'components' of forgetfulness and 'the role of women, or, to give the subject the broad context its complex development deserves, between Titanic aspiration and idealized harmony' (Manning, *Byron and His Fictions*, p. 71).

[6]   We might suggest, with Martin, that *Manfred* 'continued the attempts to show an interest in landscape begun in *Childe Harold* III', since Byron claimed that he wrote *Manfred* 'for the sake of introducing the Alpine scenery in description' (letter to Thomas Moore of 25 March 1817, in *BLJ* V, p. 188). However, as Martin goes on to point out, 'very few descriptive passages are to be found' in the text of the play itself (*Byron: A Poet Before His Public*, p. 111).

largely overwhelmed by the sway of other texts, not least a host of Byron's earlier works.

As a result, *Manfred* turns away not only from Wordsworth, but from *Childe Harold* III's comic impulse. It returns instead to the figure of the Byronic hero and to the 'tragic vision' of Byron's early tales. In particular, Byron 'virtually took over the basic elements of *The Giaour*, to create his new "dramatic poem"',[7] but the character of Manfred 'is Childe Harold' as well as the 'the Giaour', and 'like Selim ... [and] Conrad'.[8]

This puts *Manfred* outside one of the major concerns of this study: Byron's struggle to detach his writing from his earlier 'tragic vision'. But *Manfred* is a major site of experimentation and for this reason we should look at it. *Manfred* is not simply a return to the concerns of earlier works, despite the fact that Byron himself said of the poetic drama as a whole that it 'is too much in my old style'.[9] In many ways, *Manfred* offers a strikingly new vision of the Byronic hero, in which Manfred is 'the consummation of the Byronic hero-type'.[10] And in order to achieve this consummation, Byron drew on, explored, and experimented with a vast array of new kinds of writings and traditions. He looked to these for new ways of imagining and imaging his hero, and for new kinds of fictions that could be interpolated into, and which could be used to expand, his own. In *Manfred*, we see Byron seeking out new ideas through which to filter the 'tragic vision' of his early verse narratives, and we can begin this chapter by turning to the extensive range of criticism that has addressed itself to finding out the sources of those ideas.

'Critics since Wilson and Jeffrey have related Manfred to Prometheus, to both the Fausts, to Mrs. Radcliffe's dark villains, and to Walpole's Manfred.'[11] But there have been three ground-breaking studies of the models with which Byron experiments in *Manfred*. In 1915, Chew began the long scholarly search for influences, sources, models, and precursors, starting off with the source of Manfred's name: 'probably got from the Manfred of Walpole's *Castle of Otranto*'.[12] His seminal list of other sources appears as the starting point for many later source studies.[13] 'The most direct source of *Manfred*, apart from *Faust*, is Chateaubriand's *René*', says Chew, with Amelia as the 'Ur-Astarte'. *Manfred* also shows a 'more or less definite indebtedness'

---

7   Gleckner, *Ruins*, pp. 257–258.

8   Chew, *The Dramas of Lord Byron*, p. 66.

9   Letter to John Murray of 9 March 1817, in *BLJ* V, p. 185.

10   Chew, *The Dramas of Lord Byron*, p. 67. A number of critics seem to be in general agreement with Chew here. For Corbett, 'Conrad ... is clarified in Manfred' (*Byron and Tragedy*, p. 27), while Rutherford, though claiming that 'there is little or no advance on the morality and characterization of *The Giaour*', admits that Manfred presents the 'same vision' as *The Giaour* 'more fully' (*Byron*, p. 90). For Rutherford, as for Chew, the poem is the 'culmination' of much that precedes it, and is, Rutherford argues, Byron's 'supreme attempt to claim significance for the character of the Byronic hero' (*Byron*, p. 78).

11   Bertrand Evans, 'Manfred's Remorse and Dramatic Tradition', in *PMLA* 62 (Sept. 1947), p. 752.

12   Chew, *The Dramas of Lord Byron*, p. 60.

13   See, for example: Thorslev, *The Byronic Hero*, p. 166; Evans, 'Manfred's Remorse and Dramatic Tradition', p. 752; and McGann, who states that the 'best introduction to the poem is still Chew's *Dramas* (59–84)' (*Works* IV, p. 467).

to Shelley's *St Irvyne*, and is 'direct' in its 'descent' from Walpole's *The Mysterious Mother*. Minor sources, continues Chew, include Coleridge's *Remorse*, Maturin's *Bertram*, Beckford's *Vathek*, Lewis's *Monk*, and Shelley's *Alastor* and *Queen Mab*. The last, Chew argues, is a possible source for the second act in particular, though 'Manfred's visit to the Hall of Arimanes vaguely resembles Macbeth's last interview with the Weird Sisters'. Finally, Chew adds Moliere's *Don Juan*.[14]

The second of our three source studies is Bertrand Evans's 'Manfred's Remorse and Dramatic Tradition'. Evans's contention is that 'the common denominator' in the sources of *Manfred* is 'Gothic tradition': 'the conventional materials of that tradition' and 'the stock-pile of elements built up after Walpole'. He traces Manfred's hidden guilt and the play's slow and partial revelation of that guilt ultimately to *The Mysterious Mother*. The 'technique' of confronting Manfred with objects 'from which he can recoil "in great agitation"', Evans traces back to Robert Jephson's *The Count of Narbonne*, and Manfred's suffering for his past to 'Manuel, in Bertie Greetheed's "tragedy" of *The Regent*'. His remorse, argues Evans, has its origins in Francis North's *Kentish Barons*.[15]

Evans presents a convincing and thorough account of Manfred's literary ancestry. The major study of the sources of Byron's supernatural *dramatis personae*, on the other hand, is Maurice Quinlan's 'Byron's *Manfred* and Zoroastrianism'. Quinlan turns not to the Gothic tradition, but to Byron's reading of 'eastern religions, and, more especially, his interest in Zoroastrianism'. He suggests that Arimanes is a 'borrowing from Zoroastrianism', and that the seven spirits of Act I are a 'poetic parallel' to the 'demons of Arimanes'. He attributes the spirits that surround Arimanes in Act II, at least partly, to the same tradition, and suggests that references to Manfred as a 'Magian' may echo the priestly tradition of the followers of Zoroaster. Manfred's tower, Quinlan argues, recalls the 'Towers and temples ... built by the Ghebers as receptacles of sacred fire', and adds that 'dark towers are ... a favourite haunt of the demons of Arimanes'. Finally, and perhaps most surprisingly, Quinlan suggests that Montesquieu's *Persian Letters* is 'the source for Byron's Astarte', and that letter 67, in which a character called Astarte is in love with her brother, demonstrates clear parallels with the history of Manfred and Astarte.[16]

These three studies clearly establish the fact that *Manfred* was generated from a myriad of sources, a fact that must inform any reading of the poem.[17]

---

[14]   See *The Dramas of Lord Byron*, pp. 60–66, 78.

[15]   See 'Manfred's Remorse and Dramatic Tradition', pp. 753–759, 764–765.

[16]   See 'Byron's *Manfred* and Zoroastrianism' in *Journal of English and Germanic Philology* 57 (1958), pp. 726–734. Quinlan suggests that Byron's knowledge of Zoroastrianism may have begun with Pliny's *Natural History* and Plutarch's *Morals*. According to Quinlan, however, Byron 'also reveals an acquaintance with several recent authorities, such as D'Herbelot, William Jones, and John Richardson' (p. 728).

[17]   As Gleckner points out, even if we argue that Manfred is a vision of 'the human condition', we must acknowledge that Byron articulates that vision 'through the mouth of tradition and [the] accepted forms' of 'Gothicism, Prometheanism, and Faustianism' (*Ruins*, pp. 256–257).

But it has encouraged at least one critic to conclude that from the outset the play was doomed to become little more than a spectacular miscellany of set pieces or an incoherent collection of dramatic moments that juxtaposes reworkings of elements drawn from unnecessarily disparate precursors and incompatible traditions. This critic is Philip Martin, for whom *Manfred* is 'absurdly eclectic', and no more than 'a string of empty stage mannerisms ... hopelessly divorced from the contexts that gave them meaning'.[18]

Martin's revival of the charge of incoherence sounds old-fashioned in view of recent theories of intertextuality, but it can nevertheless be answered on its own terms.[19] We have time in this chapter to do so, and good reason given our larger concern with Byron's experimentation with all kinds of writing. For Martin's indictment of the play is an interpretation of Byron's experimental practice, implying as it does that Byron created his poetic drama by borrowing at random from contexts he did not respect, and without creating a coherent new context that might gather together those borrowings and give them new meaning in their new relation to each other.

We have already noted in the case of *The Giaour* that Byron could and did collect material and ideas for a new work 'magpie fashion', valuing what came fortuitously to mind or hand. In *Manfred* he goes much further than this, but his experimentation with new kinds of writing and thinking might seem collected together in a similarly random way. If so, then this is only part of Byron's practice, and *Manfred* gives us an ideal opportunity to scrutinize some of the kinds of compositional processing that accompanied Byron's seemingly haphazard exploration of new idiomatic possibilities. As Byron borrowed for *Manfred*, he incorporated what he was borrowing into an already existing, but evolving, context. Byron's Faustian borrowings, for example, are incorporated into the play's distinctively Byronic and essentially dramatic 'study' of what Corbett calls 'the incomprehensible power that directs our fate'.[20] They are combined with Byron's Zoroastrian borrowings, challenged by a distinctively Promethean defiance, and implicated in the plight of Byron's own fictional hero. All of Byron's borrowings combine to create a battle between a supernatural machinery which bodies forth a dramatic vision of externalized 'Evil', and Manfred, part tragic hero, and partly offered as a universally representative 'Man'.[21] In the unfolding relationship between Byron's supernatural machinery and Manfred, we witness an imaginative exploration of various ideas about free will, the nature of evil in relation to

---

[18]   *Byron: A Poet Before His Public*, pp. 133, 110.
[19]   The charge that the play is 'incoherent' is a long standing one. Byron himself described the play as 'inexplicable' to John Murray (letter of 15 February 1817, in *BLJ* V, p. 170), and a number of critics have added their endorsement to this opinion. Rutherford, for example, insists on 'the hopeless confusion of the supernatural machinery' of *Manfred* (*Byron*, p. 90), and recalls T. S. Eliot's famous claim that 'It is ... impossible to make out of [Byron's] diabolism anything coherent or rational' (*On Poetry and Poets* [London: Faber and Faber, 1957], p. 195, quoted by Rutherford in *Byron*, p. 90).
[20]   Corbett, *Byron and Tragedy*, p. 22.
[21]   Byron calls Arimanes 'the Evil principle' in a letter to Murray written on 15 February 1817 (*BLJ* V, p. 170), and I shall be arguing in the following that all the spirits serve Arimanes.

man, and about the nature of man's relation to the cosmos, but we need not try
to grapple with Byron's metaphysics here, or with what he means by 'Evil'.
Rather, what will concern us is the creation of a coherent dramatic context that
holds together a multitude of imaginative modes and brings all those modes to
bear on the same thematic focus. I am suggesting that Byron did create such a
coherent dramatic framework out of the range of disparate other writings he
drew on and experimented with,[22] but precisely how did he do so?

In the first place, Byron experimented in order to open up possibilities but
ensured that his experimentation with new models of procedure never became
an unmodified imitation of those models. No part of the play is simply one
thing or another. The opening scene of *Manfred* draws quite specifically on the
Faust legend as Manfred conjures up spirits.[23] And yet, the fact that Byron did
not want to simply write a Faustian play is made quite clear when the adjured
spirits appear. There is no Mephistopheles, but seven spirits of a very different
kind, akin, as we have seen, to the attendants of Zoroastrianism's Arimanes.
Two of Byron's models are brought together almost from the outset, then, and
their meeting holds this opening part of the poem off from an absorption into
either. On the other hand, the context their meeting creates is as yet unknown,
perhaps even to Byron at this point, and this is exactly the kind of open site of
possibility that Byron liked to write himself into. What potential for new kinds
of coherence there is in this combination is to be sought after in the act of
imagining that combination.

Focusing in on the ways in which just these two traditions come together
will help us to gain a purchase on Byron's experimental composition of
Manfred. We can begin by first isolating a few of Byron's more obvious
borrowings from one of them. What does Byron make of, or do with, the
features of Zoroastrian mythology he borrows? And how does he combine
these with his Faustian borrowings to create a single context larger than either
and able to contain both?

The play's 'Zoroastrianisms' concentrate in Act II, scene iv, around the
figure of Arimanes, who we see surrounded by spirits and addressed as 'our
Master – Prince of Earth and Air' (II, iv, 1). Nemesis comes forward to speak
for the gathered minions:

> Sovereign of Sovereigns! we are thine,
> And all that liveth, more or less, is ours,
> And most things wholly so; still to increase
> Our power increasing thine, demands our care,
> And we are vigilant – Thy late commands
> Have been fulfilled to the utmost. (II, iv, 23–28)

---

[22] I am also suggesting that this is one of the ways in which *Manfred*, as O'Neill
puts it, 'displays a compulsion to call to mind other works yet insist on its own distinctness'
(O'Neill, *Romanticism and the Self-Conscious Poem*, p. 94). For O'Neill's discussion of
some of the other ways in which it does this, see pp. 94–97.

[23] Byron claimed that he had 'never read' Goethe's *Faust*, but told John Murray that
'Matthew Monk Lewis in 1816 at Coligny, translated most of it to me *viva voce* – & I was
naturally much struck with it'. Byron also conceded quite freely that 'the first Scene' of
Manfred '& that of Faustus are very similar' (letter dated 7 June 1820, in *BLJ* VII, p. 113).

This campaign to 'increase / Our power increasing thine' hangs over the whole poem, and especially haunts Manfred's relation to the supernatural. Byron borrows from Zoroastrianism a 'ready made' means of imagining 'Evil', and a supernatural machinery that can be used as a means of dramatically setting up the notion of a whole supernatural order intent on gaining possession of 'all that liveth' for the 'Evil principle'.[24] This is the basic structural frame into which Byron incorporates all his spirits, and the play's supernatural diversity is gathered into this coherent overall structure from the outset, as Byron has the spirits that appear in Act I, and long before we meet Arimanes, hint that they are part of some larger 'diabolic hierarchy'.[25] In the play's opening scene, the seventh spirit tells Manfred that it has been

> Forced by a power (which is not thine,
> And lent thee but to make thee mine)
> For this brief moment to descend. (I, i, 126–128)

We naturally suspect, once we have read Act II, that the seventh spirit, in threatening to make Manfred his own, is doing so in the service of Arimanes. We are never actually told this, but even if we take the opening scene on its own terms, rather than view it in the light thrown on it by Act II scene iv, we are tantalized by the idea that some larger power than the seventh spirit is involved in some way. Why, for example, does the seventh spirit need to be 'Forced ... to descend' if he stands to gain by that descent? And by the power of whom or what is he forced? Similarly, a mysterious 'something more' seems to be implied when another of the spirits tells Manfred that it is 'to thy bidding bow'd' (I, i, 50) and, again, that it is 'To thine adjuration bowed' (I, i, 58). This spirit is not bowed 'by' Manfred's bidding but 'to' it, and while this may be nothing more than a slightly odd or unusual grammatical usage of 'to', it nevertheless suggests various kinds of questions in the reader's mind. Most pointedly, both of the details we are isolating here open up the possibility that some other supernatural authority, greater than any we meet in the opening scene, has 'bowed' these spirits 'to' Manfred's bidding: that they have been sent rather than called.

We may well be curious to know, at the end of scene, what or who might be lending Manfred power and bowing the spirits to his adjuration. Indeed, we might be curious to know if anything is doing so, but we can do little more than notice the details we have focused on. When we come to Act II, scene iv, however, our curiosity seems at last to be answered. The spirits of Act I, it would seem, now reappear revealed as minions of Arimanes and part of the diabolic campaign we learn about in this scene. We should perhaps make this assumption cautiously and advisedly, however. Rutherford insists that

---

[24] The framework borrowed from Zoroastrianism is always kept flexible enough to accommodate figures from other traditions. Most notably, at this point, Byron 'adds' Nemesis and the Destinies.

[25] Rutherford, *Byron*, p. 91.

> Byron's supernatural characters do not all exist on the same level of reality. Some are more or less allegorical in nature, others mythological.[26]

For Rutherford, only 'some' of those characters 'purport to be members of an actual divine or diabolic hierarchy'.[27] Similarly, David Eggenschwiler criticizes those readers who, 'seeking a philosophical consistency in the play commonly assume that' the spirits in Act I 'are the same as that appear in Act II'. This assumption substitutes, he argues, 'a philosophical order for the dramatic structure of the play and ignores the impressions that the spirits of Act I give of themselves and their function'.[28] But there is also a danger of being too timorous here. Various details catch a curious eye in Act II, scene iv, and encourage us to make precisely the assumption that Eggenschwiler criticizes.

The first is the fact that we are told in the opening stage direction that Arimanes is 'surrounded by the spirits'. He is not surrounded simply by 'spirits'. Surely 'the spirits' refers to the seven of Act I? Byron might, of course, mean all spirits, or 'the spirit world', but this is made more unlikely than likely, as we shall see, by the number of spirits it is implied are present. The definite article seems rather to suggest that the spirits that now appear are known to the 'audience', and since we have met no others, we can surely assume, despite Eggenschwiler's criticism, that we are to being asked to read the spirits of Act I into this scene.[29] And other details in Act II, scene iv further encourage us to do so. When the spirits hymn in unison, for example, they do so in the same metre as the spirits of Act I, who speak together in Act I, scene i, lines 132–135. This point is worth stressing because the spirits are distinguishable from each other only by the metre in which each speaks. A particular metre, it seems, is the mark of a particular presence.

Having spoken in unison, the spirits of Act II speak individually. Some spirits are numbered: 'SECOND SPIRIT' (II, iv, 30), 'THIRD SPIRIT' (II, iv, 32), 'FOURTH SPIRIT' (II, iv, 36), 'FIFTH SPIRIT' (II, iv, 42). Is this numbering significant? It peters out here, and the next spirits to speak on their own are simply 'A SPIRIT' (II, iv, 158) and 'ANOTHER SPIRIT' (II, iv, 160), but if Byron's initial numbering is significant, then perhaps it is also significant that seven spirits seem to speak in all. If so, then it is worth noting that according to Quinlan, the Arimanes of Zoroastrianism has only 'six high-ranking attendants'.[30] It is entirely possible that Byron has his own seven spirits from Act I in mind, rather than the six of Zoroastrian tradition.

---

[26]   Ibid.

[27]   Ibid.

[28]   'The Tragic and Comic Rhythms of *Manfred*', in *Studies in Romanticism* 13 (1974), pp. 65–66.

[29]   A similar situation arises in Revelation, where we encounter 'the seven angels who stand before God' (8.2). As Charles Homer Giblin points out, 'the definite article supposes they have been mentioned before', and so, as Giblin goes on to argue, we presume that 'the seven spirits before his throne' of 4.2 're-appear in 8.2 in a new guise for a further, new function' (*The Book of Revelation: The Open Book of Prophecy* [Collegeville, Minnesota: Liturgical Press, 1991], p. 41, n.).

[30]   'Byron's *Manfred* and Zoroastrianism', p. 729.

One final correspondence deserves attention. The fifth spirit of Act I, the 'Rider of the wind' (I, i, 100), says:

> To speed to thee, o'er shore and sea
>   I swept upon the blast:
> The fleet I met sailed well, and yet
>   'Twill sink ere night be past. (I, i, 104–107)

As the Destinies gather in Act II, scene iii, we hear a voice, not designated as one of those Destinies, but simply as a 'Second Voice, Without' (II, iii, 26), say:

> The ship sail'd on, the ship sail'd fast,
> But I left not a sail, and I left not a mast. (II, iii, 26–27)

Martin recalls E. H. Coleridge's suggestion that the spirit here refers to Thomas Lord Cochrane and belongs to a tradition in which supernatural agents are put to satirical use.[31] Thus, Martin can dismiss the song of each gathering spirit as simply part of a 'peculiar interlude of mild political satire'.[32] Perhaps there is a degree of satirical intention here, but it is difficult to resist the idea that this 'ship' is of the same 'fleet' referred to earlier, and that the 'Rider of the wind' is reporting the fulfilment of his promise in Act I: 'The fleet ... will sink ere night be past'. Even if the ship is not of this fleet, it would be perfectly reasonable to attribute two disasters at sea to the same malevolent spirit. Again according to Quinlan, in the Zoroastrian tradition each of Arimanes's attendant spirits is 'charged with some vicious task and consequently come to symbolize a specific evil'.[33] There is no reason why this should not be true of Byron's spirits too.

The evidence is accumulatively persuasive and we can, I suggest, assume with some confidence that one set of 'spirits' makes various appearances in *Manfred*. Thus we can also assume that our suspicions of a greater power behind their appearance in Act I are likely to be well founded. The initiating action of the play, rather than set in motion an 'empty string of stage mannerisms', appears to mark the point at which the whole supernatural and evil order of Act II, much of which is imported from Zoroastrianism and all of which is intent on taking possession of 'All that liveth' for its master, 'the Evil principal', turns its attention on Manfred.

How, then, does the campaign described by Nemesis proceed? We have discussed Byron's basic Zoroastrian substructure for his spirits, and the threat posed by the various forces of 'Evil' that this substructure organizes. Yet Zoroastrianism did not supply Byron with an idiom for his supernatural machinery or its campaign of universal dominion. Rather, the Faustian tradition is brought into play here and used to extend Byron's Zoroastrian

---

[31]   See *Byron: A Poet Before his Public*, p. 128.

[32]   Ibid. Here Martin follows Jeffrey's review of the poem in the *Edinburgh Review* 28 (September 1817), in which Jeffrey described the same songs as 'satirical and political' (quoted in *Byron: The Critical Heritage*, p. 117).

[33]   'Byron's *Manfred* and Zoroastrianism', p. 729.

supernatural order into a direct and personal relation to humanity. Let us look at the Witch of the Alps, whose tactics are more overt than those of the other spirits. Her strategy, I suggest, offers a glimpse of the supernatural campaign as a whole.[34]

Manfred adjures the Witch of the Alps at a cataract in 'A lower valley of the Alps' (II, ii, opening stage direction). His motive is to 'look upon thy beauty – nothing further' (II, ii, 38), but the witch has her own agenda. She has 'expected' him (II, ii, 37), and seems intent upon making him retell 'the core' of his 'heart's grief' (II, ii, 99).[35] Twice, as he holds back, she encourages him: 'Proceed' (II, ii, 97); 'Spare not thyself – proceed' (II, ii, 104). By doing so, she finally drives him back to the memory of his failure and despair:

> ... Forgetfulness
> I sought in all, save where 'tis to be found,
> And that I have to learn – my sciences,
> My long pursued and super-human art,
> Is mortal here – I dwell in my despair –
> And live – and live for ever. (II, ii, 145–150)

Only now does the witch suggest that 'It may be / That I can aid thee' (II, ii, 151–152). And there is a price for this aid:

> ... if thou
> Wilt swear obedience to my will, and do
> My bidding, it may help thee to thy wishes. (II, ii, 155–157)

The witch drives Manfred back to his failure, frustration, and despair precisely in order to sharpen and reintensify his desire for escape. The more desperate he is for a way out, the more likely he is to be susceptible to offers of aid. And the more likely he is to pay the price for that aid. The witch's offer is not an act of altruism, after all, but aimed at exacting what looks suspiciously like a Faustian self-sacrifice.

We can usefully draw a parallel here between what happens in Act II, scene ii and what happens in Act I, scene i, and by doing so point out how consistent the various spirits are in their relation to Manfred. The seven spirits tell

---

[34] It is not obvious that the Witch of the Alps serves Arimanes, but there is good reason to suspect she does. Manfred himself lumps the witch with the other spirits, seeing obedience to her as obedience to 'the spirits' in general (see II, ii, 158–160), and if we are assuming that the spirits who appear in Act I are the same spirits who serve Arimanes in Act II, we can offer evidence to support him. For Arimanes is 'Prince of Earth and Air' (II, iv, 1), and 'his the spirit of whatever is' (II, iv, 16). Evil indeed, it seems, holds sway over the whole natural universe, especially tempests (II, iv, 5), 'thunder' (II, iv, 6), 'earthquakes' (II, iv, 8), and 'volcanoes' (II, iv, 9), but also 'Earth, ocean, air, night ... winds' (I, i, 132), and, finally, 'mountains' (I, i, 132).

[35] In a way, the witch is quite like a Greek chorus here. Compare, for example, her prompting of Manfred with the Chorus's prompting of Prometheus in *Prometheus Bound* (see *Prometheus Bound*, in *Greek Tragedies*, vol. 1, ed. by David Greene and Richmond Lattimore (Chicago and London: University of Chicago Press, 1968), lines 196–198, 631–633).

Manfred that they cannot give him the oblivion he asks of them, but follow this up by offering him various consolations: 'subjects, sovereignty, ... power' (I, i, 140), and 'Kingdom, and sway, and strength, and length of days' (I, i, 168). This, like the witch's 'deal', smacks of a Faustian pact.

Similarly, the spirits seem to employ the witch's strategy of driving Manfred back to, and holding him in, his despair in an attempt to induce him to accept the deals they offer. This adds a particularly Byronic twist to the Faustian tradition from which Byron is borrowing. Take, for example, the vision thrust upon Manfred by the seventh spirit in the opening scene. The spirits Manfred has adjured to ask of them 'forgetfulness', 'cannot ... or will not' bestow it upon him (I, i, 164), claiming that it is 'not in our essence' (I, i, 147). At precisely this point of frustration and disappointment, he is 'given painful memory':[36]

> SEVENTH SPIRIT. [appearing in the shape of a beautiful
>   female figure]. Behold!
> MAN.   Oh God ! if it be thus, and *thou*
>   Art not a madness and a mockery,
>   I yet might be most happy. – I will clasp thee,
>   And we again will be –   [The figure vanishes
>   My heart is crush'd!
>   [MANFRED falls senseless. (I, i, 188–191)

While we can only really infer the meaning of this, Corbett seems right to have 'no doubt that what Manfred sees here is an apparition of Astarte'.[37] But she is restored only to be taken away: her apparition is a means of inflicting a particularly vindictive reminder of his loss. And that reminder is thrust upon Manfred by the seventh spirit, who is silent throughout Manfred's conversation with the spirits, but who now bursts forward as the 'most powerful of ye' (I, i, 186), evidently intent on crushing Manfred: 'Behold!'.

This episode is not an isolated act of malice. It is part of a larger strategy. For it is precisely this recollection which drives Manfred to look for forgetfulness in death, and to attempt to jump from the Jungfrau. He is prevented, it seems, by an absolutely terrestrial event – the arrival of the Chamois Hunter. Yet Manfred himself offers a more interesting possibility when he later reviews the situation:

> ... the cold hand
> Of an all-pitiless demon held me back,
> Back by a single hair, which would not break. (II, ii, 137–139)

This, to my mind, is a potentially pivotal revelation. It helps to explain the fact that the events of Act I, scene ii and Act II, scene i almost precisely repeat the pattern of the first scene. In each case, Manfred arrives at a possible site of oblivion only to find that oblivion denied. And in each instance, the aftermath

---

[36] Corbett, *Byron and Tragedy*, p. 25. As Manning has it, 'the spirits offer ... total recall' (*Byron and his Fictions*, p. 78).

[37] Corbett, *Byron and Tragedy*, p. 25.

of this discovery is not simply that Manfred is thrown back upon himself, but that he is suddenly overwhelmed by painful memory. If indeed Manfred is held from death by some unseen supernatural agent, then is recollection thrust upon him for a second time by this 'all-pitiless demon', as it is thrust on him first by the seventh spirit in Act I, scene i? It is certainly possible. Painful memory drives Manfred to the extremity of seeking oblivion in death, but here it drives him one step further, to Arimanes's hall. If we attribute Manfred's failure to find oblivion and death to a supernatural cause, as Manfred himself does, then he begins to look deliberately tortured. But if also we attribute each instance of painful recollection to the spirits, then Manfred also looks decidedly herded: pushed step by step towards Arimanes.[38]

Each movement of the argument is plausible and the coherence we are discovering exerts its own authority. Each 'dramatic moment' can be seen as an integral part of something larger than itself, and a patterning can be seen tying them altogether. Manfred is driven to suicide by the spirits' refusal to help him ('Ye cannot, or ye will not, aid me' [I, i, 164]), denied death by 'an all-pitiless demon', but repeatedly 'given painful memory'. The witch's strategy seems writ large by the spirits generally, as Manfred is repeatedly pricked into doing something, and repeatedly offered the option of a Faustian pact. Zoroastrian borrowings, Faustian motifs, and distinctive Byronic additions to this mixture fuse to create a vast supernatural campaign devoted to torturing Manfred into sacrificing himself to 'the Evil principle' in return for some kind of supernatural favour. And *Manfred* is a play about the threat posed by Arimanes 'as much as it is about Manfred and his remorse'.[39] It hurls that threat at its hero and is interested in dramatically rendering notions of how 'Evil' might gain dominion over humanity.

Yet it is equally interested in how 'Evil' might be fought off. Manfred is determined to do battle and fight the spirits. They pile frustration upon frustration on him, and drive him towards and beyond hopelessness. They hold him in his despair as he struggles to escape it. In the hunter's cabin, however, Manfred manages to extricate himself from the desperation that threatens to overwhelm him. He distracts himself from his own despair by focusing instead on his ability to bear that despair, and here we hear a distinct echo of Byron's early tales. But that echo is filtered through a second fiction. This second fiction is introduced in the opening scene of the play, when Manfred claims the status of Prometheus (I, i, 154–157), and his power to bear torture becomes increasingly Promethean in its defiance of whatever 'his superhuman torturers' might throw at him.[40] In the hunter's cabin, Manfred's image of himself as a kind of superhuman Prometheus is his salvation.[41] It

---

[38]   Corbett, who divides the play into 'three movements', collects the 'three encounters' I am discussing here together as the play's first 'movement'. He notes the fact that each encounter 'follows a similar pattern', but suggests that only two of these encounters are in any way with 'supernatural beings', and that these two encounters simply 'flank a meeting with a fellow human, the Chamois Hunter' (*Byron and Tragedy*, p. 20).

[39]   Ibid., p. 22.

[40]   Ibid., p. 39.

[41]   Byron wrote to John Murray that 'The Prometheus – if not exactly in my plan – has always been so much in my head – that I can easily conceive its influence over all or

distracts him from suffering itself by obscuring it with his own ability to bear suffering, and as a result Manfred finds a kind of temporary relief from the tortures of memory. He clearly wants to hold on to this, but Manfred's Promethean self-elevation is not sustained. When he pauses at the cataract of Act II, scene ii, and calls the witch only to 'gaze on thee a moment' (II, ii, 32), this pause is mutated by the witch into yet another fraught stage in Manfred's projected demise. The witch, as we have seen, deliberately draws Manfred out of his detachment, encouraging him to retell, and so once again to 'approach', his grief and despair. Reminded yet again of what it is he wishes to forget, he is finally driven to resort to the 'one resource / Still in my science – I can call the dead' (II, ii, 177–178).

The battle rages on, then, and we approach what should have been the culmination of the supernatural campaign we have been following. For in order to call the dead, Manfred needs supernatural aid in two ways. Firstly, he cannot call the dead himself, but must ask Nemesis to do it (II, iv, 79). Secondly, it seems he needs Arimanes to give Nemesis his express permission:

> NEM.   Great Arimanes, doth thy will avouch
>   The wishes of this mortal?
> ARI.   Yea. (II, iv, 80–81)

We can certainly 'read the whole of the quest for Astarte as a strategy of ... [Manfred's] superhuman torturers',[42] but the aim of those torturers, as I have suggested, is not simply to torture Manfred. They have a more specific aim in mind: to force or entice Manfred into accepting supernatural aid, thereby forcing him to damn himself to their dominion by buying that aid with his submission. Up to this point we have seen him refuse all aid offered, but we have also seen him driven to a final extremity that requires supernatural aid.

Yet Manfred seems to have jumped the gun and caught the spirits off their guard. The spirits are surprised to see him: 'What is here?' cries one on seeing him, 'A mortal!' (II, iv, 28–29). And when it comes to the crunch, Arimanes aids Manfred without demanding any kind of compact. Why does he give Manfred the very favour for which the spirits seem to have been forcing him to ask in order to demand of him his submission in return? Does the structure of *Manfred* break down here?

I suggest, rather, that Byron is quite consciously subverting the Faustian tradition and that Arimanes gives Manfred his aid for a reason. What is impressed upon us perhaps more than anything else is Manfred's 'power'. It is referred to four times in Manfred's initial dialogue with the spirits: by the second spirit on his entrance (II, iv, 31), twice by the First Destiny (II, iv, 55, 72), and finally by Manfred himself (II, iv, 74). I suggest that Arimanes 'avouch[es] / The wishes of this mortal' (II, iv, 80–81), without laying claim to anything in return, out of respect for this power.

---

anything that I have written' (letter dated 12 October 1817, in *BLJ* V, p. 267). While the model of Prometheus may not be new to *Manfred*, Byron certainly does new things with it here, as we shall see.

    [42]   Corbett, *Byron and Tragedy*, p. 39.

We can build a more precise picture of what is going on in this scene by noting that Manfred appears before Arimanes in the guise of 'Prometheus in his earlier and more active form, the type of Faustus, the poet-magician, who by his science' dares to aspire beyond the mortal.[43] 'Evil', in other words, is confronted with Prometheus, and for Byron, as the final act demonstrates, 'Evil' meets its match in this confrontation.

There we see Byron's vision of evil challenged and out-faced by defiant Promethean self-assertion. Manfred's tutelary spirit appears 'like Mephistopheles, to claim Manfred as his own',[44] in an attempt to 'dupe' (III, iv, 138) Manfred into thinking that he has 'forfeited' (III, iv, 97) himself simply by accepting Arimanes's aid. The spirit is met with a tremendous outburst of defiance:

> MAN.   I do defy ye, – though I feel my soul
> Is ebbing from me, yet I do defy ye;
> Nor will I hence, while I have earthly breath
> To breathe my scorn upon ye – earthly strength
> To wrestle, though with spirits; what ye take
> Shall be ta'en limb by limb. (III, iv, 99–104)

This defiance lays bear the spirit's Faustian claim on Manfred as 'forfeited', and in the end sends the spirit away empty-handed. As Manfred goes on to insist, he has entered no compact to gain the 'grace' which Arimanes has been 'accorded' (II, iv, 167) him.[45] Yet Manfred's defiance is not simply an act of righteous denial. It is also a Prometheanesque assertion of equality and absolute autonomy:

> MAN.   ... my past power,
> Was purchased by no compact with thy crew,
> But by superior science – penance – daring –
> And length of watching – strength of mind – and skill. (III, iv, 113–116)

A Promethean note is powerfully struck by Manfred's utter refusal to yield to the spirit,[46] but it is his 'daring' and his 'strength of mind' that are most relevant to us at this point. It is the 'mind' and its 'spirit' of daring aspiration

---

[43]   Stuart Sperry, 'Byron and the Meaning of *Manfred*', in *Criticism* 16:3 (Summer 1974), p. 193.

[44]   Ibid., p. 197.

[45]   There is no equivalent in *Manfred* to Faust's acceptance of the terms of Mephistopheles' 'bond' in Goethe's *Faust* (*Faust: A Tragedy*, trans. by Walter Arndt; ed. by Cyrus Hamlin [New York and London: Norton, 1976], Part 1, 1656–1659, 1710), nor any point equivalent to that at which Ambrosio has 'signed the fatal contract' and the Daemon cries 'I have triumphed! You are mine past all reprieve' in Matthew Lewis's Faustian novel, *The Monk* (Matthew Lewis, *The Monk*, ed. by Howard Anderson [Oxford and New York: Oxford University Press, 1980], pp. 437, 438). Manfred does have a sense of owing Arimanes' something for the conjuration of Astarte, though: 'for the grace accorded / I now depart a debtor' he says as he leaves the Hall of Spirits (II, iv, 167–168).

[46]   See *Prometheus Bound*, 180 and 322, in which the Chorus and Oceanos pinpoint Prometheus's 'unyeilding' determination.

that Manfred singles out as 'the Promethean spark' in the opening scene (I, i, 154), where he claims it is 'as bright / Pervading, and far darting' as the spirits themselves (I, i, 155–156). Returning, then, to Act II, I am suggesting that Arimanes sees, in Manfred's 'power', this same 'Promethean spark' and is forced to recognize the 'truth' of Manfred's claim to equality, 'though coop'd in clay' (I, i, 157). 'Evil' does have one last go at tricking Manfred into giving himself up in Act III, but for Byron, Manfred (and by extension mankind) has a power of mind and spirit over which evil can have no dominion. In Act II he has 'the Evil principle' recognize and acknowledge this.

We can, of course, only really infer that this is what is happening because Arimanes's motives remain hidden. But *Manfred* does not descend into incoherence because we cannot, finally, pin Arimanes down. All of the elements we are looking at are still interrelated in a coherent and meaningful way. Manfred still achieves his Promethean subversion of the Faustian conventions employed to trap him by the Zoroastrian 'Evil principle' and his minions: Manfred dares to ask for aid while refusing to bow himself before the spirits and his daring pays off, whatever Arimanes's reasons are for allowing it to do so.[47] Byron repeatedly evokes Faustian conventions to encourage us to assume, or better yet to fear, that to win the supernatural aid he seeks, Manfred must place himself irrevocably under the dominion of 'Evil'. And we are, I suspect, meant to assume with Corbett that when they appear in Act III, the spirits 'have come to collect the debt – the price of the conjuration of Astarte'.[48] But the closing scene brings together the play's Faustian, Zoroastrian, and Promethean elements precisely to expose these assumptions and attack the self-damning habits of mental submission before supposed absolutes which they manifest. Manfred has dared to challenge such absolutes and found that they do not exist: he 'strikes no bargains' yet still has won supernatural aid – even from 'Evil' itself.[49]

Here we begin to bring into focus one of the central thematic concerns of the battle between Manfred and the minions of 'the Evil principle'. For Byron, Prometheus's 'crime' was to 'strengthen Man with his own mind' ('Prometheus', 35–38), and the Promethean myth teaches 'Man ... A mighty lesson':

> Thou art a symbol and a sign
> To Mortals of their fate and force;
> Like thee, Man is in part divine,
> A troubled stream from a pure source;
> And Man in portions can foresee
> His own funereal destiny;
> His wretchedness, and his resistance,
> And his sad unallied existence:
> To which his Spirit may oppose
> Itself – an equal to all woes,
> And as firm will, and a deep sense,

---

[47]   It should be noted that the crime for which Prometheus is originally punished is his having 'dared' (*Prometheus Bound*, 236).

[48]   *Byron and Tragedy*, p. 46.

[49]   O'Neill, *Romanticism and the Self-Conscious Poem*, p. 95.

> Which even in torture can descry
> Its own concentred recompense,
> Triumphant where it dares defy,
> And making Death a Victory. ('Prometheus', 45–59)[50]

Manfred thrusts this 'lesson' in the face of the 'Evil' which besieges and then claims him. His insistence on it underpins, and makes possible, both his daring to confront Arimanes and his frustration of the spirits' Faustian attempts to dupe him into submission. To put this another way, Byron's Faustian and Zoroastrian borrowings are used to help create a dramatic context in which Promethean ideals can assert their power. The play, in other words, brings together what it borrows in order to dramatize, and explore further, the 'mighty lesson' offered by the Promethean myth.

Once again, then, we see Byron working along the 'same grooves of thought' he has worked along in previous poetry: *Manfred* recasts ideas first articulated in 'Prometheus' in a highly eclectic dramatic form. Furthermore, those ideas themselves are a means of reimagining and rethinking other concerns brought forward from previous works. The most important of these is the Byronic hero. In *Manfred*, Byron returns to the Byronic hero and his own previous depictions of him, but he also looks to a host of other writings for new ways of situating, imaging, and imagining the plight of his hero. And Byron's borrowings from these writings certainly offer new perspectives from which to view the suffering and heroism of the Giaour or Conrad, and expand Byron's 'tragic vision' well beyond the perimeters of his early tales.

Equally, however, we have been concerned with the idea that the end result of Byron's exploration of new ways of imaging the plight of his hero is an incoherent literary text. I have been arguing that, on the contrary, Byron's borrowings contribute to the battle between Manfred and 'Evil' that is played out by the play, and that they are given new meaning by their coherent inter-relation. I have focused exclusively in the foregoing on Byron's Zoroastrian, Faustian, and Promethean borrowings, but have, I hope, substantiated my contention against the charge of incoherence.

I suggest we end this reading of *Manfred* here. We have followed Byron some considerable way from the struggle to detach his writing from the 'tragic vision' of tales like *The Giaour* and *The Corsair* – a struggle which runs through the works that precede *Manfred*, and which resumes immediately after it. In the next chapter we will turn to its progress in canto IV of *Childe Harold*.

---

50   Quotations from Byron's 'Prometheus' are taken from *Works* IV.

CHAPTER SIX

A 'More Beloved Existence'

As we saw in the previous chapter, by the time Byron was writing *Manfred*, the idealism of *Childe Harold* III had entirely faded, to be replaced with a kind of Promeatheanesque humanism.[1] *Manfred* projects and insists upon the power of the will, the autonomous self, and individual endurance. But there is something lost in this exchange, as the intuitive sense that the self exists in a vital and revivifying connection with something larger than self is pushed to one side. In canto IV of *Childe Harold*, Byron returns to this intuition, having re-examined and rethought it, and intent on continuing to do so. For while *Childe Harold* IV is, on the face of it, quite different from *Childe Harold* III, both cantos put their trust in the idea that something outside the self can renew the self, indeed is perpetually 'watering the heart' and 'replenishing the void' (*CHP* IV, 44–45). Both cantos attempt to identify the source of this replenishment and attempt to lyrically dramatize its ministration. We will be looking at *Childe Harold* IV as, in some ways, a continuation of *Childe Harold* III and, in other ways, a revision of it.

Before we do so, however, we should note that in the light shed on Byron's thinking by *Childe Harold* IV, we can look back to *Childe Harold* III and suspect that Byron was then actually distracted from the endeavour described above by the very importation of Wordsworthian ideas which characterizes the earlier canto. These did not finally fit Byron's own intuition. In *Childe Harold* IV, Byron often looks back, nostalgically, to the idea that man lives in a vital, spiritual, and revivifying connection with nature,[2] but brings in no 'ready made' set of ideas. Rather he trusts, let us say, more to his own instinct, and feels his own way forward towards an articulation of that instinct. Nevertheless, the idea that Wordsworth in some sense distracted Byron might help us to explain why, after *Childe Harold* III, Byron progressively lost touch with the intuition, or complex of intuitions, that I am trying to isolate. That he did so is made clear by the fact that, in *The Prisoner of Chillon*, 'The Dream', and *Manfred*, the Byronic hero slowly but powerfully retakes the centre stage of Byron's poetry. The Byronic hero belongs to a world of emotional devastation and void replenished only by the poisonous vitality of remorse, and this mythology exercized a powerful pull on Byron's imagination, a pull that in 1816 returned briefly to overwhelm all else. Perhaps it was able to do so, for a while, because Wordsworthian ideas obscured, and pulled Byron away from, his own sense of a power of renewal.

These ideas can only have the status of speculations, but they offer a context for the fact that in *Childe Harold* IV, Byron once more focuses in on

---

[1]   The title of this chapter is taken from *CHP* IV, 40.
[2]   As Martin points out, if a little scathingly, 'towards the end of the canto' Byron 'goes through the Wordsworthian motions once again' (*The Poet Before His Public*, p. 97).

his instinctive sense of external sources of actual replenishment, and with renewed vigour. In order to do so, Byron clearly recognized that he not only had to steer clear of Wordsworth, but once again had to try and exile, temporarily at least, the Byronic hero from *Childe Harold*. He was not entirely successful, even in the short term, but he was at least spasmodically and temporarily successful. And when, in *Childe Harold* IV, Byron wins himself a space free of his hero-figure and his 'tragic' fate, he manages to secure a much firmer hold than ever before on the intuited 'truth' which in *Childe Harold* III and IV he is trying to make manifest. The comic *Beppo*, as we shall see, is partly a consequence of this fact, since it is a celebration of, and a delighting in, a seemingly inexhaustible source of vitality and plenitude. In this sense, *Childe Harold* IV opens up a new way forward in Byron's verse: a way forward into comedy.

How Byron pulls away from the 'tragic' Byronic hero in *Childe Harold* IV will certainly concern us in this chapter. His doing so plays a pivotal role in his movement into comedy. Indeed, many things became possible after *Childe Harold* IV that were not possible before, and became so partly as a result of the increasing distance Byron managed to put between himself and his hero. But this chapter will also focus, particularly towards the end, on the fact that *Childe Harold* IV 'helps to bridge the amazing gulf between *Manfred* and *Beppo*',[3] and will attempt to describe how it does so.

Let us begin, then, by looking at just how Byron struggles to clear a space for himself that is free of the Byronic hero and at what Byron does in the space he clears. In the first instance, of course, Byron drops the Byronic hero by dropping Harold. The Preface prepares us for his disappearance –'there will be found less of the pilgrim than in any of the preceding' (*CHP* IV, Preface, 49–50) – and while Harold does make a token appearance at the end of the canto, he is entirely absent until stanza 164, when he 'cometh late' (*CHP* IV, 1470).

However, this is only part of the story. We can certainly argue that Byron is, as Joseph puts it, 'laying aside the mask of Harold',[4] but what is thereby revealed often looks disconcertingly like another Byronic hero. Towards the beginning of the canto, for example, Byron presents himself, as often before, as a 'ruin' (*CHP* IV, 219) who suffers emotional 'Torture' (*CHP* IV, 171):

> The thorns which I have reaped are of the tree
> I planted, – they have torn me, – and I bleed:
> I should have known what fruit would spring from such a seed. (*CHP* IV, 87–90)

This certainly sounds like a Byronic hero, and if Byron is speaking here, then he seems to have slipped, momentarily at least, into the voice of a Manfred or a Giaour. It would be too much to say that Byron simply drops his interest in the Byronic hero when he drops Harold, then, but it would not be too much to claim that Byron also articulates a very different kind of consciousness in *Childe Harold* IV. The canto opens with a voice very different from Manfred's or Azo's. In the canto's opening stanza, for example, the canto's speaker is 'gladdened' by Venice, where

---

3   Rutherford, *Byron*, p. 102.
4   *Byron the Poet*, p. 75.

> A thousand years their cloudy wings expand
> Around me, and a dying Glory smiles
> O'er the far times. (*CHP* IV, 5–7)

Similarly, he 'reaps' 'joy' – and is heard doing so in the hyperbole of 'all', 'of the earth', and 'of Italy' – from Venice as

> The pleasant place of all festivity,
> The revel of the earth, the masque of Italy! (*CHP* IV, 26–27)

This is not the Byronic hero speaking, and the voice we hear opening the canto is the voice that closes it. At the end of the canto, Byron tells us that he

> ... can yet feel gladden'd by the sun,
> And reap from earth, sea, joy almost as dear
> As if there were no man to trouble what is clear. (*CHP* IV, 1581–1584)

Childe Harold IV returns to, recovers, holds on to ('can yet feel gladden'd by') a mood of joyful celebration despite objects, like the Palatine, that draw Byron into melancholy despondency. This marks *Childe Harold* IV as very different from almost all of Byron's previous work, and marks its voice as certainly not that of a Byronic hero. In *Childe Harold* IV Byron is still drawn to the Byronic hero and his fate, and though he does lay aside the mask of Harold, he often picks it up again and begins to dramatize that fate. But he is also and increasingly interested in this other, very different, kind of consciousness. Indeed, he seems to pick up the old Byronic 'mask' almost inadvertently, out of habit, so to speak.[5] And it is a habit he is determined to break. As in *Childe Harold* III, it seems that Byron does not want to write himself into the role or fate of the Byronic hero, but rather, once again, wants to discover a way of writing a new kind of poem entirely, and of creating a new persona and voice for himself. His success in *Childe Harold* III was finally overwhelmed by the retrogression of *Manfred*, and the voice of the suffering Byronic hero returned to oust the voice of the jubilant 'nature poet'. In *Childe Harold* IV, Byron returns again to the task of reinventing himself as a poet, and of discovering for himself a new kind of lyric voice and form.

Byron's determination to push past the tempting idea of returning to the familiar Byron voice of suffering and endurance is clearly demonstrated by the way in which that voice repeatedly rises up in *Childe Harold* IV only to be pushed to one side. The idea of suffering that is 'like a scorpion sting' (*CHP* IV, 200) surfaces in stanza 23, for instance. It appears as the climax of a series of associations that begins with the idea that 'Existence may be borne' (*CHP* IV, 181), but quickly moves off towards the idea of 'some' (*CHP* IV, 194), who

> ... bow'd and bent,
> Wax grey and ghastly, withering ere their time,

---

[5]   This is especially true when Byron 'breaks out ... in wild indignation and self-pity', or in 'ranting pessimism' (Rutherford, *Byron*, pp. 94, 96).

> And perish with the reed on which they leant;
> Some seek devotion, toil, war, good or crime,
> According as their souls were form'd to sink or climb. (*CHP* IV, 194–198)

The first type recalls Azo, Conrad, and the Giaour, while the second recalls more precisely Manfred's quest for 'forgetfulness' in 'Philosophy and science' (*Manfred* I, i, 13), doing 'good' (*Manfred* I, i, 17), and war: 'I have had my foes' (*Manfred* I, i, 19). All of these 'avail'd not' (*Manfred* I, i, 19, 21). Byron may well have Manfred in mind here,[6] but he goes on to say:

> But ever and anon of griefs subdued
> There comes a token like the Scorpion's sting. (*CHP* IV, 199–200)

If Byron has Manfred in mind, then he is also recalling *The Giaour*.[7] In fact, we might suggest that Byron is here drawn to the phenomenon that dominates a host of works, from *The Giaour* to 'The Dream'. He has slipped back into a vocabulary that is recognizably that of *The Giaour* and *Manfred*, and has become distracted back to the subject matter of these earlier works: 'things which bring / Back on the heart the weight which it would fling / Aside for ever' (*CHP* IV, 202–204); the 'chain wherewith we are darkly bound' (*CHP* IV, 207); 'the blight and blackening' (*CHP* IV, 211). Yet, in stanza 25:

> But my soul wanders; I demand it back
> To meditate amongst decay, and stand
> A ruins amidst ruins; there to track
> Fall'n states and buried greatness, o'er a land
> Which *was* the mightiest in its old command,
> And which *is* the loveliest ... . (*CHP* IV, 217–222)

Byron seems to have a positive sense of some new poetic venture here that is distinct from that into which he has wandered. He holds in check his tendency to slip back to the concerns that have hitherto occupied him by recalling his attention when it slips, and the Byronic hero is kept at bay by many such small acts of poetic self-discipline. Another instance can be found in stanza 35, where Byron's attention has wandered back to Manfred and the idea of 'demons' who 'seek their prey / In melancholy bosoms' (*CHP* IV, 298–300), but is refocused on 'Ferrara' (*CHP* IV, 307).

By dropping Harold in the first instance, then, but also by once again wilfully resisting the pull of the Byronic hero on his imagination, Byron struggles to detach himself from much that has hitherto governed his writing. He is reasonably successful, and wins himself enough room to set in motion a

---

6   *Manfred* may well have been 'still fresh' in Byron's mind, since 'he had just rewritten the third act in late April and early March of 1817' (Gleckner, *Ruins*, pp. 286–287) when he began *Childe Harold* IV on '19 June 1817' (McGann, *Works* II, p. 317). Thus, it 'is perhaps not surprising', argues Gleckner, to also 'find Byron universalizing the death of poets and the circumstances of his own life to date in terms reminiscent of the "triumph" of Manfred' in stanza 32 (Gleckner, *Ruins*, p. 287).

7   See *The Giaour*, 422–432: 'The Mind, that broods over guilty woes, / Is like the Scorpion girt with fire ... Whose venom ... darts into her desperate brain'.

new kind of poetic enterprise: 'To meditate amongst decay, to stand / A ruin amidst ruin, there to track / Fall'n states and buried greatness'. This enterprise is, unavoidably it seems, infected by what went before it, but the sense of being a 'ruin' as the Giaour, Lara, and Manfred are 'ruins', is put to one side, over and over again, in favour of tracing, firstly, other 'Fall'n states', but ultimately 'buried greatness'.

But why do we find, in this meditative venture, not only a marked departure from both Byron's earlier narrative mode and the dramatic mode of *Manfred*, but a considerable departure from cantos I–III of *Childe Harold* as well? Cantos I–III range across Spain, Greece, Albania, Turkey, France, Germany, and Switzerland. Each arrival is inevitably followed by a departure and this unrootedness helps to produce an attitude that becomes the central concern of *Childe Harold* I–III: even in canto III, it is the attitude itself, or the 'mindset' of the 'gloomy exile', that Byron's quest for a communion with nature seeks to overcome.

No ranging across Europe is suggested by the verb 'stand', and *Childe Harold* IV is not a poem about unrootedness, or even about the search for some kind of rootedness. It does not traverse the continent but stays in Italy, and the speaker is no 'gloomy wanderer' and certainly no 'exile'. Why this radical departure? We can only really speculate, but from the very beginning of the canto, Byron presents himself as being quite at home in Italy, in Venice, and, especially, in Rome: 'Oh Rome!' he cries in stanza 78, 'my country!' (*CHP* IV, 694). We might, then, hazard that in *Childe Harold* IV, we hear a real and new sense of belonging on Byron's part, which began to draw him away from his long-standing and self-dramatizing interest in the idea of exile. At the very least, we have to acknowledge that in this canto, Byron is more powerfully interested in the idea of a sense of belonging to something and to somewhere than in any of his previous works, and much less interested in the idea of always being excluded and always having to move on.

When Byron manages to clear himself a free space, what does he do in it? This will take time to answer. We can make a start, though, by saying that Byron fills the spaces he makes for himself with a 'collection of lyrics' which explore 'the implications of images supplied by the European journey' which the canto, at least in part, describes.[8] This, of course, is true of *Childe Harold's Pilgrimage* generally, but in cantos I and II Harold's narrative gives 'some connexion to the piece' (*CHP* I and II, Preface, 11–12), while in canto III Byron's quest gathers his numerous lyrics into stages of that quest.

With Harold largely absent, and without the kind of project that would give it an apparent internal structure, *Childe Harold* IV is 'the most loosely organized ... section' of *Childe Harold's Pilgrimage*, and more obviously a collection of lyrics than previous cantos.[9] Each of Byron's meditative lyrics

---

8   Nellist, 'Lyric Presence', p. 46.
9   Rutherford, *Byron*, p. 97. We should, of course, note that Byron's trip 'from Venice to Rome provides the basic [though very loose] structure of the work' (Rutherford, *Byron*, p. 93), but in previous cantos, other structures were built into this basic journey structure that effectively took those cantos over. Such structures are lacking in canto IV. For further discussions of the structure of *Childe Harold* IV see Gleckner (*Ruins*, pp. 277–294)

focuses on a single object or location. And yet we find, according to critics like Joseph and Gleckner, a predominance of one kind of lyrical response or tone, and for them this tone defines the canto as a whole: it is a lament 'for lost empire ... for the decay of love, ... the triumph of time over human mortality, ... as Joseph claims'.[10] *Childe Harold* IV does lament these things, but I resist the idea that *Childe Harold* IV is a vast lament. Byron's journey from Venice to Rome inspired many other kinds of lyric too, and the poem celebrates and delights in as much as it laments.

That *Childe Harold* IV is not simply a lament we have already seen from brief quotations taken from the beginning and end of the canto. But much critical emphasis has been put on the canto's tendency to lament, not least by Gleckner and Joseph. Less attention has been given to the canto's impulse to celebrate.[11] Accordingly, let us begin here, and establish precisely what it is that Byron wants to commemorate and, in most cases, revere. As Byron laments a great number of things, so he celebrates a great number of things, but we can gather together what he laments under umbrella phrases like 'the fate of man' or 'the human condition'. We can do the same for the things Byron celebrates, or better, we can trace a 'theme' running through the many instances we find of celebration in the canto. Later we can situate the canto's jubilance in the terms of poem as a whole, but for now let us isolate the central theme of that jubilance.

It is introduced after 'the initial vision of the "dying Glory" of Venice', and is, to borrow Gleckner's phrase, 'the theme of creation':[12]

> The beings of the mind are not of clay;
> Essentially immortal, they create
> And multiply in us a brighter ray
> And more beloved existence: that which Fate
> Prohibits to dull life, in this our state
> Of mortal bondage, by these spirits supplied
> First exiles, then replaces what we hate;

---

and Joseph, who gives a purely descriptive account of the poem's 'surface structure' in Appendix B of *Byron the Poet* (pp. 144–145).

[10] *Ruins*, p. 271, quoting Joseph, *Byron the Poet*, p. 27. 'The entire canto is', Gleckner argues, 'built around ... central images, or rather scenes and lines that Byron builds into images'. In these 'striking image clusters, or to use Ezra Pound's term, "radiant nodes"... Byron finds "the moral of all human tales", the same "rehearsal of the past", first life and freedom, then vice and corruption, at last barbarism and desolation', and, for Gleckner, Byron builds the whole poem around this 'moral' (*Ruins*, pp. 288–289). For a slightly different perspective see Rutherford, who suggests that in *Childe Harold* IV 'we have a new mood and new theme – the elegiac' and that 'Canto IV is best regarded as a long meditation on Time's works, defeats, and victories' (*Byron*, p. 97).

[11] A number of critics do emphasize some positive elements in the canto, however. Most notable among these are McGann (in *Fiery Dust*), Newey (in 'Authoring the Self') and Kipperman, who reads the canto as 'life-affirming': 'The pilgrimage that began in malaise and despair over the irreconcilable demands created by human freedom ends in an affirmation of possibilities' (*Beyond Enchantment*, pp. 193, 195). I will be keeping these critics in view.

[12] *Ruins*, p. 272.

Watering the heart whose early flowers have died,
And with a fresher growth replenishing the void. (*CHP* IV, 37–45)

For Gleckner, this stanza 'contains the seeds of the transition from hope ... to a renewed realization of the futility of even that hope',[13] but at this point at least, Byron's tone is celebratory. What he is celebrating is creativity, and in particular literary creativity, as manifested by the literary characters mentioned in the previous stanza: 'Shylock and the Moor / And Pierre' (*CHP* IV, 33–34). And what he claimed to find in a communion with nature – revitalization, renewal, spiritual 'growth' – he now recognizes is actually supplied by the imagination. More precisely, it is found in the imagination's creation of fictions, since it is these fictions, 'the beings of the mind', who supply 'that which Fate / Prohibits to dull life'. In our relation to our fictions, we might say, we are renewed and replenished and find some kind of vitality otherwise lacking. Perhaps the Wordsworthian idea of 'benevolent Nature' is one such fiction, but, if so, then it is a fiction which creates 'in us ... a ... more beloved existence'. The speaker's attitude to such fictions, at least to the literary fictions he mentions, is one of gratitude and celebration, and Byron is isolating and celebrating the mind's capacity to create, and its ability to supply us with vitality by doing so.

Or at least in stanza 5 he is, but can we say that a celebration of creativity runs through the whole canto and balances Byron's lament over the fate of man? The very next stanza suggests not, because in it the whole business of artistic creation comes under attack. To note this is to keep in view an important feature of the canto, namely, that it is always unstable, and flows through distractions, assertions, doubts, and fears, without ever finding a site of stability which it can occupy unassailed. Especially important here, however, given our present focus on the canto's celebratory elements, is the fact that in stanza 6 a celebratory attitude towards creativity seems to fall prey to a sudden outburst of hostility and contempt, and so seems to be no more than a local feature of the poem. In stanza 6, we can provisionally suggest, we see Gleckner's 'renewed realization of ... futility'. The attitude that wells up is offered as the voice of 'Reason' (*CHP* IV, 61):

Such is the refuge of our youth and age,
The first from Hope, the last from Vacancy;
And this worn feeling peoples many a page,
And, may be, that which grows beneath mine eye:
Yet there are things whose strong reality
Outshines our fairy-land; in shapes and hues
More beautiful than our fantastic sky,
And the strange constellations which the Muse
O'er her wild Universe is skilful to diffuse. (*CHP* IV, 46–54)

The third line of this stanza reminds us of the fact that writing and literary creation are the immediate objects of stanza 5's paean, and it is such imaginative writing that is now mocked by words like 'refuge', 'Vacancy' and

---

13   Ibid.

'worn'. The poem, it seems, turns from what it now calls fantasy, and with some contempt, to 'things' of 'strong reality': 'for waking Reason deems / Such over-weening phantasies unsound, / And other voices speak, and other sights surround' (*CHP* IV, 61–63). However, I suspect that there is a considerable degree of irony in all this that Gleckner does not pick up on. Before we assume too readily that Byron's celebratory attitude towards creativity is actually scorned here, we might just have a look at Byron's later lyric sequence on the Venus de Medici, a piece of art and so another example of the creativity Byron seems to be scorning in stanza 6:

> There ... the Goddess loves in stone, and fills
> The air around with beauty; we inhale
> The ambrosial aspect, which, beheld, instils
> Part of its immortality; the veil
> Of heaven is half undrawn; within the pale
> We stand, and in that form and face behold
> What Mind can make, when Nature's self would fail;
> And to the fond idolaters of old
> Envy the innate flash which such a soul could mould. (*CHP* IV, 433–441)

The statue is a 'thing' whose 'strong reality', indeed, its 'immortality', is seen and felt in the 'blood – pulse – and breast' (*CHP* IV, 450).[14] It 'bodies forth' 'love', but also 'Mind' – and in 'Mind', an 'innate flash'. The very word 'flash' recalls both the 'brighter ray' of fiction and fantasy, and the even brighter ray of 'strong reality' which 'Outshines our fairy-land'. In fact it combines the two. In the Venus, Byron finds the 'strong reality' Reason seeks, but he finds it in an example of the imaginative creativity dismissed by 'Reason' as 'phantasy'. For the Venus is 'another "Being of the Mind"' like Shylock, the Moor, and Pierre:[15] it began as a thought, a flash innate to Mind. When we come to Venus de Medici, the voice of 'Reason' we hear in stanza 6 is silenced.

The Venus should convince us that a consistent theme does run through Byron's sporadic jubilation.[16] And his lyrical reaction to the Venus is worth looking at in some detail, since in it, Byron further articulates what it is he wants to celebrate about creativity in general. To begin with, the statue's 'eyelids, brow, and mouth' (*CHP* IV, 459) carry the trace of their conception, and are

---

[14]   The statue is presented, in Cooke's words, as one of those 'things which penetrate the mind from without, filling it with *their* existence instead of its own notions' (*The Blind Man*, p. 122).

[15]   Joseph, *Byron the Poet*, p. 87.

[16]   The Venus de Medici 'reveals an interesting shift in Byron's attitude to sculpture, at least within the framework of the poem. For he was normally inclined to be disparaging towards it; in describing this Florentine visit to Murray, he referred to sculpture as one of the "two most artificial of the arts" (the other being painting); and later, in *Don Juan*, he was to ridicule the sculptors with their "stone ideal" as "a race of mere impostors"' (Joseph, *Byron the Poet*, p. 87, quoting Byron's letter to Murray of 26 April 1817 (*BLJ* V, p. 218), and *Don Juan* II, 944, 942 (*Works* V).

> Glowing, and circumfused in speechless love,
> Their full divinity inadequate
> That feeling to express, or to improve,
> The gods become as mortals, and man's fate
> Has moments like their brightest. (*CHP* IV, 460–464)

The word 'inadequate' is odd. Byron seems to be celebrating the fact that the statue reaches after an expression of 'love', but falls short of it. Put the other way around, however, the statue brings to mind the love it cannot express: it communicates a sense of being inadequate. Similarly, though the statue has its own 'full divinity', in it 'the gods become as mortals'. The Venus reduces the gods to something mortal, we might want to say, but is not Byron rather saying that it manages to bring to mind a sense of a 'divinity' that is beyond its reach? Surely this is what he means when he says that in looking at the statue, 'man's fate / Has moments like' the 'brightest' of 'the gods'. If so, then despite the fact that Love and 'the gods' are both beyond the statue's reach, Byron is claiming that they are nevertheless communicated by it. The statue points to, and draws our attention to, something else and greater than itself.

How does it do so? To answer this, it seems, we have to look once again at the originary 'flash' of inspiration in the sculptor's mind. This is what we are being invited to focus on as we behold the statue. And for Byron, that 'flash' reveals something divine: it has 'half-withdrawn' the 'veil / Of Heaven'. As we are invited to behold the creative capacity of the human 'Mind' in the statue, so we are invited to behold something more than the human mind in that capacity; to see 'heaven', 'divinity', 'immortality' in the 'innate flash' with which the statue's conception began: 'The beings of the mind are not of clay', but 'Essentially immortal'. Thus, it is 'the loveliest dream / That ever left the sky on the deep soul to beam' (*CHP* IV, 476–477) that Byron celebrates when he celebrates the Venus.

Similarly, in the 'delicate form' (*CHP* IV, 1450) of the Apollo Belvedere, Byron sees

> All that ideal beauty ever bless'd
> The mind with in its most unearthly mood,
> When each conception was a heavenly guest –
> A ray of immortality. (*CHP* IV, 1454–1457)

This should put it beyond doubt that again and again in *Childe Harold* IV, Byron turns to delight in and celebrate art and the creative processes that, for him, art 'bodies forth'. For Byron, the Apollo, like the Venus, expresses the 'mind' at the moment of its conception. Like the Venus and Egeria, the Apollo is 'a beautiful thought' (*CHP* IV, 1035), or series of beautiful thoughts, 'softly bodied forth' (*CHP* IV, 1035). We are invited to imagine the 'mood' in which the statue was conceived, and to see each thought that conveys it to the mind of the sculptor as 'a heavenly guest'.[17] This visitation is 'expressed' in the statue,

---

[17] 'The poem reaches here a point of repose, a sacramental repose before an unearthly perfection witnessing to the numinous and man's sharing in it' (Newey, 'Authoring the Self', p. 175).

which ultimately, 'if made / By human hands, is not of human thought' (*CHP* IV, 1464).

Ideas about artistic and imaginative creation which were only implied as Byron looked at the Venus, are much more fully articulated here. More generally still, we later learn that 'Thought', for Byron in *Childe Harold* IV, is 'the faculty divine' (*CHP* IV, 1139), into which 'the beam' of something more than the human 'pours' (*CHP* IV, 1143). This is 'evidenced' by the examples of creative 'thought' supplied by Byron's journey. Creative thought is a benediction from somewhere beyond the human – it is 'not of human thought' – but through it mortality has some access to immortality, or rather is touched by and guided by, something immortal. In *Childe Harold* IV, what Byron wants to celebrate more than anything else is the 'fact' that there is some kind of 'faculty divine' that receives that guidance or inspiration. It is this inspiration which creates for us, and in us, the 'beings' which supply us with vitality, and so it is through our 'faculty divine', that is, our capacity for 'conceiving and bodying forth the Ideal', that the heart is watered, the void endlessly replenished.[18] By our fictions are we revitalized, and our fictions come to us 'each' as 'a heavenly guest'. By its connection, via the 'faculty divine', to something immortal but beyond even the nature of *Childe Harold* III, mortality is sustained and energized.

Let us put the canto's celebratory impulse back into context, then, since what we have said so far does not amount to a reading of the canto, though it will go some way to help us with the question of how *Childe Harold* IV moves Byron towards the writing of *Beppo*. But we cannot argue that the whole of *Childe Harold* IV is celebratory. We should recall the critics we mentioned earlier, for whom the 'central theme' of the canto is its lament, and must concede that while the poem is not wholly 'built around' images that articulate this theme, it is at least in part. To put this another way, *Childe Harold* IV occupies, at various times, the two extreme moods of despair and delight, and demonstrates that both are equally inhabitable. Indeed, to inhabit one is to detach oneself entirely from the other. Any mood is transitory. On the one hand, we can 'gaze' at and delight in 'beauty', but must 'turn away' eventually, if only because 'the heart / Reels with its fulness' (*CHP* IV, 442–444). On the other hand, though Byron is forced to 'turn away' from 'beauty' and delight, he is always won back by these things eventually. The Arno, to give just one of many examples, 'wins' his attention from its engrossing lamentations and to 'the fair white walls' of Florence (*CHP* IV, 425).

Consciousness is never still in *Childe Harold* IV, but constantly moving from desolation to beauty, being drawn from despondency to enthusiasm, and slipping from delight to dismay. One lyric sequence in particular helpfully suggests an image that accurately describes this never ending movement of consciousness: the sequence that describes the Terni waterfall. The movement of this sequence is circular, and moves 'round' from the 'torture' below the speaker, up to the 'unemptied' cloud above him, then back down, with the 'unceasing showers', to 'an eternal April' from which the eye is drawn by the 'fall of waters' back to the 'gulf' below (*CHP* IV, 617–627). The whole canto,

---

18   Ibid., p. 167.

we might say, also traces a circle.[19] It begins with Byron's delight at Venice, follows as he is drawn, ultimately, to the Palatine and a 'shrine' to human grief (*CHP* IV, 953), then moves with him as he returns to 'joy' (*CHP* IV, 1583) at the end of the canto, when he is 'gladdened' (*CHP* IV, 1582) by the sun.

Within this large circular progress, numerous other circles are traced, or, more accurately, the same circle is repeatedly traced. Stanza 42, for example, begins a lament for 'Italia! Oh Italia!' (*CHP* IV, 370) that runs to stanza 47. Arno then distracts Byron from that lament, and leads him to Florence and the Venus de Medici. By stanza 57 he is berating 'Ungrateful Florence' (*CHP* IV, 505) and lamenting her neglect of the ashes of the 'all Etruscan three' (*CHP* IV, 496). But by stanza 66, he is once more delighting, this time in 'Clitumnus ... sweetest wave / Of the most living crystal' (*CHP* IV, 586–587).

This circular movement of consciousness, from delight, 'round' to lament, and then back 'round' from lament to delight, does not end with the poem. '*Childe Harold* ... ends, and issues, in resolute irresolution',[20] so that Byron's 'reward' is not to have successfully found a final 'coherent vision of fragments' to 'sustain' him 'in his dying'.[21] Rather, it is to be found in the continued existence of 'moments' in which 'man's fate' is like the gods' 'brightest' moments, and in which Byron discovers that he 'can still feel gladden'd'. He can occupy such moments only briefly, since they will always come to an end: 'the weight / Of earth recoils upon us' (*CHP* IV, 464–465). But such moments are, nevertheless, repeatedly encountered and, though briefly, enjoyed. Byron's final moment of 'joy' in *Childe Harold* IV is found in solitude, and could only be sustained by continued solitude: 'Oh! that the Desert were my dwelling place ... That I might forget the human race' (*CHP* IV, 1585–1587). But sustained solitude brings with it the threat of loneliness, so that Byron must imagine living in his 'desart' retreat with 'one fair Spirit for my minister' (*CHP* IV, 1585). In any case, his solitude is not to be continued, since there are, after all, men 'to trouble what is clear' (*CHP* IV, 1584), but while this hits a gloomy note, it does not hit a finally gloomy note. We should recall, for instance, that while society might 'trouble' solitude, it also brings with it the prospect of 'festivity' and 'revel' (*CHP* IV, 26–27).

Childe Harold IV lyrically dramatizes moments of both near despair and moments of intense joy, and presents us with a speaker who is desolated, at times, by his fate, and at other times 'dazzled and drunk' with 'what Mind can make'.[22] But, while that speaker is 'dramatically presented to the reader in a

---

[19] McGann has suggested that the canto is actually about 'constant development and painful growth' (*Fiery Dust*, p. 49), and this is clearly true. But as Newey points out, it also dramatizes 'arrestment and fragmentation, the mind collapsed back upon itself or pointlessly meandering' ('Authoring the Self', p. 169). McGann's ideas about development, movement forward and spiritual 'increase can be applied to ... [the] poem, and the mental life it expresses, only if we recognize that process as simultaneously involving repetition and circling, bewilderment and loss, the dilemmas of consciousness and the dissolution of gains' (Newey, 'Authoring the Self', p. 179).

[20] Newey, 'Authoring the Self', p. 182.

[21] Gleckner, *Ruins*, p. 271.

[22] 'He alternates between periods of hopefulness and expectancy ... and spells of terrible despair' (McGann, *Fiery Dust*, p. 48).

succession of virtually present moments',[23] all those moments exist in a continuity, a kind of lyric flow, which 'bodies forth' a complex and ever changing consciousness. And it is difficult, on the face of it, to say that the poem is 'built around' any one 'central theme', or even around one dominant kind of response or tone precisely because it is 'built around' the writing subject in all his variability.[24] The canto is a lyric dramatization of selfhood, in which we see Byron responding emotionally to the scenes and sights he passes through, 'making and recognizing images' of what he sees and experiences, 'and moving about' those images 'in manners appropriate to their characters and with various degrees of aptitude'.[25]

A number of critics would disagree with the idea that *Childe Harold* IV is self-dramatization, but it is vital that we see the canto as precisely this, if we are to see how *Beppo* is, at least in one vital respect, a natural development of *Childe Harold* IV. We should meet opposition head-on, then, and especially that which comes from the idea that in *Childe Harold* IV, Byron 'returns ... more firmly than ever to the mode of eighteenth-century topographical poetry'.[26]

While we could argue with Tilottama Rajan that Romantic literature is 'a literature involved in the restless process of self-examination',[27] and with Paul Michael Privateer that 'in romanticism, poetic writing *is* the poet who speaks',[28] it would be more difficult to argue that the same is true of the eighteenth-century tradition of topographical poetry. And *Childe Harold's Pilgrimage* clearly does belong to that tradition, and not least canto IV.[29] Furthermore, while he was writing canto IV, Byron was telling Murray about his discontent with 'Romanticism' and his admiration of Pope.[30]

---

[23]   Ibid., p. 40.

[24]   Correspondingly, 'There is ... no one style in canto IV' and the 'tone isn't governed ... by a singleness of feeling in the author' or his poetic self (Rutherford, *Byron*, p. 101).

[25]   Michael Oakeshott, 'The Voice of Poetry in the Conversation of Mankind' in *Rationalism in Politics and other Essays* (London: Methuen, 1962), p. 204. Oakeshott calls this 'imagining' and argues that the self 'appears as' precisely this kind of 'activity': 'It is not a "thing" or a "substance" capable of being active; it is activity ... [and] I shall call this activity "imaging"' (p. 204).

[26]   Joseph, *Byron the Poet*, p. 75. Joseph adds, however, that in *Childe Harold* IV Byron surpasses 'most' of that tradition 'in the solid authenticity of his material, and in the range and flexibility of his technique' (*Byron the Poet*, p. 75).

[27]   *Dark Interpreter: The Discourse of Romanticism* (Ithaca: Cornell University Press, 1980), p. 25.

[28]   *Romantic Voices: Identity and Ideology in British Poetry, 1789–1850* (Athens and London: University of Georgia Press, 1991), p. 1.

[29]   The reader of *Childe Harold* 'will be impressed by the number of old familiar motifs in Byron's poem: invocation, address, order in variety, praise of the women of the district, genre scenes, water-mirror, storm and calm, and graveyard and ruin sentiment thoroughly digested by the poet, "a ruin amidst ruins"' (Robert Aubin, *Topographical Poetry in XVIIIth Century England* (New York: Modern Languages Association of America, 1936), p. 256.

[30]   'With regard to poetry in general I am convinced the more I think of it – that ... *all* of us – Scott – Southey – Wordsworth – Moore – Campbell – I – are all in the wrong –

But none of this should distract us from the obvious fact that in *Childe Harold*, eighteenth-century topographical traditions undergo a 'highly Romantic transformation'. As McGann puts it, in *Childe Harold*, Byron is 'personalizing the topographical poem',[31] and we can say that Byron is transforming the tradition by moving the self in towards its centre. And the composition of *Childe Harold* IV offers one particularly valuable opportunity to give a detailed local analysis of how this transformation came about. At an early stage in the canto's composition, the canto's sequence of 'Natural Scenes' was organized around a crescendo building up to a climax in the sublime.[32] As Byron edited the sequence, however, he turned it into something much more 'Romantic', especially if by that we mean something that is ultimately concerned with the self.

The sequence begins in stanza 61, in which Byron turns from 'Art in galleries' to 'Nature ... in the fields' (*CHP* IV, 546–547). What follows is a series of snapshots of natural sights: 'Thrasimene' (sts 62–65); 'Clitumnus' (sts 66–68); 'Velino' (sts 69–72); and 'The infant Alps', especially 'Soracte's ridge' (sts 73–77). The sequence begins, then, with a lake: 'a sheet of silver' on a 'plain' (*CHP* IV, 578). 'A little rill of scanty stream' (*CHP* IV, 582) is followed up with 'the most living crystal' (*CHP* IV, 586–587) of Clitumnus, running alongside a 'mild declivity of hill' (*CHP* IV, 597). In terms of sublime effect, the 'plain' is surpassed by the 'hill', which in turn is surpassed by the 'infant Alps' (*CHP* IV, 650), and here we begin to see the crescendo that runs through the whole sequence. That crescendo seems to be heading towards a climactic view of 'the Alps' themselves, but the sequence originally found its climax in the falls at Terni, as we shall see. Firstly, however, the river, which has surpassed in 'dignity' (*CHP* IV, 664) the lake, is now surpassed, oddly, by Soracte's ridge, which is like 'a long-swept wave about to break, / And on the curl hangs pausing' (*CHP* IV, 668–669). In the original version, 'about to' looks forward to Terni, where the waters 'fall' (*CHP* IV, 615), since Byron originally put the Velino section at the end of the sequence as its climax. Similarly, the crescendo which runs through 'plains', 'hills', and 'infant Alps' climaxed, in the original version, in the 'headlong height' (*CHP* IV, 613) of the precipice from which the waters of the Velino fall.

This sequence, then, and especially in its original conception, looks much more like a piece of eighteenth-century landscape poetry than an early

---

one as much as another .... I am the more confirmed in this – by having lately gone over some of our Classics, particularly *Pope* ... and I was really astonished ... and mortified – at the ineffable distance in point of sense – harmony – effect – and even *Imagination*, Passion – & *Invention* – between the little Queen Anne's Man, and us of the lower Empire – depend upon it [it] is all Horace then, and Claudian now, among us – and if I had to begin again – I would model myself accordingly' (letter of 15 September 1817 to John Murray, in *BLJ* V, p. 265).

[31] McGann, *Works* II, p. 271.

[32] Joseph, *Byron the Poet*, p. 144. Joseph divides the canto into 'two almost equal halves', and subdivides the first half into 'two unequal sections: the first of these describes cities and towns (Venice, Arqua, Ferrara, Florence); the second, natural landscapes (Trasimene, Clitumnus, the cascades of the Velino, Mount Soracte)' (*Byron the Poet*, pp. 83–84). It is this second 'section' I am isolating here.

nineteenth-century 'Romantic' poem of 'self-examination' or self-projection. Indeed, the climax of the sequence we have described draws strongly on Thomson's *Seasons*. Byron follows the general movement of Thomson's waterfall in 'Summer', and appropriates a number of details.[33] For Thomson, the waterfall is a 'tortur'd Wave' ('Summer', 599), while for Byron the waters suffer an 'endless torture' (*CHP* IV, 618). The eye in *Childe Harold* IV, like the eye in Thomson's poem, follows the mist thrown up by the waterfall, and notes the resulting 'unceasing shower' (*CHP* IV, 623) as Thomson notes 'a ceaseless Shower' ('Summer', 598). In neither poem does the attention 'find Repose' ('Summer', 599) on the ground watered by this shower. Rather, in both cases the eye is drawn back to 'the gulf' (*CHP* IV, 627): 'Nor can the tortur'd Wave find Repose / But raging, still amid the shaggy Rocks' ('Summer', 599–600). Then, while Thomson's poem follows the water 'falling fast from gradual Slope to Slope' ('Summer', 603), Byron's follows it as it 'leaps' (*CHP* IV, 628) from 'rock to rock' (*CHP* IV, 628). Finally, Byron follows Thomson by following the water to 'the vale' (*CHP* IV, 636): in 'Summer', the water 'steals, at last / Along the Mazes of the quiet Vale' ('Summer', 605–606). Of course, Byron adds a great deal to Thomson's much shorter description of a waterfall, most noticeably, the 'Iris' (*CHP* IV, 642) sitting 'Like Hope upon a death-bed' (*CHP* IV, 643).[34] Yet the similarities are striking, and suggest that Byron was consciously using Thomson as a model for this part of *Childe Harold* IV.

The sequence as a whole, then, and its climax in particular, belong very much to the eighteenth-century 'loco-descriptive tradition',[35] though we should note that it always contained a few 'Romantic' motifs. It always focused in on the writing subject and his faltering inspiration in the section on Soracte's ridge, for example, though even here there is something of an eighteenth-century manner to Byron's apology to Horace. But any Romantic touches were originally subordinated to the larger crescendo described above, and appeared, at most, to be incidental. Then Byron decided to insert the Velino section where it now stands, and so to end the whole 'Nature sequence' of the canto with the address to Soracte. This single change 'modified' the 'loco-descriptive' cast of the sequence more than any other,[36] since it broke down the previous ordering of landscapes as a crescendo of sublimity. And, instead of ending with a sublime climax, the poem's 'Nature sequence' now ends with a personal anticlimax. Soracte's ridge, Byron implies, should inspire

---

[33] All quotations from 'Summer' are taken from James Thomson, *The Seasons*, ed. by James Sambrook (Oxford: Clarendon Press, 1981). Line references will be given after each quotation in the text.

[34] It seems that Byron adds to Thomson by drawing on Shakespeare: Jonathan Bate suggests that the simile 'Hope upon a death-bed', 'may derive from Pericles' awakening, where Marina looks "like Patience gazing on king's grave and smiling / Extremity out of act" (v. i. 138)'. Furthermore, the 'broader comparison which Byron goes on to make conjures up Shakespeare's other great scene of awakening: "Resembling, 'mid the torture of the scene, / Love watching Madness with unalterable mien"' (*Shakespeare and the English Romantic Imagination*, p. 232).

[35] McGann, *Works* II, p. 317.

[36] Ibid.

homage, and certainly calls for it. Horace's 'classic raptures' should be 'quoted', and the hills woken with echoes of 'the lyric Roman'(*CHP* IV, 666):

> ... not in vain
> May he, who will, his recollections rake
> And quote in classic raptures, and awake
> The hills with Latian echoes. (*CHP* IV, 669–672)

The poet cannot answer his own sense of what is needed here. He 'abhorr'd / Too much, to conquer for the poet's sake, / The drill'd dull lesson' (*CHP* IV, 672–674), and so cannot quote Horace's 'classic raptures', or 'awake / The hills with Latian echoes'. Therefore, Soracte and Horace go unsung: 'fare thee well – upon Soracte's ridge we part' (*CHP* IV, 693) Byron says to Horace's memory, and there is a real sense of being at fault in this parting, of regret, and of having failed.

By deciding to fix as the (anti)climax of the canto's 'Nature section' the image of the floundering poet rather than the sublime image of Terni, Byron supplies the poem at this point with a kind of continuity it did not have before. When stanzas 61–77 ended with the Terni passage, they came to an obvious end, and when the poem turned to Rome it did so abruptly. Nothing connected the two sequences and this made the poem, at this point at least, look very like a collection of essentially separate lyrics. In the final version, however, the poem's turn to Rome can be explained in almost narrative terms. Nature suddenly ceases to inspire the poet, who turns to Rome for an alternative source of poetic inspiration. As a result of Byron's changes to this one sequence, the figure of the poet, and even the precariousness of writing itself, gives 'some connexion to the piece' in the absence of Harold. Correspondingly, poetic self and poetic inspiration take up a new centrality and significance: they structure the poem overtly and, at this point at least, they explicitly dictate the direction taken by the poem, rather than, say, a 'central theme', a fictional narrative, Byron's journey, or the poet's external subject matter.

At some point in the poem's composition, this 'Romantic' foregrounding of self seems to have become deliberate policy. In the canto's dedication, Byron says that *Childe Harold* IV is

> a composition which in some degree connects me to the spot where it was produced, and the objects it would fain describe. (*CHP* IV, Dedication, 40–42)

The canto is self-representing and self-asserting, written, as we have seen, to 'stand / A ruin amidst ruins'. In it, Byron interpolates himself into the scenes he describes, and this is true from the very beginning of the canto: it opens with the word 'I'. The continued first-person address ensures that the figure of the poet commands as much attention as Venice as he becomes almost visually central to the scene:

> A thousand years their cloudy wings expand
> Around me, and a dying Glory smiles
> O'er the far times. (*CHP* IV, 5–7)

Everything centres 'around me', and the viewing consciousness does not simply view, but commands our attention in his viewing, so that while we are invited to view Venice, we are equally invited to view the speaker in Venice.[37] If at some point Byron resolved to write a poem in a more eighteenth-century mode, then the resolution was short-lived despite Byron's many local eighteenth-century practices. Rather, the canto is a dramatization of self which foregrounds a profound sense of man's lamentable fate and an intense sense of gratitude for the 'divine benediction' of thought, as well as the self's movement between these.

This seems a reasonable description of the canto, but it is one that still does not go far enough. We can and should take this argument a step further. We especially need to reconsider our earlier statement that the canto as a whole cannot be described as celebratory. This is still true, but our way of saying it obscures the fact that, in a sense, the opposite is also true. By the end, though it has not sustained its celebration throughout, it has recovered its celebratory attitude and in this sense has remained, overall, a celebratory poem. Indeed, the whole canto seems to have been conceived as a celebration, and fights to sustain its faith in what it celebrates.[38] It dramatizes Byron as he moves through the scenes and experiences of his journey, in order to dramatize the benediction and reception of 'thought' in a wider sense than its local celebrations of the Venus and Apollo allow. To put it another way, the poem is not simply offered as a lyric account of a journey, but also as a vast lyric extension of its local claims for creative thought, extending those claims to 'thought' generally. It is motivated by the powerful conviction that its insights into the fate of man, and even its sophisticated lamentations over that fate, contain, or record, instances of precisely what Byron wants to celebrate in the Venus, the Apollo, and Egeria, namely, flashes of inspiration and thoughts that seem to come as heavenly guests.

We have not yet looked at the poem from this angle because we have implicitly read the poet-figure as a tourist.[39] We should now stress that Byron does not only represent himself as this. He also represents himself as an artist and a thinker. As a thinker, he is creating 'images' of what he saw on his

---

[37]   The 'speaker is as much an object of attention as the scene which he surveys – he is an important figure in the foreground of his own composition, which would hardly be complete without him there as an observer and participant' (Rutherford, *Byron*, p. 98).

[38]   'Byron does seem always to have begun writing a poem with a fairly precise idea of what he wanted to say. But the completion of the work in its first form also seems to have had the effect of clarifying the substantive issues and artistic problems for him, enabling him finally to formulate an aesthetic unit whose total form and meaning he did not fully comprehend at first (though in every instance the eventual product can be seen to be implied in certain undeveloped images and ideas that existed in the original form of the poem)' (McGann, *Fiery Dust*, p. 122).

[39]   The canto, of course, encourages us to do this: as Rutherford points out, Byron 'comes nearer' in *Childe Harold* IV 'than he had ever done before to the methods of a guide book, trying to include everything of interest to the tourist' (*Byron*, p. 98).

journey from Venice to Rome, and as a poet, he is creating a poem out of those images and out of his own making of them. When he says that 'we can recal such visions, and create' (*CHP* IV, 466), he is describing what he is doing as he writes.[40]

Byron the poet, then, is dramatizing Byron the thinker, and he is doing so in a mode we should recognize from earlier cantos. In *Childe Harold* IV, as in much of the rest of *Childe Harold*, we see Byron 'letting things happen' and the canto is a witness to 'what happens on the page when ... [Byron] picks up the pen'.[41] *Childe Harold* IV, in other words, is a record of whatever thoughts occurred to Byron as he ranged through the memories of objects and locations supplied by the journey from Venice to Rome, and in this sense it is a dramatization of Byron thinking: indeed, of thought itself. But in *Childe Harold* IV, thought is seen as both the activity of a self, of an 'I' contemplating, and a manifestation of something other than self. At its best, this something else is 'divinity': creative thought, especially, is seen as a divine benediction. This divinity is not limited to any one kind of thought, as we shall see, but to read *Childe Harold* IV is, in the first instance, to witness the creation of a poem. And for Byron, the creative process is, in many essential respects, passive: ''Tis to create, and in creating live / A being more intense, that we endow / With form our fancy, gaining as we give / The life we image' (*CHP* III, 46-49). To create is to 'gain' what is created, which comes to, not from, the creating subject. Byron only touches on this idea in *Childe Harold* III, but in *Childe Harold* IV he develops and refines it. He focuses our attention on the fact that by 'letting things happen' he is dramatizing, in its own now, his own reception of 'what happens' as he meditates on art, history, time, and humanity. To put this another way, he focuses our attention on the fact that his poem gives artistic, literary, and linguistic form to all kinds of thoughts as they 'pour ... in' (*CHP* IV, 1143) from somewhere unknowably outside the self:

> ... let us ponder boldly – 'tis a base
> Abandonment of reason to resign
> Our right of thought – our last and only place
> Of refuge; this, at least, shall still be mine;
> Though from our birth the faculty divine
> Is chain'd and tortured – cabin'd, cribb'd, confined,
> And bred in darkness, lest the truth should shine
> Too brightly on the unprepared mind,
> The beam pours in, for time and skill will couch the blind. (*CHP* IV, 1135–1143)

In *Childe Harold* IV, we see Byron 'ponder'. He knows well that his meditations, like any other meditations, often lead to 'error and illusion' and 'mis-takings',[42] and that thinking is always beset by 'Demons / who impair the strength of better thoughts' (*CHP* IV, 298–299). The 'beam' of 'truth' is, as

---

40 The poem was written in Venice on Byron's return from the trip to Rome. For the most part, therefore, it recalls what it describes.

41 Nellist, 'Lyric Presence', p. 42.

42 Newey, 'Authoring the Self', p. 169.

often as not, lost in 'darkness', and Byron is 'beset with the constant danger of despair from his own vigorous scepticism'.[43] Yet he insists that despite all this, the 'beam' of 'truth' nevertheless 'pours in', and *Childe Harold* IV is written to catch and record that 'beam'. It is written to become a lyrical monument to the benediction of 'truth', and to stand as a poetic companion to the visual testimony of the Venus and the Apollo to the 'divine' benediction of 'beauty'. Where the Venus half-withdraws the 'veil of Heaven', and the Apollo records the visitation of 'thoughts that were each a heavenly guest', *Childe Harold* IV at its best, or when it achieves 'that mood' it so wants to achieve and which it fights to sustain, shows, Byron would persuade us, 'mortality touched by the divine'.[44]

This seems a natural point at which to turn to the question of how *Childe Harold* IV moves Byron towards the writing of *Beppo*, but I want to stay with *Childe Harold* IV a little longer. For it would still be a misrepresentation of the canto to simply emphasize its insistence that 'thought itself, the capacity for creation and self-creation, for reflection and acts of decision, of knowing and understanding' is 'in part something given, a beam pouring in'.[45] *Childe Harold* IV is also a kind of 'call to arms': 'Let us ponder to boldly'. It seeks to engender and encourage thought on the part of its reader. It is 'an affirmation of possibility',[46] and sees thought as an activity which can be entered into, 'learned and worked at with skill' to become 'a possible basis for action, and for growth'.[47] Indeed, the canto champions the activity of thought as a real and practical redemption of man's lamentable fate. Before looking forward to *Beppo*, then, I want to pause and explore this practical redemption argued by *Childe Harold* IV.

For Byron in *Childe Harold* IV, the activity of thought offers the subject a means of transcending, or, at the very least, taking 'refuge' from, his fate. As McGann tells us,

> From his earliest to his latest work, ... [Byron] cherished the idea (or the hope) that he could stand above or beyond the contradictions of his age: not merely as a 'grand Napoleon of the realms of rhyme' (*Don Juan* XI, St. 55) but a superb *Citoyen du Monde* who could survey, as from 'a tower upon a

---

43   McGann, *Fiery Dust*, p. 40.
44   Joseph, *Byron the Poet*, p. 91.
45   Newey, 'Authoring the Self', p. 168.
46   Kipperman, *Beyond Enchantment*, p. 195.
47   Newey, 'Authoring the Self', p. 168. The theme of growth is important, though I only touch on it here and in note 19. It runs through Byron's lyric contemplation of literature at the beginning of the canto, and through the contemplations of art and sculpture I have been talking about. It culminates in the section on St Peter's, where 'cumulative acts of limited perception ... eventuate in a general sense of comprehension' (McGann, *Fiery Dust*, p. 40): 'we thus dilate / Our spirits to the size of what they contemplate' (*CHP* IV, 157–158). For a full discussion of the growth and expansion of both consciousness and spirit which is looked for in *Childe Harold* IV, but which is only ever partially and intermittently achieved, see McGann, *Fiery Dust*, pp. 36–40 and Newey's answer to McGann in 'Authoring the Self', pp. 178–180.

headlong rock' (*Childe Harold* III, st. 41), the world of dispute and turmoil below.[48]

The idea that it is possible to 'stand above or beyond' the 'dispute and turmoil below' finds its most powerful expression in *Childe Harold* IV, and in more senses than McGann's commentary would suggest. Not only does Byron cherish the idea of standing above 'the contradictions of his age', but in *Childe Harold* IV he cherishes the idea of standing above the contradictions of his being, and, in some sense at least, of even standing above 'man's' lamentable existential fate. And in *Childe Harold* IV, Byron has replaced the Wordsworthian idealism he rejected in *Childe Harold* I and II, but to which he returned in *Childe Harold* III, with his own idealism. It is through thought, if through anything, that transcendence is to be achieved, as we see when he gazes at Palatine and sees written there

> ... the moral of all human tales;
> 'Tis but the same rehearsal of the past,
> First Freedom, and then Glory – when that fails,
> Wealth, vice, corruption, – barbarism at last.
> And History, with all her volumes vast,
> Hath but *one* page, – 'tis better written here,
> Where gorgeous Tyranny had thus amass'd
> All treasures, all delights, that eye or ear,
> Heart, soul could seek, tongue ask – Away with words! (*CHP* IV, 964–972)

Byron's own tale dissolves into 'all human tales', and he is already written into the Palatine, pre-empted and foreshadowed. All 'tales', it would seem, be they histories of races, of cultures, or of individuals, are ultimately fated to be 'the same rehearsal of the past': never adding anything to what is already 'written here'. Even the act of writing 'volumes vast' only repeats History's 'one page', so that Byron cries 'Away with words'. But he does not stop writing, and his act of writing does add something not written on the Palatine: self-knowledge. And it is precisely this self-knowledge that Byron's poem wants to foreground here. While the Palatine cannot know that it is 'the same rehearsal of the past', a human spectator can; and can know that he or she is yet another rehearsal of the same past.

In one sense, of course, this is actually a part of the repetition that is lamented here. All humans can 'know' their fate in the sense that Byron 'knows' his here, but knowing that one simply repeats the past does not help prevent one from being such a repetition. Yet Byron is not claiming any kind of escape from his fate as a human being. Rather, he is interested in the idea that in knowing that fate, the mind can somehow 'stand above or beyond' it even while the self enacts it.

In *Childe Harold* IV, Byron implicitly accepts his fate simply to repeat 'the moral' figured in the Palatine, but articulates a 'mind' which, though it is tied to a mortal existence that must rehearse the same old moral, and though it cannot escape its fate, can transcend it in one way at least. The mind can stand

---

48 *The Romantic Ideology*, p. 138.

outside the mortal existence it is chained to, stand 'above or beyond' it, and know it.

This is, for Byron, a kind of victory: tragic repetition can be intellectually (if not actually) mastered, contained, and conquered. But, I suggest, the mind's ability to know its fate also offers, for Byron, the 'last and only place / Of refuge' he mentions in stanza 127. Unfortunately, Byron does not expand on what he does mean by this refuge, but we can speculate. And other thinkers help us here. For Hegel, for example, the self 'excludes itself from essential Being' in an 'independent Self-existence' that is 'the knowledge', or the knowing, 'of itself on the part of essential being'.[49] In the light of this quotation, we might recall Oakeshott's claim that the self 'appears as activity' and suggest that the intimate relationship between self and mind somehow enables the self to 'ideally model itself after and take form as an objective knowing that ... liberates the individual' from,[50] let us say, 'subjective suffering'. Does Byron have something like this in mind when he claims that thought is a 'refuge'? Or does he mean something less fraught with philosophical pot-holes? Either is possible. He may simply mean, after all, that consciousness finds a 'refuge' in the activity of 'objective knowing', or 'the activity of groping thought' which aims at objective knowing,[51] because whilst absorbed by that activity, it is distracted from subjective suffering.

Either way, the 'refuge' is a temporary one. Neither the self nor consciousness can ultimately escape either 'the turmoil below' or 'suffering', and both remain 'coop'd in clay'. If indeed 'the self' can 'take form as an objective knowing', and transcend the 'vice, corruption, ... [and] barbarism' of being human, then it can only do so temporarily. Self and consciousness are always drawn back to suffering, and out of the 'refuge' of objectively knowing it. They are drawn out of that objective knowing by fatigue, if by nothing else: 'the weight / Of earth recoils upon us'. But thought and the act of thinking are also assailed by doubt, or rather 'the fear that its genius may be a demon or a tyrant, and its paradise an illusion (or worse)':[52] 'Of its own beauty is the mind diseased, / And fevers into false creation' (*CHP* IV, 1090–1091). Even the idea that thought might be a refuge is haunted by the fear that thought itself simply tortures us with the 'unreach'd Paradise of our despair / Which o'er-informs the pencil and the pen' (*CHP* IV, 1096–1097).

However, even though Byron seems to lose faith from time to time in the very 'truth' his poem attempts to dramatize, we must emphasize that the poem is not finally as gloomy as McGann seems to suggest it should be:

> In the end Byron's poetry discovers what all Romantic poems repeatedly discover: that there is no place of refuge, not in desire, not in the mind, not

---

[49] G. W. F. Hegel, *The Phenomenology of the Mind*, trans. by J. B. Baillie (London: George Allen and Unwin, and New York: Humanities Press, 1910, revised 1931, 8th impression, 1971), p. 767.

[50] Privateer, *Romantic Voices*, p. 29. For Kipperman, the liberation is from time: 'through our created ideals we can stand outside the round of time, infinitely reflective' (*Beyond Enchantment*, p. 197).

[51] McGann, *Fiery Dust*, p. 46.

[52] McGann, *The Romantic Ideology*, p. 103.

in imagination. Man is in love and loves what vanishes, and this includes
– finally, and tragically – even his necessary angels.[53]

McGann is, I presume, referring to much later works, though even in *Childe
Harold* IV we can see how precarious Byron's hold on this 'refuge' was, even
in 1817. Yet Byron's assertion that thought is a refuge testifies to a refusal
simply to lament fate, or to accept that this fate is 'redeemed only' by man's
'indomitable spirit and mind'.[54] Instead, as I have tried to argue throughout this
chapter, *Childe Harold* IV attempts to demonstrate, and in doing so celebrate
and delight in, despite its own doubts, the fact that man's fate is redeemed by
the benediction of thought. The mind can know its fate, and it can create things
which 'look like gods below' (*CHP* IV, 469).

With this assertion about the real force of celebration in *Childe Harold* IV
in place, we can now go on to ask: how does all this move Byron forward
towards writing comic verse, or, to put it another way, how does *Childe
Harold* IV 'help bridge the amazing gulf between *Manfred* and *Beppo*'? It does
this and more. To begin with, it successfully detaches Byron's poetry from the
Byronic hero. By doing so, it helps Byron to recover, in *Beppo*, the ironic
detachment from this figure with which *Childe Harold* I and II began. Beppo is
a Byronic hero in many respects,[55] but is also made to look rather ridiculous.

Hand in hand with this manoeuvre goes another. *Childe Harold* IV once
again attempts to hand Byron's poetry over to the impulse to celebrate, and
delight in, something more than man's endurance. But *Childe Harold* IV also
opened up the possibility of comedy for Byron in a more profound sense than
either of these. In it, Byron recovers and crystallizes his instinctive sense of a
source of renewal which revitalizes human existence. And on the basis of that
intuition he builds a vision of the human condition which in many ways
resolves the dilemmas of his tragic vision. Where Manfred is 'coop'd in clay',
and forced to suffer remorse and grief, *Childe Harold* IV insists that thought
offers a transcendence of, and refuge from, this suffering. And where the
heroes of the early tales must suffer the 'Vitality of poison' in order to fend off
the void of their desolated being, *Childe Harold* IV asserts that through the
human capacity for thought, divinity replenishes, inspires, and redeems that
void.

Here we find Byron on the threshold of writing comic verse which revels
in the fecundity of creative thought as both a refuge from, and a redemption of,
man's lamentable fate. *Childe Harold* IV effects a radical change in Byron's
practice as a poet. As a direct result of its insistence on thought as 'our last and
only place of refuge', Byron's subsequent poetry becomes fascinated with the
very fact of thought. In *Beppo*, thought is contemplated in its appearing, in its
coming into being, and the powerful attraction to images of tragic suffering is
now overwhelmed by a fascination with the mind's capacity to generate those
images. But reposing, as he does in *Beppo*, in the very appearance of images
naturally draws Byron's attention to both the multiplicity and the mixed nature

---

[53]   Ibid., p. 145.
[54]   Gleckner, *Ruins*, p. 271.
[55]   As Joseph points out, 'Beppo's life as a slave, renegade and pirate ... would have
made the experience of an early Byronic hero' (*Byron the Poet*, p. 135).

of what appears. It is at this point that he moves into comedy. Comedy is founded in precisely this kind of multiplicity and mixture. It eliminates the distinction between the high and low, between what is trivial and what is profound, between the worth of Beppo's adventures and his hairstyle.

That is why Byron remains engaged with the fact of creative thought throughout *Beppo* and *Don Juan*, revelling in that thought's redemption of each moment from the threat of death and silence. So engaged, his imagination is turned away from the horror of emotional void and of being 'cabin'd, cribb'd, confined' in clay. It is turned away, too, from the idea that each human is subject to the tragic destiny written on the Palatine. In *Beppo*, Byron discovers his way into comedy by celebrating the mind's power to distract itself from its own tragic imaginings.

We end at *Beppo*, and at Byron's first sustained foray into comedy. It is the pull to, and arrival at, comic form that concerns us, rather than what Byron goes on to do with it. We began with cantos I and II of *Childe Harold* and Byron's first extended exploration of new kinds of writing and imagining. Various ideas began to take hold of him here: tortured exile, the ruins of history, bereavement, and alienation. Such ideas culminated, in the verse narratives which followed *Childe Harold* I and II, in a vision of human existence devastated by tragic fate. The exploration of new forms and idioms now became a search for new representions of this image of tragedy, and Byron remained almost entirely occupied with that search until 1816. Here he began to pull away from the tragic, first by exploring Wordsworth's preoccupation with nature, but finally by carrying Wordsworth's idealism forward towards a comic vision in which he could uncover his own instinctive hold on connectedness rather than alienation, of plenitude rather than devastation, of benediction rather than a tragic fate. This impulse towards an idealism in some ways like Wordsworth's (though in other ways very different), and to ideas of redemption and renewal, faded in the face of Byron's powerful attraction to the tragic in the poems which followed *Childe Harold* III, until, in *Manfred*, Byron entered definitively his own distinctive tragic world. But comedy was pushed to one side only temporarily. Byron recovered that earlier intuition of connectedness in *Childe Harold's Pilgrimage* IV, and confidently moved in the direction of comedy. In this last instalment of *Childe Harold*, his attention is pulled away from his own tragic fictions by the very fact that the mind can create fictions at all. It is a major contention of this study that Byron's comic verse, which delights in the plenitude of human creativity, in the fecund play of fancy, is born in this shift of focus. Here is the path to Byron's greatest poem, *Don Juan*. But here we might also find, on further enquiry, a path to Byron's later mastery of the tragic form in *Marino Faliero* and *The Two Foscari*.

Bibliography

Primary Sources

Aeschylus, *Prometheus Bound*, in *Greek Tragedies*, ed. by David Greene and Richmond Lattimore, vol. 1 (Chicago and London: University of Chicago Press, 1968), pp. 61–106

Aristotle, 'Poetics', trans. by M. E. Hubbard, in *Ancient Literary Criticism*, ed. by D. A. Russell and M. Winterbottom (Oxford: Clarendon Press, 1972), pp. 85–131

Beattie, James, *The Minstrel, in Two Books: with Some Other Poems* (Edinburgh and London: [n.pub.], 1771; reprinted London: [n.pub.], 1784)

Byron, George Gordon, Lord, *The Complete Poetical Works of Lord Byron*, ed. by Jerome J. McGann, 7 volumes (Oxford: Clarendon Press, 1980–1993)

The Works of Lord Byron (poetry), ed. by Ernest Hartley Coleridge, 7 volumes (London: John Murray, 1898–1904; revised and enlarged edition, 1905–1922)

Byron's Poetry, selected and ed. by Frank D. McConnell (New York and London: Norton, 1978)

Byron: Childe Harold's Pilgrimage, ed. by H. F. Tozer (Oxford: Clarendon Press, 1916)

Byron's Don Juan: A Variorum Edition, ed. by Truman Guy Steffan and Willis W. Pratt, 4 volumes (Austin: University of Texas Press, 1957)

Lord Byron: The Complete Miscellaneous Prose, ed. by Andrew Nicholson (Oxford: Clarendon Press, 1991)

Byron's Letters and Journals, ed. by Leslie A. Marchand, 12 volumes (London: John Murray, 1973–1982)

Medwin's Conversations of Lord Byron, ed. by Ernest J. Lovell (Princeton: Princeton University Press, 1966)

Byron: Interviews and Recollections, ed. by Norman Page (Basingstoke: Macmillan, 1985)

Galt, John, *Letters from the Levant* (London: [n.pub.], 1813)

Goethe, Johann Wolfgang von, *Faust: A Tragedy*, trans. by Walter Arndt, ed. by Cyrus Hamlin (New York and London: Norton, 1976)

Hegel, G. W. F., *The Phenomenology of the Mind*, trans. by J. B. Baille (London: George Allen and Unwin, and New York: Humanities Press, 1910; revised 1931; 8th impression, 1971)

Lewis, Matthew, *The Monk*, ed. by Howard Anderson (Oxford and New York: Oxford University Press, 1980)

Rogers, Samuel, *The Poems of Samuel Rogers* (London: [n.pub.], 1834)

Shakespeare, William, *The Complete Oxford Shakespeare*, ed. by Stanley Wells, Gary Taylor, John Lowett, and William Montgomery (Oxford: Clarendon Press, 1986)

Thomson, James, *The Castle of Indolence*, in *James Thomson: The Castle of Indolence and Other Poems*, ed. by Alan Dugald McKillop (Lawrence: University of Kansas Press, 1961), pp. 70–119

'Summer' in *The Seasons*, ed. by James Sambrook (Oxford: Clarendon Press, 1981), pp. 58–43

Wordsworth, William, *The Poetical Works of William Wordsworth*, ed. by Ernest de Selincourt, 5 volumes (Oxford: Clarendon Press, 1940–1949)

The Prelude 1799, 1805, 1850: Authoritative Texts, Contexts and Reception, Recent Critical Essays, ed. by Jonathan Wordsworth, M. H. Abrams, and Stephen Gill (New York and London: Norton, 1979).

The Prose Works of Wordsworth, ed. by W. J. B. Owen and Jane Worthing Smyser, 3 volumes, (Oxford: Clarendon Press, 1974)

Secondary Sources

Abrams, M. H., *The Correspondent Breeze: Essays on English Romanticism* (New York: Norton, 1987)

Arnold, Matthew, 'Byron', in *Essays in Criticism*, 2nd series (London: Macmillan, 1888; reprinted 1900), pp. 163–204

Aubin, Robert, *Topographical Poetry in XVIIIth. Century England* (New York: Modern Language Association of America, 1936)

Baker, Nigel, 'Byron and Childe Harold in Portugal', in *The Byron Journal* 22 (1994), pp. 43–50

Barber, Cesar Lombardi, *Shakespeare's Festive Comedy: A Study of Dramatic Form and its Relation to Social Custom* (Princeton: Princeton University Press, 1959)

Barthes, Roland, *Image-Music-Text*, trans. by Stephen Heath (Glasgow: Fontana, 1977)

Bate, Jonathan, *Shakespeare and the English Romantic Imagination* (Oxford: Clarendon Press, 1989)

   Romantic Ecology: Wordsworth and the Environmental Tradition (London: Routledge, 1991)

   'Apeing Romanticism', in *English Comedy*, ed. by M. Cordner, P. Holland, and J. Kerrigan (Cambridge: Cambridge University Press, 1994), pp. 221–240

Bate, Jonathan (ed.), *The Romantics on Shakespeare* (London: Penguin, 1992)

Beatty, Bernard, 'Lord Byron: Poetry and Precedent', in *Literature of the Romantic Period 1750–1850*, ed. by R. T. Davies and B. G. Beatty (Liverpool: Liverpool University Press, 1976), pp. 114–134

   Byron's Don Juan (London: Croom Helm, 1985)

   'Fiction's Limit and Eden's Door', in *Byron and the Limits of Fiction*, ed. by Bernard Beatty and Vinvent Newey (Liverpool: Liverpool University Press, 1988), pp. 1–38

   'Lord Byron', in *A Handbook to English Romanticism*, ed. by J. Raimond and J. R. Watson (Basingstoke: Macmillan, 1992), pp. 45–55

Beatty, Bernard, and Vincent Newey (eds), *Byron and the Limits of Fiction* (Liverpool: Liverpool University Press, 1988)

Berry, Francis, 'The Poet of *Childe Harold*', in *Byron: A Symposium*, ed. by John Jump (London and Basingstoke: Macmillan, 1975)

Bloom, Harold, *A Visionary Company: A Reading of English Romantic Poetry* (Ithaca: Cornell University Press 1961; revised and enlarged, 1971)

Bloom, Harold (ed.), *George Gordon, Lord Byron* (New York: Chelsea House, 1986)

Butler, Maria Hogan, 'An Examination of Byron's Revisions of *Manfred* Act III', in *Studies in Philology* LX (1963), pp. 627–636

Butler, Marilyn, 'The Orientalism of Byron's *Giaour*', in *Byron and the Limits of Fiction*, ed. by Bernard Beatty and Vincent Newey (Liverpool: Liverpool University Press, 1988), pp. 78–96

Cave, Terence, *Recognition: A Study in Poetics* (Oxford: Clarendon Press, 1988)

Chase, Cynthia (ed.), *Romanticism* (London and New York: Longman, 1985; 2nd edition, 1992)

Chew, Samuel, *The Dramas of Lord Byron: A Critical Study* (Gottingen: Vandenhoeck and Ruprecht, and Baltimore: Johns Hopkins University Press, 1915; reprinted New York: Russell and Russell, 1964)

Chew, Samuel (ed.), *Childe Harold's Pilgrimage and Other Romantic Poems* (New York: Doubleday, Doran and Company, 1936)

Christensen, Jerome, 'Perversion, Parody and Cultural Hegemony: Lord Byron's Oriental Tales', in *South Atlantic Quarterly* 88 (Summer 1989), pp. 570–603

Cooke, Michael G., *The Blind Man Traces the Circle: on the Patterns and Philosophy of Byron's Poetry* (Princeton: Princeton University Press, 1969)

Corbett, Martyn, *Byron and Tragedy* (Basingstoke: Macmillan, 1988)

Cordner, M., P. Holland, and J. Kerrigan, (eds), *English Comedy* (Cambridge: Cambridge University Press, 1994)

Cronin, Richard, 'Mapping *Childe Harold* I and II', in *The Byron Journal* 22 (1994), pp. 14–20

Culler, Jonathan, *Structuralist Poetics: Structuralism, Linguistics and the Study of Literature* (London: Routledge and Kegan Paul, 1975)
>   *The Pursuit of Signs: Semiotics, Literature, Deconstruction* (London: Routledge and Kegan Paul, 1981)
>   *On Deconstruction: Theory and Criticism after Structuralism* (London: Routledge and Kegan Paul, 1983)

Curran, Stuart, *Poetic Form and British Romanticism* (New York and Oxford: Oxford University Press, 1986)

Davies, R. T., and B. G. Beatty (eds), *Literature of the Romantic Period* (Liverpool: Liverpool University Press, 1976)

de Man, Paul, *Blindness and Insight: Essays in the Rhetoric of Contemporary Criticism* (New York: Oxford University Press, 1971)
>   *The Rhetoric of Romanticism* (New York: Columbia University Press, 1984)
>   *Romanticism and Contemporary Criticism: The Gauss Seminar and Other Papers*, ed. by E. S. Burt, Kevin Newmark, and Andrzej Warminski (Baltimore: Johns Hopkins University Press, 1993)

Derrida, Jacques, *Margins of Philosophy*, trans. by Alan Bass (Brighton: Harvester Press, 1982)

Doherty, Francis M., *Byron* (London: Evans, 1968)

Edwards, Philip, *Shakespeare: A Writer's Progress* (Oxford and New York: Oxford University Press, 1986)

Eggenschwiler, David., 'The Tragic and Comic Rhythms of *Manfred*', in *Studies in Romanticism* 13 (Winter 1974), pp. 63–77

Eliot, T. S., 'Byron' in *Poetry and Poets* (London: Faber, 1957), pp. 193–206

Elleridge, Paul W., *Byron and the Dynamics of Metaphor* (Nashville: Vanderbilt University Press, 1968)

Evans, Bertrand, 'Manfred's Remorse and Dramatic Tradition', in *PMLA* 42 (September 1947), pp. 752–773

Everett, Edwin M., 'Lord Byron's Lakist Interlude', in *Studies in Philology* 55 (January 1958), pp. 62–75.

Fischer, James R., '"Here the Story Ends": Byron's *Beppo*, a Broken Dante', in *The Byron Journal* 21 (1993), pp. 61–70

Fry, Christopher, 'Comedy', in *The Tulane Drama Review* 4:3 (March 1960), pp. 77–79

Frye, Northrop, *The Anatomy of Criticism: Four Essays* (Princeton: Princeton University Press, 1957)

Giblin, Charles Homer, *The Book of Revelation: The Open Book of Prophecy* (Collegeville (Minnesota): The Liturgical Press, 1991)

Gleckner, Robert F., *Byron and the Ruins of Paradise* (Baltimore: Johns Hopkins University Press, 1967)

Griffiths, Eric, *The Printed Voice of Victorian Poetry* (Oxford: Clarendon Press, 1989)

Hartman, Geoffrey, *Beyond Formalism: Literary Essays 1958–1970* (New Haven and London: Yale University Press, 1970)

Holmes, Richard, *Shelley: The Pursuit* (London: Weidenfeld and Nicolson, 1974)
Iser, Wolfgang, *The Implied Reader: Patterns of Communication in Prose Fiction from Bunyan to Beckett*, trans. by Wilhelm Fink (Baltimore: Johns Hopkins University Press, 1974)
James, D. G., *The Romantic Comedy* (London: Oxford University Press, 1948)
Jamil, Tahir, *Transcendentalism in English Romantic Poetry* (New York: Vantage Press, 1989)
Joseph, M. K., *Byron the Poet* (London: Gollancz, 1964)
Jump, John D., *Byron* (London: Routledge and Kegan Paul, 1972)
Jump, John D. (ed.), *Byron: A Symposium* (London and Basingstoke: Macmillan, 1975)
Kidwai, Abdur Raheem, *Orientalism in Lord Byron's 'Turkish Tales'* (Lampeter: Mellen University Press, 1995)
Kipperman, Mark, *Beyond Enchantment: German Idealism and English Romantic Poetry* (Philadelphia: University of Pennsylvania Press, 1986)
Knight, G. Wilson, *Lord Byron: Christian Values* (London: Routledge and Kegan Paul, 1952)
Kroeber, Karl, *Romantic Narrative Art* (Madison: University of Wisconsin Press, 1960)
Langbaum, Robert, *The Poetry of Experience: The Dramatic Monologue in Modern Literary Tradition* (London: Chatto and Windus, 1957)
Leech, Clifford, *Tragedy* (London: Methuen, 1969)
Lindley, David, *Lyric* (London: Methuen, 1985)
Manning, Peter J., *Byron and his Fictions* (Detroit: Wayne State University Press, 1978)
Marchand, Leslie A., *Byron: A Biography*, 3 volumes (London: John Murray, 1957)
    Byron: A Portrait (London: John Murray, 1970)
    Byron's Poetry: A Critical Introduction (London: John Murray, 1965)
Marchant, W. Moelwyn, *Comedy* (London: Methuen, 1972)
Marinelli, Peter Vincent, *Pastoral* (London: Methuen, 1971)
Marshall, William, 'The Accretive Structure of *The Giaour*', in *Modern Language Notes* 76 (1961), pp. 502–509
    The Structure of Byron's Major Poems (Philadelphia: University of Philadelphia Press, 1962)
Martin, Philip W., *Byron: A Poet Before His Public* (Cambridge: Cambridge University Press, 1982)
McFarland, Thomas, *Shakespeare's Pastoral Comedies* (Chapel Hall: University of North Carolina Press, 1971)
McGann, Jerome J., *Fiery Dust: Byron's Poetic Development* (Chicago: University of Chicago Press, 1968)
    'Byron's First Tale: An Unfinished Fragment', in *Keats–Shelley Memorial Association Bulletin* 19 (1968), pp. 18–23
    The Romantic Ideology: A Critical Investigation (Chicago: University of Chicago Press, 1983)
    The Beauty of Inflections: Literary Investigations in Historical Method and Theory (Oxford: Clarendon Press, 1985)
    'Byron and the Anonymous Lyric', in *Byron Journal* 20 (1992), pp. 27–45.
Moore, Thomas, *Life of Lord Byron: With his Letters and Journals*, 6 volumes (London: John Murray, 1830; reprinted London: [n.pub.], 1854)
Nellist, Brian, 'Lyric Presence in Byron from the *Tales* to *Don Juan*', in *Byron and the Limits of Fiction*, ed. by Bernard Beatty and Vincent Newey (Liverpool: Liverpool University Press, 1988), pp. 39–77
Newey, Vincent, 'Authoring the Self: *Childe Harold* III and IV' in *Byron and the Limits of Fiction*, ed. by Bernard Beatty and Vincent Newey (Liverpool: Liverpool University Press, 1988), pp. 148–190

Oakeshott, Michael, 'The Voice of Poetry in the Conversation of Mankind', in *Rationalism in Politics and other Essays* (London: Methuen, 1962), pp. 197–247

O'Neill, Michael, *Romanticism and the Self-Conscious Poem* (Oxford: Clarendon Press, 1997)

Pafford, Ward, 'Byron and the Mind of Man: *Childe Harold* III and IV and *Manfred*', in *Studies in Romanticism* 1 (Winter 1962), pp. 105–127

Page, Norman, *A Byron Chronology* (Basingstoke: Macmillan, 1988)

Panofsky, Erwin, *Meaning and The Visual Arts: Papers in and on Art History* (New York: Doubleday, 1955)

Peckham, Morse, *Beyond the Tragic Vision: the Quest for Identity in the Nineteenth Century* (New York: George Braziller, 1962)

Pite, Ralph, *The Circle of Our Vision: Dante's Presence in English Romantic Poetry* (Oxford: Clarendon Press, 1994)

Privateer, Paul Michael, *Romantic Voices: Identity and Ideology in British Romantic Poetry* (Athens and London: University of Georgia Press, 1991)

Quinlan, Maurice, 'Byron's *Manfred* and Zoroastrianism', in *Journal of English and Germanic Philology* 57 (1958), pp. 726–738

Raimond, J., and J. R. Watson (eds), *A Handbook to English Romanticism* (Basingstoke: Macmillan, 1992)

Raïzis, M. Byron, 'Byron's Promethean Rebellion in 1816: Fictionality and Self-projection in his Poetry of that Year', in *The Byron Journal* 19 (1991), pp. 41–52

Rajan, Tilottama, *Dark Interpreter: The Discourse of Romanticism* (Ithaca: Cornell University Press, 1980)

Rice, Philip, and Patricia Waugh (eds), *Modern Literary Theory* (Basingstoke: Macmillan, 1990)

Robson, W. W., 'Byron as Poet', in *Critical Essays* (London: Routledge and Kegan Paul, 1966), pp. 148–188.

Rutherford, Andrew, *Byron: A Critical Study* (Edinburgh: Oliver and Boyd, 1961)

Rutherford, Andrew (ed.), *Byron: The Critical Heritage* (London: Routledge and Kegan Paul, 1970)

   Byron: Augustan and Romantic (Basingstoke: Macmillan, 1990)

Saglia, Diego, 'Spain and Byron's Construction of Place', in *Byron Journal* 22 (1994), pp. 30–42

Salinger, Leo, *Shakespeare and the Traditions of Comedy* (London and New York: Cambridge University Press, 1974)

Seed, David, '"The Platitude of Prose": Byron's vampire fragment in the context of his verse narratives', in *Byron and the Limits of Fiction*, ed. by Bernard Beatty and Vincent Newey (Liverpool: Liverpool University Press, 1988), pp. 126–147

   '"Disjointed Fragments": Concealment and Revelation in *The Giaour*', in *Byron Journal* 18 (1990), pp. 14–27

Soderholm, James, 'Dorothy Wordsworth's Return to Tintern Abbey', in *New Literary History* 26:2 (Spring 1995), pp. 309–322.

Sperry, Stuart M., 'Byron and the Meaning of *Manfred*', in *Criticism* 16:3 (Summer 1974), pp. 189–202

Sundell, Michael G., 'The Development of *The Giaour*', in *Studies in English Literature 1500–1900* 9 (1969), pp. 587–599

Steiner, George, *The Death of Tragedy* (London: Faber and Faber, 1961)

Swann, Karen, 'Literary Gentlemen and Lovely Ladies: the Debate on the Character of Christabel', in *English Literary History* 52:1 (Spring 1985), pp. 397–418

Thorslev, Peter L., *The Byronic Hero: Types and Prototypes* (Minneapolis: University of Minnesota Press, 1962)

Watson, J. R., *English Poetry of the Romantic Period 1789–1830* (London: Longman, 1985)

West, Paul, *Byron and the Spoiler's Art* (London: Chatto and Windus, 1960)
West, Paul (ed.), *Byron* (Englewood Cliffs: Prentice Hall, 1963)
Wilson, Peter B., '"Galvanism upon Mutton": Byron's Conjuring Trick in *The Giaour*', in *Keats–Shelley Journal* 24 (1975), pp. 118–127

Index